Michael Ross, Manfred Grauer, Bernd Freisleben (eds.)
Digital Tools in Media Studies

The series "Medienumbrüche | Media Upheavals" is edited by Peter Gendolla.

MICHAEL ROSS, MANFRED GRAUER, BERND FREISLEBEN (EDS.)
Digital Tools in Media Studies
Analysis and Research. An Overview

[transcript] Medienumbrüche | Media Upheavals | Volume 27

This book was produced by the Collaborative Research Centre 615 "Medienumbrüche / Media Upheavals" at the University of Siegen with funding by Deutsche Forschungsgemeinschaft (German Research Foundation).

Bibliographic information published by Deutsche Nationalbibliothek
Deutsche Nationalbibliothek lists this publication in Deutsche Nationalbibliographie; detailed bibliographic data are available on the Internet at http://dnb.d-nb.de

© 2009 transcript Verlag, Bielefeld

All rights reserved. No part of this book may be reprinted or reproduced or utilized in any form or by any electronic, mechanical, or other means, now known or hereafter invented, including photocopying and recording, or in any information storage or retrieval system, without permission in writing from the publisher.

Cover design by Kordula Röckenhaus, Bielefeld
Cover photograph by Janis Zinke (www.janis-zinke.de;
   source: www.photocase.de)
Edited and typeset by Michael Ross
Printed and bound in Great Britain by Marston Book Services Ltd, Oxfordshire
ISBN 978-3-8376-1023-9

Contents

Introduction 7

Louis Pelletier, Pierre Véronneau
Databases for Early Cinema Research 17

Harry van Vliet, Karel Dibbets, Henk Gras
Culture in Context
Contextualization of Cultural Events 27

John Sedgwick
Measuring Film Popularity
Principles and Applications 43

Jaap Boter, Clara Pafort-Overduin
Compartmentalisation and its Influence on Film Distribution and Exhibition in The Netherlands, 1934-1936 55

Deb Verhoeven, Kate Bowles, Colin Arrowsmith
Mapping the Movies
Reflections on the Use of Geospatial Technologies
for Historical Cinema Audience Research 69

Michael Ross, Roger Sennert, Jens Wagner
Putting Itinerant Cinemas on the Map 83

Yuri Tsivian
Cinemetrics, Part of the Humanities' Cyberinfrastructure 93

Ralph Ewerth, Markus Mühling, Thilo Stadelmann, Julinda Gllavata, Manfred Grauer, Bernd Freisleben
Videana: **A Software Toolkit for Scientific Film Studies** 101

Vera Kropf, Matthias Zeppelzauer, Stefan Hahn, Dalibor Mitrovic
First Steps Towards Digital Formalism:
The Vienna Vertov Collection 117

Warren Buckland
Ghost Director
Did Hooper or Spielberg Direct *Poltergeist?* 133

Christoph Brachmann, Hashim Iqbal Chunpir, Silke Gennies,
Benjamin Haller, Philipp Kehl, Astrid Paramita Mochtarram,
Daniel Möhlmann, Christian Schrumpf, Christopher Schultz,
Björn Stolper, Benjamin Walther-Franks, Arne Jacobs,
Thorsten Hermes, Otthein Herzog
**Automatic Movie Trailer Generation
Based on Semantic Video Patterns** 145

Leonardo Boccia, Peter Ludes
**Key Measures and Key Visuals
in Brazilian and German TV Annual Reviews** 159

Margret Schild
Text-Based Film Retrieval 2006
A New Concept to Index, Manage and Present Films,
Their Content and Context 171

Rolf Kloepfer
How to Capture Offers of Filmic Effectiveness
AKIRA III as an Aid.. 177

Introduction

From the Study of Media Upheavals to an Upheaval in Media Studies

Looking at the history of media in the past 150 years or so, we can observe a long succession of developments and refinements on the technological level as well as on the levels of production and reception, including cultural adaptations and social acceptance. At some points in time, these developments seem to gain momentum and bring about a change so radical that it reflects on society at large. At the research centre "Media Upheavals", based at the University of Siegen and funded by Deutsche Forschungsgemeinschaft, we take into view two periods that stand out for their far-reaching technological change and the impact they have had on society: At the beginning of the 20th century, a radical change was perceived and commonly pinpointed on film and other media for recording and reproducing 'life'. Today, at the beginning of the 21st century, we feel the impact that digital technology and media have on our lives, from personal communication and new forms of entertainment to a radically globalized world.

One of the assets of the Siegen research centre is the participation of projects from a range of disciplines, including media studies, sociology, and informatics. The two projects that joined forces for this volume are a film-history project dealing with the emergence of cinema in Germany around 1900, and an informatics project which develops 21st century methods and tools for all researchers at the centre. Since the use of digital tools is a fairly recent development in media studies, and one which opens up a whole range of new research areas and opportunities for collaboration and result presentation, it might actually be considered to be a kind of media upheaval in its own right. To discuss both potentials and problems arising from the new tools, we invited researchers from all over the world for a workshop. The response to our call for papers, and the lively discussions during the workshop, held in 2007 at Siegen, showed us that we struck a chord when addressing the subject. While many scholars and scientists have already made use of digital tools with considerable success, there still is a great interest in alternative approaches and in the discussion of the scope of possible applications. With this volume, we aim to provide interested parties from both media studies and the informatics an overview of current areas of research and areas of application for digital tools in order to give orientation and to encourage further projects along these lines.

Collecting Data

Perhaps the most basic way to make use of digital tools in media studies is the collecting of data. For decades now, word processing and spreadsheet software have been used to store information electronically for easy access and simple analysis. With database software becoming increasingly flexible and user-friendly, and with huge storage capacity being available at small cost, the collection of large data corpora has become fairly simple, creating an increasing interest in empirical studies. Like in so many other areas, the Internet has played an important role in refining the techniques of data collecting. Firstly, it allows for decentralized data entry: data can be entered from any computer connected to the Internet, and on more than one computer at the same time, allowing for fast and convenient working conditions, especially in a team of researchers. Secondly, the Internet serves as a perfect place for the publication of data collections: it allows world-wide distribution at minimal cost, while at the same time being vastly superior to printed data collections in terms of usability (searching, analyzing etc.) and updating.

Louis Pelletier and Pierre Véronneau describe the genesis of such a database project in some detail, from an original local database created in the mid-1990s to today's Internet-based portal on the history of silent film in Quebec. They show that rapid technical development can even challenge a previous digital project: Is it still necessary to have a "handmade" database-driven index to film-related articles in newspapers and journals of a particular place and time, once these periodicals are available as fully-searchable digital reproductions on the Internet? Pelletier and Véronneau answer in the affirmative, stressing the superiority of human indexation over simple text search routines. One might argue that this is certainly true at the moment, but in the face of current research into digital information retrieval and text mining may look quite differently another decade or so from now. Still, the examples and reasons Pelletier and Véronneau provide, from misprints in the original source to ambiguous names and scores of now obsolete synonyms do not let it seem likely that we will be able to dispense with a kind of human supervision for some time to come. It is a conclusion that will turn up again and again in the course of our discussion.

It must be stressed that the Quebec project greatly profited from the digitalization of its primary sources: it allowed them to expand their corpus and to simplify access to the texts themselves – both for the researchers on the project and the later users of the database. This was made possible by a co-operation between the academic film history project, the local Cinemathèque, and the national library. The example shows that co-operations like these can be extremely fruitful, and they are often seen as a major goal of a networked academic community. Harry van Vliet, Karel Dibbets, and Henk Gras elaborate on this particular issue a bit further. It is their aim to connect information on cultural events of the past, like film screenings and theatre performances, to the contextual materials still available in archives and museums. Based on two fundamental data collections on Dutch cinema and theatre which in themselves are of great use to historians in the field, the authors are currently working on an ontology to allow database connections between the institutions involved, for what they call "semantic interoperability". Standardization like this is a key issue for any data collecting project that is interested in either incorporating external data or linking the own data with that of others. The problems range from developing rules for indexing personal names or place names to the definition of core databases to which others may refer. As can be seen in the field of libraries, which had to develop standards for cataloguing well before the digital age and were among the first to adapt their rules to the conditions of computers and electronic databases, standardization processes are difficult and can take a lot of time – and may still differ significantly between institutions from different countries or cultural backgrounds.

Even if film and theatre studies can build on standards developed for libraries or other pertinent institutions, the task is still far from elementary, especially where single historical events (e.g., a theatrical performance) are concerned. The Dutch example shows a promising approach by building on an existing collection of core data which is set as a standard and may be referred to by other data collections. While an obvious approach, its success depends greatly on the solution to one substantial problem: It only works if the existing data collection is both sufficiently comprehensive and thoroughly reliable, since it will have to be accepted by all partners of the project. While reliability may be ascertained to some degree by academic supervision, the comprehensiveness of a data collection is naturally limited by the resources available. Especially with international co-operations, existing data collections often turn out to be too limited, most of them having originated from a national context. Examples of non-academic data collections on the Internet show that collections are best accepted that make use of a co-operative data collecting model (e.g., the Internet Movie Database at www.imdb.com, or Wikipedia and its many variants). Thus, projects combining one or more existing core databases with a secure multi-user collaborative platform to form an "Academic Social Web" might be best-suited for academic data collecting in the future. There are plans to advance this concept within the Siegen research centre in the near future, both in theory and practice.

Measuring Success

Collecting data is not the actual aim of scholarship, of course, but rather the means to be able to analyse a particular situation in respect to particular questions. Pelletier and Véronneau describe how the Canadian project started out as a tool for cinema historians to simply find relevant information within the individually unmanageable scores of contemporary periodicals, to become a platform for academic research as well as teaching. Van Vliet, Dibbets and Gras stress the fact that joint databases result in an "enrichment" of information that can be used to re-assess long-held assumptions, e.g. on audience composition in relation to theatrical genres. An area which particularly lends itself to the analysis of collected data is their statistical evaluation. In empirical media studies, the success of a medium, a genre or even a single product is a popular field of research, and it is only natural that this kind of research is made much easier with the help of digital tools, both for collecting the data to be analysed and for the mathematical operations necessary to get at the results.

Today, box-office takings are pretty well documented, so one can get a good idea of the success of particular films or genres compared to others at the same time. Things become more difficult the further one goes back in time. For the first decades in movie history, data is scarce and conclusions will have to be tentative. Even fairly basic data like the number of screenings of a film are difficult to ascertain, and the number of actual viewers is quite impossible to tell. Once the cinema industry gets a little more ordered, and feature films come into the focus of the audience (and of the researcher), things become a little easier. John Sedgwick chose 1930's British cinema to develop his tools for measuring film popularity. His starting point is the rare example of a source which gives insight into audience numbers and revenues at a particular cinema in Portsmouth. To put the data from this source into relation to cinema-going practices in Portsmouth in general, Sedgwick developed a formula to measure success when the available data is limited to newspaper advertisements, resulting in a so-called POPSTAT value for each film. By applying statistical methods to a data collection, Sedgwick discovers discrepancies in audience reception between first-run and other cinemas and offers an approach to explain these discrepancies.

Jaap Boter and Clara Pafort-Overduin look at the same phase of cinema history, in their case in the Netherlands, but focus on the aspect of film distribution rather than reception. By applying Latent Class Analysis to an extensive dataset covering Dutch cinema programmes between 1934 and 1936, they come up with seven clusters of films in relation to the cinemas where they were screened. Contrary to popular belief, however, no clear pattern could be found that relates particular films to particular geographic regions and their dominant social group – a factor previously thought to be highly formative on Dutch cinema attendance as well as on Dutch culture as a whole. Instead, film distribution seems to follow other rules than the social composition of a cinema's trading area.

The examples of both Sedgwick and Boter/Pafort-Overduin show the potentials of advanced statistical analysis, and at the same time make 'traditional' media scholars aware of the need to get statistical expertise for their empirical research from the outset of their projects. Actually, both papers show the advantages of transdisciplinary research in media studies, in that both John Sedgwick and Jaap Boter are economists who have enhanced the film scholars' understanding of cinema culture with their particular expertise.

Geographical Data

The geographical aspect introduced by Boter and Pafort-Overduin in the context of their socio-geographic analysis is further elaborated by Deb Verhoeven, Kate Bowles, and Colin Arrowsmith. They discuss some of the general questions of using geospatial technologies in cinema studies, drawing on their own project on Greek cinema-going in Melbourne as a case in point. While arguing very much in favour of a geographical approach to audience research, they point out the many challenges that have to be overcome, especially when dealing with historical data. Given the immense amount of data necessary for a thorough analysis of, for example, socio-geographical factors for cinema-going, one of the first questions has to be where to get the data from. Digital data is only available for the most recent times, and even that varies greatly in scope and quality, not to mention compatibility and rights issues. To collect relevant data within a film-related research project will often be far too time-consuming, so that a strategic collaboration with interested parties from other fields of science and scholarship appears to be desirable.

Once these challenges are overcome, researchers are rewarded with new insights into their field that might otherwise have escaped them. This view is reinforced by Michael Ross, Roger Sennert, and Jens Wagner, who present a pragmatic solution to the problem of visualizing the stations of itinerant cinemas in the first decades of cinema. By combining information from a trade journal with a visualization tool based on Google Maps, film researchers were not only able to get a better idea of the actual routes of carnies, and of the areas particularly frequented by itinerant cinemas at the time, but they were also able to enhance their own data by resolving ambiguous identifications, especially with place names referring to more than one place. Considering the possibilities of geospatial tools discussed by Verhoeven et al, the itinerant cinema tool is only a very early step towards a comprehensive use of its potentials, but as such has proved to be useful already. Again, the lack of available existing data in digital format (including historical maps adjusted to up-to-date cartographic standards and historical census data) is the primary challenge for any further development here, and one can only hope that the significance of such data is recognized by funding institutions to allow for their coordinated digitalisation, for the benefit of geographers, historians and other scholars from all kinds of fields, including media studies.

Old Wine in New Wineskins?

Before we turn to the second part of our collection, which deals with digital tools for film and video analysis and annotation, and the results which can be achieved by this, we would like to address a point raised during our workshop regarding the actual innovation of media research with digital tools. It can be argued, of course, that the kind of research described so far could have been achieved without any digital tools at all: indices can be kept (and sometimes are indeed still kept) on index cards, counting and calculating are possible without computers, and a good printed atlas can provide the information needed to analyse any geographical data. This is certainly true, but it is also somewhat beside the point. Nobody will argue that the digital tools are doing something completely new and hitherto impossible. However, they can do operations so fast, and can re-do them over and over again with new or updated data, that much research only becomes feasible now that digital tools are available.

As a case in point, another database supervised by the film-history project at Siegen stores information on more than 40,000 films available on the German market between 1895 and 1920. The data ranges from film titles and countries of origin to the films' length and genre, as well as actors and crew members working on a film. The fairly simple database, available on-line at www.fk615.uni-siegen.de/earlycinema/fg/, allows statistical analyses on the film market in Germany for a variety of factors, including the changing dominance of some production countries over others within the covered time span, or the development of average film lengths in time and/or in relation to particular genres. With data collections of this size, it instantly becomes obvious that there are great limitations for analysis without the help of digital tools. Considering that the information from the filmography database can be linked to other data, e.g. on programming in particular cinemas, which again might be connected to census data on the social composition of particular areas, the tremendous possibilities of digital tools compared to traditional "handmade" analysis are even more obvious. Digital tools allow for results that in theory can be achieved by other means, but in practice would almost never have been achieved for pragmatic reasons. At the same time, the new tools require skills for handling them to get the best results from their application.

Tools for Film and Video Analysis

The database-related tools presented so far were more concerned with the context of media and their reception, rather than media products themselves. In the second part of this volume, we turn to tools that help with the analysis of audio-visual media products, i.e. films, videos etc. Classical film scholarship has been very much concerned with "reading" and interpreting films, looking for subtexts, an ulterior meaning or artistic merits. At first, it may seem difficult to imagine how this might be an area for applying digital tools, being so much related to cultural knowledge and human thinking. As we will show, there are plenty of fields where digital tools can at least assist media scholars in their work.

Not surprisingly, the branch of formalist film studies lends itself to digital tools particularly well. In his paper, Yuri Tsivian introduces a self-developed tool which, for all its apparent simplicity, is a powerful tool for anyone who has ever faced the task of counting recurring themes in a film or measuring the lengths of particular items. Tsivian's Cinemetrics software was originally designed, and is most useful for establishing the average shot length of a film, i.e. the average length of film shots between cuts. With Cinemetrics, the actual work of identifying cuts has still to be done manually by the scholar himself, while watching the film, but the simple measuring and counting tool provides all relevant information within seconds after the entering work is completed. What makes Cinemetrics even more important is its design as an Internet-based community tool: results of an analysis can be uploaded into an already impressive database where they immediately become available to other researchers. The collaborative approach allows comparative work on a much larger scale than would be possible for a single researcher.

Ralph Ewerth et al have a more ambitious goal in mind. Their software toolkit Videana was trained to detect film cuts and certain kinds of content in audiovisual material, without human interference. Automatic video analysis has been given much attention lately, and the Videana software scored very impressive results at international contests for shot boundary detections (i.e. cuts) as well as recognition of camera movements, textual elements, and faces. Those sceptic of automatic analyses are able to check Videana's results very easily and correct any mistakes the software may have made. Given recognition rates of 80% to 97% for cut detection, one does not have reason for too much scepticism, however; especially considering that human annotation reaches very similar scores.

Employing similar technologies from a slightly different angle is the Digital Formalism project introduced by Vera Kropf, Matthias Zeppelzauer, Stefan Hahn, and Dalibor Mitrovic. By focusing on the films by Russian formalist filmmaker Dziga Vertov, the project has an excellent reason to apply tools for detecting formal elements in film to their material. Apart from shot cuts and camera movements, the project aims to reveal patterns in the director's work hitherto unrecognised, using data mining techniques. Furthermore, the researchers expect some help for archives in determining similarities and differences between variant copies of the same film. The technical work is reflected within an advanced film theoretical framework discussing formalism and the digital, and putting the results of the analyses into context.

Another field of application for digitally-assisted formal analysis is introduced by Warren Buckland, who intends to settle a question of authorship by a comparison of directors' film styles. Was *Poltergeist,* Buckland asks, directed by its official director, Tobe Hooper, or its writer and producer, Steven Spielberg? Again, parameters like average shot length, number of camera movements, and shot scales are considered to determine the characteristic style of the two potential directors, which then are matched to the parameters of the film in question. Buckland bases his argument on statistics derived from a relatively small sample: the first 30 minutes from two films of each of the two directors and the first 30 minutes of *Poltergeist*. In view of the good results of automatic detection of at least some of the formal elements examined by Buckland, it is obvious that its use for research of this kind can greatly help to broaden the basis for a statistical analysis and make the results even more convincing.

While the applications presented by Buckland, Kropf et al and Tsivian are primarily academic, Christoph Brachmann et al show a more practical application of film analysis in their paper. The authors have analysed the pattern of trailers for action films and have formalised them in such a way that they are now able to generate similar trailers automatically. The fact that these get comparatively good ratings with test audiences shows the extent to which (a) a formalisation of this particular kind of trailer is possible, and (b) an automatic detection of formal elements can be achieved. Even if film studios will probably stick to their practice of creating trailers manually, the authors' approach is an important step towards processing semantic patterns in audiovisual material.

An important element in the generation of action trailers is the use of sound in films. Leonard Boccia and Peter Ludes elaborate a bit further on this theme, taking into closer view the importance of music in TV broadcasts, here in annual reviews of Brazilian and German TV. The authors introduce the concept of Key Measures and thereby provide future scientists with helpful instruments to detect particular kinds of sound elements and the semantics involved. At the same time, the intercultural approach by Boccia and Ludes also shows the limitations of any automatic analysis: A precise detection of semantic elements will always depend on the cultural background of the media product analysed, for a particular kind of music might have quite different connotations in different cultural contexts.

Film Annotation

Apart from statistical evaluation, a film analysis – be it automatic or manual – can reveal a wealth of information on a film. The question is how this information is stored to be easily retrieved when needed. The automatic detection tool developed by Ewerth et al already incorporates an annotation tool which allows users to enter free information to any particular frame of the analysed film. For some cases, however, it makes sense to develop more sophisticated solutions.

Margret Schild introduces a solution from the point of view of the librarian and archivist. With the software she describes, it becomes possible to link printed materials like books, advertising materials etc. not only to a film, but to particular scenes of a film. Thus, interested parties can be directed to pertinent literature while watching a film. The software can be used for exhibitions, where the screening of a film can be accompanied by further textual information, or on the Internet, where the viewer of an on-line film, or even of a personally-owned DVD, is pointed to materials relevant to a particular scene.

Rolf Kloepfer's annotation tool AKIRA III brings us back to the question in how far digital tools can assist film scholars in reading and interpreting a film. Kloepfer argues that much of film reception happens on a subconscious level and has to be carefully extracted from the film by a minute examination. His analysis tool allows for manual annotation of films in a way based on the notation of musical scores. When consistently applied, AKIRA III can bring to light patterns of meaning, of repetition, and of coherence which – even though formative on the reception of a film – are so elusive that they often escape the attention of the researcher. Using both a classic and a fairly recent example of film art, Kloepfer successfully shows the potentials of digital tools even for the most sophisticated ways of dealing with media.

Special Thanks

We would like to thank a number of people and institutions involved in the success of this volume. As mentioned earlier on, the volume can be traced back to a workshop held at Siegen in 2007. Annemone Ligensa and Joseph Garncarz provided significant input to the concept of the workshop, and Katrin Barkhausen, Ralph Ewerth, Ingo Köster, Roger Sennert, and Jens Wagner were of particular help in organizing the event. We would also like to thank all the contributors for their lively discussions at the workshop, their co-operation and their patience during the editorial process. Finally, we would like to thank the Deutsche Forschungsgemeinschaft and the University of Siegen for funding and housing the workshop, this publication, and the work of the research centre in general.

Siegen, October 2008

Michael Ross
Manfred Grauer
Bernd Freisleben

Louis Pelletier, Pierre Véronneau

Databases for Early Cinema Research

Databases are one of the most common ways to link digital tools and cinema. We will show the specificity of two databases designed by GRAFICS, pointing out how they were developed by film scholars involved in various fields of research, how they contributed their own concepts to the database design, what information each database includes and how it is structured, and why those databases already helped deepening the knowledge of film activities during the silent era in Québec. At the same time, we present results of a cooperation between a university and a film archive. Finally, we will discuss new perspectives of linkage between GRAFICS, the *Cinémathèque québécoise* and the *Bibliothèque et Archives nationales du Québec* (BAnQ) in respect to a research project on early film activity in Québec as reflected in the contemporary press. The project aims at a global website with many internal links for research, reference, and documentation.

GRAFICS *(Groupe de recherche sur l'avènement et la formation des institutions cinématographique et scénique)* is a research group working on early cinema in Québec and elsewhere in the world. It was created in 1994 at the Université de Montréal, building on the pre-centennial mood that was prevailing in the western world at the time.[1] Studying the cinematographic and theatrical institutions, it developed many axes of research:

1. Reception – audiences / social practices
2. Exhibition; Theatres: buildings – programs / intermediatic practices
3. Music – Sound effects
4. Lecturer
5. Production
6. Cultural representation / identity
7. Travelling exhibition
8. Institutional discourse

---

[1] GRAFICS is headed by André Gaudreault, and Pierre Véronneau is one of the researchers affiliated to it. Over the years, it has received financial assistance from Fonds québécois de la recherche sur la société et la culture (www.fqrsc.gouv.qc.ca) and the Social Sciences and Humanities Research Council of Canada (www.sshrc-crsh.gc.ca).

One of the first research projects undertaken by GRAFICS was the Québec newspaper project. Up to that point, newspapers had occupied a paradoxical place in film historiography: though widely available in research libraries and generally acknowledged as an exceptional source of data on film exhibition and audiences, daily newspapers proved to be too intimidating a resource for many film historians. It is easy to understand why: looking for specific information in hundreds of thousands of pages is really like looking for the proverbial needle in a haystack. However, this difficulty was greatly reduced by GRAFICS' collaborative structure, which enabled several researchers sharing an interest in early cinema to pool their resources and hire a team of research assistants. The assistants were asked to systematically collect every document pertaining to moving and projected images, as well as amusement places and popular visual culture, printed between 1895 and 1915 in three Montreal newspapers: *La Presse* (still published today, and still touting itself as "America's largest francophone daily"), *La Patrie*, and *The Montreal Daily Star* – then Canada's largest newspaper. It should be noted that moving pictures had enjoyed an exceptional level of popularity and acceptance in the largely francophone province of Québec in the nickelodeon era.[2] This was reflected by the coverage given to moving pictures by the selected newspapers, which turned out to be more important and sustained than that of most American and English-Canadian newspapers of the same era.[3]

The documents collected by GRAFICS in Québec newspapers varied widely in nature and content: there were reports on screenings, exhibitor ads, opinion pieces on moving picture shows, drawings and photographs of filmgoers, news items (for instance on ladies refusing to take off their hats in moving picture theatres), etc. Even the classifieds turned out to be an exceptional source of data. By the early 1910s, not a week went by without at least one small and otherwise undocumented moving picture theater showing up in the "For Sale" section. The wealth of documents generated by the project eventually filled several filing cabinets, and soon became almost as daunting as the newspapers themselves. It was consequently decided to index the collection. This led to the creation of a FileMaker database, which by 1997 held close to 16,000 files indexing as many documents from *La Patrie* and *La Presse*. The database was subsequently copied to CD-ROM and made available, along with bound copies of the collected documents, to visitors of the *Cinémathèque québécoise*'s *mediatheque*. Over the past decade, several Canadian and international research-

---

2   On the popularity of early cinema in the province of Quebec, see: Gaudreault/Lacasse (1996).

3   In recent years, Richard Abel, in the United States, and Paul S. Moore, in Canada, have also extensively studied the coverage of silent cinema in newspapers.

ers have made the trip to the *Cinémathèque québécoise* to consult this exceptional collection.

An important development pertaining to GRAFICS' newspaper project came about in 2005 when the *Bibliothèque et Archives nationales du Québec* – one of the province's very few cultural organizations not chronically short on funds – launched a major digitization project aiming to make most of Québec's historical periodicals available online by the end of the decade. One of the first titles available on the BAnQ's website was *La Patrie*. This did not go unnoticed by GRAFICS' members, who by this point were aware of the fact that their ten year old FileMaker database was becoming obsolete, and was thus in need of a major overhaul. The situation was eventually solved with the help of the federal government's *Canadian Culture Online* program.[4] By joining forces with the BAnQ and the *Cinémathèque québécoise*, GRAFICS was able to convince *Canadian Culture Online* to provide funding for a project entitled "Silent Film in Québec, 1896-1930". The project's objectives were a) to enable the BAnQ and the *Cinémathèque québécoise* to digitize part of their collections and make these available on the Internet, and b) to give GRAFICS the means to pursue its research in these newly digitized collections, and subsequently use its discoveries to build an educational website.

During this second phase of its newspaper project, GRAFICS collected several thousands of new documents in about twenty recently digitized historical periodicals: daily big city and weekly small town newspapers, women's and fan magazines, specialized weeklies, etc. These were indexed in a new version of GRAFICS' newspaper database developed with *Ruby on Rails*, an open-source database-backed web software, and are now being made available to anybody with an Internet connection through a search engine featured on the website of the "Silent Film in Québec, 1896-1930" project. This search engine will generate results featuring the retrieved documents' bibliographical references as well as hyperlinks permitting the user to view them on the BAnQ's website.[5]

Before we launch into a detailed description of the types of researches permitted by the project's database and search engine, it is necessary to recapitulate the arguments that convinced GRAFICS to pursue its systematic survey and indexing of Québec's historical newspapers in a technological context very different from that of the project's beginnings. It is safe to say that in the early days of the project nobody at GRAFICS could have predicted – or even

---

4   *Canadian Culture Online* is part of the *Department of Canadian Heritage*'s strategy to encourage a uniquely Canadian presence on the Internet. See www.culture.ca.
5   The website of "Silent Film in Québec, 1896-1930" (www.cinemamuetquebec.ca) was launched in September 2008.

dreamed – that by 2007 an ever-growing number of historical newspapers would be available in their entirety as searchable digital files on the Internet. The phenomenal progress of digital technologies since the mid-1990s consequently forced GRAFICS to reconsider the methods, the objectives and, indeed, the validity of its newspaper project. Given the phenomenal development of digital tools, and more particularly of Optical Character Recognition software (OCR) now routinely used to convert digitized pages into searchable textual documents[6], was the systematic collecting and indexing of film-related newspaper articles and documents really worth the investment in time and money? After taking into account a variety of issues ranging from the purely technical to the epistemological, GRAFICS' members agreed that it definitely was.

There is no denying the extraordinary possibilities opened by the intersection of computerized search engines and OCR software. For researchers who had to unwind kilometers of worn-out microfilm in remote research libraries in order to locate a few interesting documents, the possibility of instantly gathering hundreds, or even thousands, of relevant documents by simply typing a few words in an on-line search engine is nothing short of revolutionary. Still, there are some tasks that OCR software cannot perform yet, and many others that in all likelihood it never will. Regarding GRAFICS' project, a first limitation of the various OCR software is that, according to tests performed by the BAnQ, they still have a relatively high error rate when dealing with old newspapers reproduced on rather less than perfect microfilms. And even when they do correctly capture the content of the printed page, the use of OCR software is still limited by the staggering amount of misprints and misspellings that can be found in historical newspapers. As opposed to the human reader, OCR software cannot – and indeed, should not be made to – see a "kinetoscope" where a "kenitoscope" has been printed. Apart from that, search engines solely relying on OCR often prove rather ineffectual when asked to perform several types of basic searches. Simple search requests involving personal names, for instance, commonly turn out to be nearly impossible. A case in point is that of Léo-Ernest Ouimet – the single most important individual in the history of silent cinema in the province of Québec. Since "Ouimet" is one of the province's most common surnames, any search using this criterion performed on a Québec newspaper will return literally thousands of irrelevant documents. (First names are not very useful for this kind of request, since – if used at all –

---

6   See, for instance the Library of Congress's *Chronicling America: Historic American Newspapers* project, part of the *National Digital Newspaper Program* (www.loc.gov/chroniclingamerica); Cornell University's *Making of America* project (cdl.library.cornell.edu/moa); *ProQuest Historical Newspapers* (www.proquest.com/products_pq/descriptions/pq-hist-news.shtml).

they tend to vary widely in form. "Léo-Ernest" can thus appear in historical newspapers as "Léo", "Ernest", "L.", "E." or "L. E.".)

Search engines relying on OCR software will also be regularly stalled by the extreme instability of the nomenclature of film-related terms and categories in the pre-institutional period covered by the project. At the same time, this instability constituted the main justification of and a great challenge to GRAFICS' indexing enterprise. In order to return a comprehensive list of results when interrogated through the website's search engine, the project's database had to rely on a strict categorization and normalization of the data entered on each document's file. Obviously, this does not sit well with silent – and more particularly early – cinema, which by definition is a period largely devoid of standardized practices: Between the 1890s and the late 1920s, films were exhibited in a variety of venues and contexts, genres and formats were ever changing, and labor division in film production had yet to stabilize in clearly denominated functions such as producer, director and cameraman. Most of the categories of information indexed in the project's database consequently had to rely on standardized lists of predetermined entries. For instance, a single unified category – "cinema" – was inscribed on the file of every document referencing "kinetographic records", "moving pictures", "motion pictures", "animated views", "photoplays", "motography", "films" or "movies" (to quote only some of the most common variations on a single type of attraction). This normalization principle most notably applied to the "function" field associated to the indexed organizations and individuals, to the fields dedicated to the types of venues and attractions mentioned by the document, as well as to another field registering some of the indexed attractions' particular features, such as the presence of lecturers and the use of sound effects or color processes. A standardized subject headings system inspired by those of the BAnQ and the *Fédération internationale des archives du film* (FIAF) has also been devised and incorporated in the project's database. Its various entries deal with issues related to the general historical context ("World War I"), with specific debates pertaining to film ("Legislation: Sunday laws"), to film audiences ("Women", "Ethnic groups: French-Canadians"), as well as to film uses and contents ("Education").

Names of individuals and organizations have also been strictly normalized according to the *Anglo-American Cataloguing Rules 2* and, as much as possible, covered by a single unified entry. The fact that the *London Bioscope Co.* – a well-known traveling company based in Montreal – is called the *London Film* in one particular article does not mean much. Film titles, however, have been systematically indexed in the exact formulations in which they can be found in the treated documents, since their variations can be very telling. For instance, when the 1902 *Edison Film Manufacturing Co.* production *Jack and the Beanstalk* is screened in Montreal under the title *Jacques et les tiges de fer* (translates *Jack and the Iron Stalk*), much is revealed about local strategies of appropriation. In order to facilitate search requests, a "normalized title" field has nevertheless been added to the database. (It should however be noted that, even with the help of such exceptional online resources as the *Silent Era Québec Filmography*, which we will cover later, and the American Film Institute's *Silent Film Catalog*, the identification of the quoted films' "original" titles has turned out to be a task far too time-consuming to be done systematically.) Finally, once again in order to facilitate search requests, the database allows entering the names of the producer(s) and director(s) of each quoted film, even if they do not appear in the indexed document. However, every piece of information not coming from the indexed document has been segregated and clearly identified as such, in order to retain the possibility of limiting a search request to documents explicitly referring to particular agents.

Apart from these normalization issues, another argument in favor of GRAFICS' indexing enterprise is that the database and search engine on which it relies can also be made to perform some forms of automated statistical analysis. For example, a researcher interested in the rise of the star system might want to see how many indexed newspaper documents from the year 1909 refer to film actors and actresses ("performers" function) and then, by repeating the same query for the subsequent years and comparing the resulting figures with those obtained for the "production" and "direction" functions, uncover some salient features of the evolution of promotional discourse. It would moreover be possible to generate figures dealing specifically with advertisements or reviews, since the types of documents, along with the types of publications, have also been indexed in the database.

Such combinations of research criteria could simply not be accommodated by search engines relying solely on OCR-generated files. Another fundamental drawback of OCR is that it greatly reduces the likeliness of an unexpected discovery. As anybody who has done historical research can testify, groundbreaking discoveries are often made by accident rather than through targeted searches. OCR only permits one to find what one is looking for. On the other hand, OCR unquestionably remains the best tool for the study of the evolution of the nomenclature of film-related terms. It can easily retrieve the earliest uses of such connoted words as "nickelodeon" and "photoplay", or identify the periods during which the use of these words peaked. It also remains extremely useful for preliminary samples aiming to gauge a newspaper's level of coverage of moving pictures. In the end, it really seems that indexing and OCR should be conceived and used as two complementary research tools. There is no arguing that in a perfect world, historical newspaper collections would all be both indexed and treated with OCR software.

We hope to have demonstrated that the phenomenal progress of digital tools did not render obsolete the type of systematic survey and indexing work pursued by GRAFICS since the 1990s. Quite on the contrary, it is our opinion that, by disseminating the rewards of this innovative enterprise outside of a small select circle, digital technologies have made it more relevant than ever. Let's now hope that this exponentially increased ease of access will stimulate researchers, but also film and history devotees, as well as anybody with a passing interest in early and silent cinema, to find new uses for the surprising variety of documents that can be found in old newspapers and magazines. Over its first decade, GRAFICS' newspaper project has generated several major research projects, such as the *Silent Era Québec Filmography* and Germain Lacasse's study of film lecturers. There is no doubt that several other projects still lie dormant in GRAFICS' newspaper database and in the digitized collections of its partners.

The filmography of the films shot in Québec during the silent era clearly illustrates the importance of local newspapers during this period.[7] Researchers analyzed all available information relating to cinema not only in the newspapers, but also in the trade press, companies catalogues, censorship files, and other archives. This research brought to light, first of all, the existence of hitherto forgotten films. Secondly, it made it possible to determine how films were produced, advertised, and received by the public and assimilated by specific communities. The copious amount of information available on film exhibition made it possible to introduce a considerable amount of documentation that is not provided in film catalogues or the trade press. The way a film's title could vary throughout the province, for example, demonstrates the importance of the exhibitor during this pre-institutional era of film history. Exhibitors re-named films in order to highlight whichever elements they thought more attractive to their own audience. The filmography is thus pre-institutional in that it provides disparate information and documents the heterogeneity of film-related activities. The filmography also embodies the period's intermediality, drawing on sources other than those of the film world and documenting the way cinema interacted with other media. We thus see the special place moving pictures occupied at the time: cinema was a new, unstable and hybrid practice which was appropriated by other practices and institutions, but it also soon freed itself from this appropriation in order to establish its autonomy and legitimacy and constitute its own specific sphere of influence

---

7   This research was subsidized by the *Social Sciences and Humanities Research Council of Canada*. It is headed by Pierre Véronneau, with André Gaudreault and Germain Lacasse as co-researchers.

within an effervescent, intermedial environment, in which large-circulation newspapers, telephony, radio and other media were also rapidly expanding.

The indexing of the newspapers led to the discovery that many films were shot in Québec and in Canada, both by Canadians and foreigners. So another project grew out of the first: a transnational filmography of films shot in Québec. For this team project, we decided to explore as many sources as possible to find information on the films in question. This first filmographic database was built in FileMaker, and a website was launched at the 2002 Domitor conference held in Montréal. Each entry provides technical information on the film (production company, date, etc.) as well as descriptions from period publications and critical commentary by members of the research team.

The goal of this filmography is two-fold: first, to establish an inventory of films shot in the province of Québec in the early years of film history and to make this information publicly available; and second, to attempt to understand how these films were received at the time they were produced and first viewed. This latter goal, of course, is much more difficult to accomplish than the former, but attempting it will allow us to demonstrate the specificity of early cinema and the transformations cinema has undergone over the past century. A study of the entries in this filmography will not only provide readers with information about the individual films but will help them to understand these films' history and, more specifically, the task of writing film history.

The filmography has been established on the basis of geographical territory. The films found here were not made by a particular production company or filmmaker, or produced in a particular country; instead, they were made within a given territory.[8] In some ways, it is a filmography that reveals the variety of films made within Québec and the diverse strategies that existed for distributing and exhibiting these films from a sort of pre-institutional and transitional era to the era of institutionalised practices and film-related government regulations. The filmography makes it possible to understand how film production and reception in Québec developed rather than simply highlighting the role of any given community or individual. It is also possible to use the filmography to study how various groups and communities responded to the appearance of a radically new apparatus and its equally novel practices and texts.

Within a comparative filmography, the research must pay attention to the origin of the production agents. During the pre-institutional period, many films were shot by foreigners wishing to show exotic locations and original situations. When the same locations and topics were shot by local agents, the

---

8   This point was elaborated by Pierre Véronneau at the 2006 Domitor conference held in Ann Arbor, Michigan.

point of view was different, as if those agents wanted to appropriate their own "foreignness", to show their own people and play on local identification. A good example for this are the films shot for the tercentenary of Québec in 1908: the one from Urban *(Québec: The Tercentenary Celebration)*, the one from Gaumont British *(Québec Pageant)*, the two from Vitagraph *(Discoverers: A Grand Historical Pageant Picturing the Discovery and Founding of New France, Canada* and *Québec Tercentenary Celebration)*, and the three shot by Léo-Ernest Ouimet *(Fêtes du tricentenaire, première série; Fêtes du tricentenaire, deuxième série: Tableaux historiques des Pageants; Fêtes du tricentenaire, troisième série: Partie indienne et de la cour)*.

There were many flaws and failures in the way the database handled the information. So in 2003 we decided to build a new database on a more rigorous and systematic basis, and import the content of the old database into it. The second database was done in Microsoft Access, and it was published on the Internet in fall 2006 at http://cri.histart.umontreal.ca/Grafics/fr/filmo/default.asp. In the final part of this article, we would like to point out some important features of this new version.

The original title is a key issue for a film. Generally, this is the title found in a producer's catalogue or on the film itself. It is important to indicate the source of the title. If the title is found in a source that is less reliable, e.g. a contemporary newspaper, the cataloguer can choose chevrons to emphasize that the title is only presumed to be the original title. In the absence of any contemporary documents, the cataloguer creates hypothetical titles, or draws on titles already attributed to the work by archivists or historians. Square brackets indicate a non-contemporary title, and a box can be checked in the case of an attribution. This small example shows how digital tools oblige us to structure and divide the information in separate and semantically well-defined data to allow the researchers to intersect the information and eventually draw their conclusions.

One of the major issues in building digital tools to handle audiovisual and film-related collections is to start with a strict analysis of the information that needs to be processed, to determine how it can be controlled with authority files, and to write elaborate cataloguing rules. The quality of information retrieval depends largely on the precision of the organization of data entry. Filmographic tools are useful in film studies that focus on production and exhibition. We are able to store information on shooting locations, screenings, persons and companies involved in the production, different kinds of sources, etc. The database also allows us to provide important content information, like the film's subject and genre. It was decided to use the FIAF subject headings as a standard. There is also a "Film Comment" field where you find comments on the film production and exhibition, and a "Film Context" field that documents the historical context of the film's subject. Sometimes even the entering of data might call for some annotation. We decided to complement many fields with a "Note" button which leads to comments on the data, transcriptions of articles and other pertinent information.

In 2004, a partnership agreement was set up between the *Cinémathèque québécoise* and the *Université de Montréal* to share some information gathered by GRAFICS. For instance, clippings and film catalogues were made available at the CQ media library. Part of the filmography was included in the CQ database *Ciné-TV*. This SQL database is divided into many modules that are linked together, for their filmographic part, by a core module called *Répertoire*, a "database" that may be a reference by itself (like the *IMDb*), and works as a point of access to all the collections (films, documents, and film-related collections like stills, posters, archives) and all the research tools of the *Cinémathèque*. The existence of this module allows the researcher to cross-cut information and to find all that is accessible at the *Cinémathèque québécoise* on a specific title, agent or topic. Four collections, *Canadian Cinema and Television, Videos, Film-Related Collections,* and *Documents*, are already on the Web (collections.cinematheque.qc.ca) and soon to be completed by the *Répertoire de la production audiovisuelle au Québec* (www.repertoireaudiovisuelquebec.ca).

In conclusion we may say that databases are among those digital tools that can have a great effect on film research and film studies, providing an in-depth indexation and standardization of the information, especially for subjects, names and titles. It is also important to interconnect between databases as much as possible to share their strength and multiply their effects. The example of the two databases of the GRAFICS (filmography and newspapers) and the one of the *Cinémathèque québécoise (Ciné-TV)* shows that through co-operation between institutions and research projects, it was possible to develop powerful tools to access and document silent cinema in Québec, and make it available on the Internet.

Bibliography

Gaudreault, André, and Germain Lacasse: *Au pays des ennemis du cinéma: pour une nouvelle histoire des débuts du cinéma au Québec*. In collaboration with Jean-Pierre Sirois-Trahan. Québec: Nuit blanche, 1996.

Harry van Vliet, Karel Dibbets, Henk Gras

Culture in Context

Contextualization of Cultural Events

Introduction

The collective memory of the Netherlands has been 'solidified' as cultural heritage in an enormous quantity of archives and collections of books, paintings, films, archaeological remains, folkloric artefacts, and other art and audiovisual objects. For primarily historical reasons, these objects have ended up in a large number of different buildings and collections. The physical restrictions to heritage material place limitations on visitors and researchers. Related objects are often stored at different locations. The consequence of this is that either the researcher or the object must make a journey, a situation which is not ideal where access to cultural heritage is concerned.

Digitization brings the promise of continuous access to cultural heritage collections because it eliminates physical preconditions for access with respect to time and place. This gives rise to all kinds of new possibilities for cultural recreation, tourism, research and education. Thus, the current ICT developments have also been taken up by government and cultural heritage institutions in order to bring into better view their public tasks pertaining to storage, availability and promotion of cultural heritage. As a result, there are currently various initiatives with respect to digitization and accessibility of collections via the Internet. One example is 'Memory of the Netherlands' ('Geheugen van Nederland'), a project at the Dutch Royal Library, which is unlocking various digitized collections.

While the access problem is receiving a good deal of attention from various national and international (research) programs, the question of how to define 'related objects' has received less attention so far. Alongside obvious cases such as 'all of a particular artist's paintings' or 'all objects found at a Roman excavation site', we can also place less obvious but equally relevant 'relations' between items such as a Dutch film distribution company and the films that were available in the Netherlands, or between membership of a cultural association and attendance of a theatrical performance. These relations are not 'more of the same', but rather require a different approach and perspective with respect to unlocking digital information 'surrounding' cultural objects. In this paper, we will provide an initial description of the *Culture in Context* research program which we have in mind.

The Cultural Infrastructure as Context

Relations between film circulation, screening history and distribution companies, or between education, membership of a cultural association and attendance of a particular theatre in Rotterdam are relations which go further than a grouping of cultural objects by artist, style, period and institutional framework. These kinds of relations touch on a much wider 'infrastructure' of the cultural and socio-economic context. This perspective on the wider (cultural) infrastructure is well suited for cultural events such as theatrical performances and film screenings.[1] These events are no longer there and can only be 'recalled' on the basis of (leftover) contextual information. The text or film stored is just one part of it; the venue of the show, the composition of the audience, staging notes, program sheets and reports in the press are objects which are at least just as important for assessing the totality of a show. Relevant information for the representation of these kinds of cultural events can be found not only in the cultural domain, but equally outside of it. It may include, for instance, tax information, geographical data, genealogical details, etc. Given the necessity of recovering lost cultural events via residual contextual information, we must have an eye for the richness of the cultural infrastructure and its larger socio-economic context, in its full width and depth. The enrichment of cultural objects by means of contextual information is no mere triviality, rather it is the only way to 'capture' the cultural 'object'.

The importance of context is perhaps most evident in a museum for the theatrical arts. This can be clearly seen at the Theatre Institute of the Netherlands (TIN). The unique aspect of its collection is that the central object, the theatrical performance, is entirely absent. A performance is an event, a meeting of players and spectators in a space. You cannot store this kind of event; not the actors or audience at any rate.[2] There are costumes, scripts and photos which commemorate a performance, but the performance is gone forever once it is over. Thus, there is a large void in the Theatre Institute of the Netherlands

---

[1] Actually, all historical events share the fact that they are no longer available. For instance, the army museum can only show the context of the Battle of Waterloo.

[2] An integral video recording of a performance also has its limitations, if only in the choice of camera angles and framing, which involves 'cutting' back and forth between different cameras in order to provide the best possible picture of the event (for an example, see: www.fabchannel.com). Furthermore, even today it is only a small number of performances that are recorded in full.

where other museums can display a plethora of works of art to demonstrate their identity. Interestingly, this vacuum is the archive's most valuable possession. In the absence of a central object, the TIN collects as many artefacts and as much information pertaining to the performance as possible: set designs, costume sketches, scripts, soundtracks, portraits, playbills, reviews, etc. This is a specialization in paraphernalia, theatrical remnants which can be used to document and reconstruct a performance. The TIN has become an expert in the collection of context. Even its database is completely geared toward contextual information: it links the most diverse objects with one another around an empty core.

Providing access to cultural heritage is of course a precondition for enabling people to familiarize themselves with it, but 'access' does not mean much unless it is access to rich information. Cultural objects did not come about in isolation and are used in a communal context. Thus, their reconstruction will also have to break through the isolation of the preserved cultural object as much as possible by weaving it into a web of relations with other cultural objects as well as contextual information. This is what we mean by the term *rich* information. The added value here is that this kind of enrichment makes the visitor's experience more profound, increasing opportunities for recognition and providing more fuel for reflection. For the latter, of course, our thoughts go mostly to the 'professional' visitor of the cultural heritage: the scholar. The researcher is able to attain a more extensive 'data pool' thanks to the richness of the information, the web that is woven around data which lack even a superficial relation. This data pool is the basis for conducting (historical) analyses which have not yet been carried out or which can accentuate or refute current notions based on fragmented, incoherent and isolated information (Gras/van Fliet 2004).

The Digital Infrastructure as Context

Incidentally, the promise of digital evolution does not immediately solve all of the problems related to access, enrichment and presentation of the cultural heritage. Digitization continuously proves to be a complex and slow (i.e. difficult) process which drains a great deal from budgets in the cultural heritage sector. The first problem with respect to access is still that, just as the physical objects are stored in independent collections, the digital equivalents are also stored in many non-interoperable databases. Even if this problem is solved, we will still have the problem of searching through millions of (heterogeneous) objects. Building on this, we have the challenge of arriving at combinations from the search results which provide more insight into, for instance, the painting being displayed or the historical performance. We then have the question of how to present the (combined) results in such a way that they respond to the needs of the person who asked the original question. And this (automatic) personalization is far from trivial.

Cultural heritage institutions scarcely meet the first challenge of digitization. For the time being, the dynamics of digital cultural heritage lie in the digitization of one's own collections within one's own walls. Thus, the *Geheugen van Nederland* website (www.geheugenvannederland.nl) is no more than a web page of handy links to isolated digital collections rather than an integral access point to Dutch cultural heritage. The dream of an integral search engine which can search straight through the archives and collections of different heritage institutions was high on the government's agenda in the year 2000, but not necessarily so on those of the institutions. Everyone seemed to concur that the user would benefit from unrestricted access to historical information. Furthermore, the development of the necessary toolkit, technically speaking, would not have to be a very formidable task. Therefore, in March of 2000, the ministry placed the *Archives on Display (Archieven in de étalage)*, as the report of the same name aptly indicated. Many heritage institutions snatched this up in order to display their treasure rooms online. They have made ample investments in the digitization and exhibition of their own collections. Yet, five years later, the wondrous search engine that can look straight through all of their databases is still a distant dream. New technology has hardly done anything to make the exchange and integration of information a reality in the heritage sector. The trends toward more convergence and transparency of information seem to be stagnating. New, opposing forces have arisen, while the old compartmentalization seems to be getting stronger. The institutions are still just making their island empires, but now digitally as well. Nor is there any (commercial) benefit in working together; instead, it is a matter of market shares and promoting one's own unique character. The interchange of feature films and documentaries between the broadcasting archive and the film museum, which has been fostered by the minister, is one of many examples. It also means that the information systems of these collections have little in common. The exchange and integration of data takes the lowest priority under such circumstances.

Yet the integration of the various collections is not an impossible task. In fact, the blueprint of the infrastructure can be sketched out on the back of a cigar box (Figure 1; taken from van Vliet/Velthausz 2002). The structure is dictated by the unification of the suppliers (cultural heritage institutions) and the users (visitors to the collections). The institutions digitize their own inventory, which will vary in size and complexity depending on the 'objects'. Specific services can be devised for each of these objects. Thus, smart algorithms can be used to determine whether there is a view of an image (visual material),

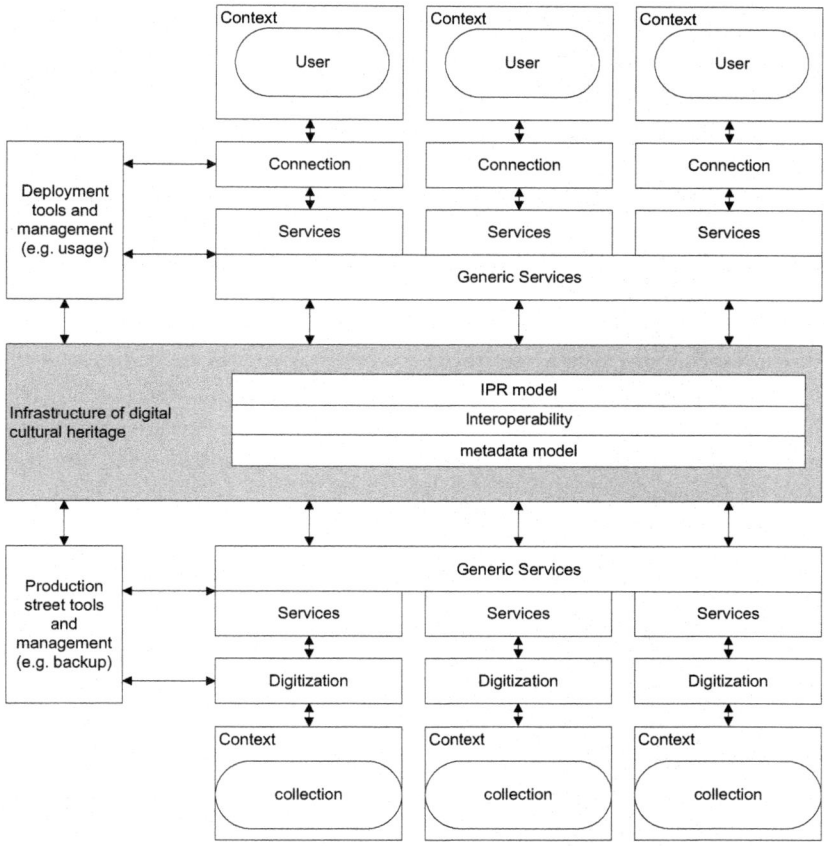

Figure 1. Blueprint of digital cultural heritage infrastructure

whether a question is asked in an audio fragment (audio material) or whether manuscripts can be converted into 'Times Roman' (text material). But in addition to these specific 'services', we also have generic 'services' which will be applicable for all institutions. They should all store the digital objects and provide them with metadata, for which ICT tools will be available for the implementation and/or administration. Agreements on these matters, such as which tools to use and what the minimal metadata will be, will already constitute an ample step towards integration. A good example of this is the DARE program (www.darenet.nl), which aims to integrate digital repositories of scientific collections. Taking steps to bring oneself into conformity with the agreements made there will provide a silent connection to a worldwide interface and access to other collections. We actually see the same pattern on the users' side: every user (group) will want to unlock the cultural information. Therefore, they will be using practically the same browser technology but will select their own channel or 'portal'. This is the case, for instance, with the scholarly researcher (essentialvermeer.20m.com), with the interested layperson (www.geheugenvan nederland.nl) or for the teacher and student (www.kennisnet.nl). It will not be long before these portals have been personalized in such a way that everyone has their own 'portal'. Here as well, specific services can be created for specific users: whether it is a matter of being able to analyze the data found via time series analyses (the scholar), of integrating the 'hits' returned into a genealogical summary (the interested layperson), or of making a PowerPoint presentation out of the figures found (the student). Again, certain services are generic for all visitors: for instance, everyone will want to be able to do searches, and anyone should be able to create a user profile to store search results and present information from them. More generic ICT tools can also be used here as well. Finally, there are a few issues that are critical with respect to integration: you must make some kind of agreement regarding the rights that come into play (known as *Intellectual Property Rights*); you will also have to make some kind of arrangement to enable the exchange of information, known as *interoperability*, which is definitely more than just a technical data issue, having ramifications for the exchangeability of the 'meaning' of information; and you should place attention on a *metadata model* so that information is described structurally and is easier to look up. Solutions (or partial solutions at least) are available for all three issues.

What you really have to bear in mind with this infrastructural blueprint is that 'the world' has its own will, is heterogeneous and complex and stays that way, and the same applies to the creation of digital collections from heritage institutions. A mandate as to how to carry out digital collection in a uniform way seems not to be viable in practice; more importantly, however, it would not do justice to the heterogeneity of the various objects. Of course standards can be agreed upon regarding how to store or describe things, but these will quickly prove to develop into 'dialects' used to capture the uniqueness of the objects: an archaeological find is something different again from a text, a film scene or a costume. The real crux of the matter lies in the standardization of the *exchange* of the data, i.e. the bridges that can be built between digital collections. This exchange touches on a technical bridge that must be built (exchange of data), a semantic bridge that must be built (exchange of meaning) and an organizational bridge that must be built (exchange of interests and rights). The latter two are by far the most onerous, the organizational bridge seemingly only passable if columns have been put in place which demonstrate the value of even talking about it all. The value is certainly there, we only need to bring it to light.

The Context of the Performance

A complex totality of solutions will have to provide an answer to the aforementioned pending issues in order to arrive at the integration of digital cultural heritage collections. Within the *Culture in Context* research program (CiC), we would like to focus on three sub issues which will be expressly investigated in connection with one another. These are the semantic interoperability, the enrichment process, and specific presentation tools for different users.

Semantic Interoperability

One characteristic of the digital heritage infrastructure is that the various collections are distributed and heterogeneous. This will not change in the future. One essential question here is how the meanings of information in the different databases can be linked up with one another. The indication 'tax' for an amount may mean something different from one database to another. Thus, the collective display (and perhaps even totaling) of the amounts as being tax amounts may result in a misrepresentation of the state of affairs. This is the problem of semantic interoperability: the meaningful interfacing of metadata. This is in fact the question of the meaning relations between different objects (and ultimately between these objects and 'the world') in different data collections and/or databases.

The solution to this that the *Culture in Context* program will develop is that of an ontology.[3] While this is not a definitive answer to the issue of interoperability, a well-directed effort can eliminate a great deal of ambiguity. This effort primarily consists in the definition of concepts and their interrelations, instances of those concepts, and attribute values.[4] The main concept for the *Culture in Context* program is the performance: the place where and the moment when a film or play is presented. The performance is related to some other concepts: places (countries, cities, cinemas, theatres), products (titles of films, plays), persons (involved in performances and other activities, such as producers, distributors and sponsors), and legal entities (companies, theatre troupes). These four terms can be used to describe and inventory the infrastructure of the film and theatre culture up to a certain extent. They are in fact the DNA of the film and theatre culture (Dibbets 2005). They enable the researcher to ana-

---

3   This may turn out to be rather a selection from existing ontologies and thesauri.

4   Ontology also essentially handles the multilingual problem because the ontology abstracts from it and the linguistic expression can be viewed as a specific phenotypical instance.

lyze networks and patterns in the film and theatre culture and to investigate the dynamics of the cultural infrastructure.

Enrichment

Fortunately, the historical event consists of the placement of meaningful combinations. These meaningful combinations are attained by making the meaning relation of the combination explicit on the one hand and by organizing the spectrum of the interrelations on the other hand. The former is resolved (in part) by the ontology, and the latter by making a lot of connections (possible) between different data sources. Enrichment is seen as both a deepening (more meaningful description of the collection) and a broadening (more meaningful 'links' with other collections and/or data) of information.

The *Culture in Context* program opts for the interlinking of a wide array of different data sources around the concept of performance and the detailed description of the data. A metadata model will be developed for this, which is related to the ontology so that (semi-)automatic metadating is possible on the basis of this ontology. Furthermore, individual records can be linked to sources and publications which contain more detailed information on that theatre, performance, person, title or project. If these sources are available online, then it is possible to make a link between the two. The solution consists solely of metadata and does not contain any digitized sources, images, etc. itself. There are sufficient instances which specialize in digital sources. The solution collects contextual information from these sources by making links to these sources and permitting these sources to make a link back. The difference between the suppliers of metadata and the providers of digitized objects is therefore relevant to further implementation. The creation and administration of these links and the addition of metadata according to a specific structure will be supported by the development of tools for allocating metadata in a coherent and transparent manner.

Users

'Meaningful' relations ultimately lie *in the eye of the beholder*. It will not suffice to merely 'ontologize' and enrich collections; instead, we must ensure that this enrichment also adds definite value for the actual use of the digital information. Various users can be anticipated who can derive added value from the enriched information surrounding 'the performance'. Historically interested parties working on, for instance, genealogical research would be able to unlock more encyclopedic knowledge regarding persons; educators would be able to use the material for illustration and further reflection on particular cultural events and/or opinions regarding them, etc. Specific analysis and presentation tools must be developed and attuned to the various needs of these distinct user groups.

One major user group is certainly the academic community which conducts research into the infrastructure of cultural life, especially the cultural offerings, the cultural participation and the cultural policy. Yet we can also distinguish a large multiformity of subgroups within this group. Contextual information on the infrastructure of cultural life is of interest to historians, e.g. due to the possibility of researching local activities with respect to film and theatrical events in light of marketing methodology, economic concentration and innovations in the context of a national industry. Social historians will gain access to detailed information on film showings and theatre performances, visitors and censorship, which offers a unique opportunity to analyze the shift in popular culture and the modernization of public entertainment. Urban historians will find information on buildings, their usage and the development of neighborhoods and cities. For social scientists, the related data on theatres and cinemas, management and presentations is a challenge to produce an analysis of social networks and development in their time. Ethnologists will enjoy a rich context of information on the treatment and reception of foreign films and theatrical repertories in a local setting, which enables cultural exchange in a comparative perspective. Finally, theatrical and cinematic scholars will be able to fulfill their hearts' desires by interlinking the relationship between programming, attendance rates, reviews and performance analyses and arriving at a unique historical study on reception, as well as a 'cross-medium comparison' study by investigating the interdependencies of theatres and cinemas.

Geographic analyses, comparison in time and comparisons between film screenings and theatre performances are some of the possibilities that come to mind. It must be clear here that the data are certainly of such a nature that complex data analyses, like time series analyses, are possible.[5] Yet not every analysis has to go in depth immediately. Researchers must have the option to pose questions at different levels and derive relevant information from them. We penetrate, as it were, deeper into the context and its relationships, for more and more detailed information. Below are a few sample questions (in ascending order of complexity):

---

5   See: Gras/Franses.

- Which films were shown and where?
- Where was *Who's Afraid of Virginia Wolf* put on with actress Ank van Moer?
- Which actors have played *George* and *Martha*?
- How many films were censured?
- Did Royaards' *As You Like It* receive more spectators in the first tier than in the gallery?
- Did it receive more spectators in The Hague than in Haarlem?
- What programming did cinemas use, and how did they differ in different cities and in what ways (genre, country, censorship)?
- How did the social make-up of the French Opera season ticket holders in The Hague size up in relation to the those of the *Haags-Franse Opera* in Rotterdam in the 1830's, and how did these compare with the German Opera 1860-1882 and the *Opera Italiana* in The Hague and Rotterdam (1933)?
- What film programming and distribution circuits can be identified and how have they changed over the course of time?

But it is not only the scholar who will find useful information. Digital context data from the cultural infrastructure of film and theatre presentations is well-suited for research projects pertaining to local history, cultural heritage and film and theatre culture. These attest to the representation of local identity and personal experience and can be used to draw links with super-regional contexts and developments. The information can be easily included in exhibitions, websites and research projects by museums, archives, schools and universities. Finally, there are also immediate practical advantages with respect to cultural heritage. In the coming years, the historical value of hundreds of thousands of objects must be appraised in order to make a decision with respect to preservation and digitization. This selection gains a great deal of validity if contextual information is available regarding the potential relevance of the object. The copyright problem can be handled in the same vein. Copyright information only refers to an individual object up to a certain extent. In many cases, this information must be derived from the relationship with other work, other authors, and the historical context. Digital context data can also provide support here by offering a rich environment in which the object was created and used.

If we refer back to figure 1, the three issues on which *Culture in Context* is focusing connect up with three basic components of the infrastructure we have outlined here.

1   On the production side, the emphasis is on the development and implementation of generic services, namely tools for enrichment of presentations via (contextual) metadata.

2   For the central infrastructure, the emphasis is on creation and administration of an ontology for 'the presentation' as a (partial) solution to semantic interoperability and the development of an associated metadata model.

3   On the side of the unlocking, specific services and/or tools for the analyses of the data files for e.g. scientific research are being developed.

We would like to stress that the *Culture in Context* program is focusing first and foremost on the enrichment, which includes the 'broadening' of scope via the stimulation and facilitation of the interfaces between various digital collections. The other two components (set-up of the central infrastructure and specific tools for unlocking) are viewed as being necessarily bound up with it in order to make the enrichment as efficient and effective as possible and to provide the necessary proof for the added value of the approach.

Two Examples

The first steps toward setting up context datahubs have already been taken for both film screenings and theatrical performances. These are the *Cinema Context Collection* of the University of Amsterdam and the *Netwerk Theaterbestanden (Theatre File Network)* of the University of Utrecht.

Cinema Context

Cinema Context is a website for research into the history of film culture.[6] The main question here is how to explain the fact that the integration of film and cinema in Dutch society deviates so strikingly from that of neighbouring countries. Cinema attendance has always been much lower compared with the normal European levels; the country also had far fewer cinemas per capita. To

---

6   In the *Cinema Context* project, researchers are cooperating with archives: the Universiteit van Amsterdam and the Universiteit Utrecht have joined forces with the Filmmuseum and The Netherlands Institute of Sound and Vision. The project was funded with an investment subsidy by the Netherlands Organisation of Scientific Research (NWO), while the technical infrastructure was developed at the Digital Production Centre of the University Library of Amsterdam. The project was completed in 2006. All data are freely accessible for researchers and the general public at www.cinemacontext.nl.

gain insight into the structure and development of Dutch film culture, it was important to find out more on the screening history of films. Almost nothing is known on this topic. As much as we know about the films that have been made, we know very little about their screening or interest in them or about cinemas, proprietors, distributors, musicians, etc.

Cinema Context is both an encyclopedic reference work and an analytical tool. Not only can you look up information in it, but you can also analyze this information. The data collected are suitable for qualitative and quantitative research. You can use *Cinema Context* to look up elementary data on a particular film, screening, censorship decision, cinema, cinema manager, lecturer, theatre company, etc. For instance, you can find out which films were first shown where and when. At the same time, all of the data are available as a complex totality. You can use them for statistical analysis, for an investigation into the growth and expansion of the local and national film culture or for a study of social networks in cinema chains and screening circuits.

It does not appear to be difficult to link the collected contextual information and/or metadata to information from entirely distinct areas of knowledge. For instance, *Cinema Context* can provide the addresses of all cinemas in the Netherlands with a geographic location, the latitude/longitude coordinates. These coordinates comprise the key to geographic information systems (GIS). They open the door to enormous data files for socio-geographic and demographic research. *Cinema Context* can link its data and analyses to private data on local film culture. For instance, it is possible to draw a relationship between the history of a cinema and the changing make-up of the population in the surrounding area. You can also visualize the geographic distribution of the cinema business in the Netherlands over the course of time. You can chart the route that a traveling cinema followed prior to the First World War. Or you display the location of a cinema via a link to a digital street plan, which was unlocked with the same coordinates. Audiovisual archives no longer enter into the matter, while the historian's radius of action is becoming much larger.

Theatre File Network

The *Netwerk Theaterbestanden* was originally set up to test the traditional exposition of theatre history. This exposition assumed that in the 18th century the elite opted for classical drama and the common populace opted for the burlesque. The first half of the 19th century witnessed the strong rise of melodrama and the elite left drama and flocked to the opera. After 1870 the bourgeois elite reconquered the theatre for themselves. By means of a series of databases in which ticket sales by circle and by theatre have been referenced to the performance (and the artists), time series analyses were applied to test whether the differentiation in taste (for instance: elite = first tier = classical and other 'high culture' whereas 'the rabble' = gallery = melodrama) was in fact as strong as purported by the traditional exposition. This proved to be incorrect when taken over the entire research period (1699-1974). From 1700 up to around 1850, the main finding was that theatre attendance was dictated almost entirely by season and audience loyalty. People hardly ever selected 'a performance', and even when they did it was not until around 1974, the end of the data series. The social characteristics of theatre-goers according to the traditional exposition were then tested by making a prosopographic database of the shareholders, season tickets, and ticket vendors. These data refute the hypotheses of the traditional exposition, albeit more so in Rotterdam than in The Hague, where the rift between opera-goers and drama-goers was much wider, due in part to the Royal Court and the centers of government.

These databases also provide encyclopedic knowledge, on the repertoire (of each theatre), the artists and the interest, as well as on persons who ran the theatre, the supporters, season ticket holders and ordinary ticket holders. Here as well, the rather detailed databases can be further linked up with existing databases with data on theatrical performances and their contexts, as well as to geographical information and thus also to the social make-up of the neighborhoods from which the audience came. Moreover, the Rotterdam prosopography has a genealogical component because they also looked up data on the parents and grandparents (provided they were born in Rotterdam, Kralingen, or Delfshaven) of participants in the theatre culture who were born in Rotterdam. This information proved to be quite meaningful for Rotterdam: the elite neighborhoods produced the most spectators known by name and this increases after 1887, when a new Groote Schouwburg (Great Theatre) was built in a new neighborhood for the business elite.

To answer the question whether the 19th century café-theatres otherwise functioned as the 'great' theatres, a database has been built for performances outside of theatres, also with rich contextual information (currently covering 1770 to 1856). This database, if further expanded, may become an important link between the 'high-culture' play and opera files and cinema culture.

What these two examples demonstrate is the added value of collecting contextual information and integrating it for new and improved analyses. Here, this concerns source material such as ledgers from film showings and theatre performances, advertising, entertainment sections, reviews and essays from newspapers, theatrical archives on theatre programs, archives with prosopographic data, director's notebooks, scripts and prompter's scripts, posters and playbills, tax data (entertainment tax in particular), shareholders' stocks and stocks from sponsors and subsidizers. The recent publications based on this material are still merely an initial taste of the many perspectives that are possible with respect to the rich material assembled, and, as far as the *Culture in Context* program is concerned, we are only yet witnessing the beginning.

The Context as Enrichment

The *Culture in Context* program must result in the integration of digital sources and contextual information into a digital knowledge infrastructure in the field of film and theatre culture. The result is a network of databases on the infrastructure of cultural life and especially cultural offerings, cultural participation, and cultural policy. The infrastructure is held together semantically by an ontology on 'the performance' and consists of metadata that have been implemented on the basis of a metadata model. Supported by enrichment tools and specific analysis tools, meaningful historical information can be provided in a user-friendly manner for different target groups such as scientists.

The enrichment of the *Culture in Context* program itself is the priority for the reinforcement of the cohesion of archives and museums by taking contextual information as the starting point and by creating a platform for information management in this field. Not only is new information added to the artefacts regarding how they were used, sold and evaluated, but new links are also made with data from other collections, which produces a more complete and sometimes surprising new picture of the artefact. Thus, contextual information is a medium that brings diverse and diffuse museum objects into relation with one another and thus serves as fuel to propel the development toward integral access.

Secondly, enrichment will enable us to break through the fragmentation and isolation of information which makes research impossible. This research is in a better and more balanced position to conduct descriptive and enlightening studies by drawing new relationships. The tools for enrichment and analysis make this quicker and easier. This also opens the door to the perspective of international research. International comparative research in the field of performance history will also finally be within reach. There are many kinds of local research in this field in various countries, but there are no methodologies or technology to consolidate and analyze the diffuse data. An initial category of questions pertains to a comparison of film and theatre culture in different European cities, regions and countries. A second group of questions focuses on border areas, where the cultural and economic boundaries are often fuzzy. Sometimes these areas are under more influence from cultural centers on the other side of the border, such that the distinction between center and periphery of the nation comes to be seen in a new light. Thirdly, research into international distribution patterns will experience a boost; thus, the question of whether American films have been distributed in the same manner throughout Europe is relevant.

Thirdly, attention for the meaning of information in different collections means that advancements can be made in the development of a common language and the transparency of the basic material. A simple but telling example here is translations of titles. Title translations are an international problem in the identification of performances in the past. We do know that many foreign plays have been performed in translation and that many films were imported from other countries, but there exists no comparative overview of these translated titles. This impedes local research, while international comparative studies are rendered nearly impossible. It also frustrates the interfacing of the national data collections with international systems. The *Culture in Context* program fulfils this need by referencing the original title with various translations. There is common interest in a data hub with a reliable concordance list of film and play titles. This interest can also be passed on to other 'attributes' and concepts and their interrelations. This motivates our attention to a presentation ontology.

Fourthly, the future of the historian also comes into play. The digitization and re-orientation toward the public role of museums and archives tap into another audience: they are currently focusing more on education, entertainment and tourism than on historical research. This is something which historical scholarship still needs to get accustomed to and find a niche in (Dibbets 2005). Historians themselves must also be reintegrated with the new digital infrastructure. The allure of a rich pool of historical information may be precisely such that the historian will again play a relevant and unique role in the relationship with archives and museums.

More concretely, the *Culture in Context* program will work to link up digital collections by creating a platform of information management in this field, a portal where the linked data take center stage instead of the individual collections. This information management will consist of the creation and administration of a presentation ontology and an associated metadata model, and the development and implementation of support tools for the allocation of metadata, (automatic) metadating of cultural context information, the ability to make (statistical) inquiries into the data pool and the (graphic) representation of these results. The organization will seek to make contact with (inter)national collections pertaining to theatre and film in order to link them up.

Information on the context of film showings and theatre performances, such as the showing, circulation, reception, etc., has not as of yet been systematically collected and recorded. Film and theatre culture do indeed have the attention of science, but historians generally focus on individual performances without examination of the context. Our knowledge of this context is particularly fragmented, incoherent and full of holes. Therefore, it is this knowledge of the context which must be prioritized in the digitization process of cultural archives and collections. Without supplemental information, a historical source has no meaning and is worthless to our understanding of the past. The examples from the *Cinema Context* website and the Rotterdam database indicate the magnitude of the (scientific) gains if this context is mapped out and linked up with pre-existing information/collections. The Culture in Context program will contribute to systematically filling in this gaping hole in contextual information. It will therefore be indispensable for current and future research on film and theatre history. It will also place the Netherlands in a unique position vis à vis the international research given that these contextual data are not systematically available in other countries either.

Bibliography

Archieven in de etalage. Zoetermeer: Ministerie van OCW, 2000.

Dibbets, Karel. "Op zoek naar een digitale conservator." *Jaarboek Stichting Archief Publicaties* 5 (2006): 189-197.

Gras, Henk, and Philip Hans Franses. "Did men of taste and civilization save the stage? Theater-going in Rotterdam 1860-1916. A statistical analysis of ticket sales." *Journal of Social History* 36.3 (2003): 615-655.

Gras, Henk, and Harry van Vliet. "Paradise lost nor regained: Social composition of theatre audiences in the long nineteenth century." *Journal of Social History*, 38.2 (2004): 471-504.

van Vliet, Harry, and Daan Velthausz. *Position paper eCulture.* Enschede: Telematica Instituut, 2002.

John Sedgwick

Measuring Film Popularity

Principles and Applications

Film popularity is an important subject for film historians and film theorists because of what it tells them about the tastes and preferences of film audiences and the strategies developed by producers to direct and satisfy them. Critical to this perspective is the assumption that filmgoers are, for the most part, attracted to the cinema primarily by the qualities inherent in the films they go to see: or, to put it another way, although there may be many reasons why filmgoers choose to see a particular film at a particular cinema, at a particular time, and on a particular date, in general these reasons are dominated by the anticipated quality of the chosen film. How else is it possible to explain the fact that in more-or-less all cinemas everywhere, attendances, and with them box-office revenues, varied (and vary today) greatly from film programme to film programme?[1] The incontrovertible fact that different films attracted varying numbers of filmgoers to the same cinema provides justification for the development of a methodology that connects levels of film popularity, empirically established, with the particular film characteristics that attracted audiences at moments in time, and over periods of time that can be shown to be characterized by life-cycle limitations that result from the persistent underlying desire for (not too off-the-wall) novelty on the part of audiences. Although this chapter confines itself to the empirical issue of how film popularity can be measured, it should be seen as a contribution to the development of such a methodology.

Of course, film popularity also matters to the agents who are instrumental in supplying movies for audience consumption – namely, producers, distributors, and exhibitors. Within a capitalist context, these agents are compelled to produce a rate of return on capital that is positive within a time frame that is, if not contractually, then implicitly, defined by the need to keep shareholders and project-specific investors confident and happy. If they are not able to do this they either go out of business or behave as benefactors. For producers, distributors and exhibitors, films represent a flow of revenue to be set against costs – the greater the popularity of a film the greater is its revenue stream. Between them these agents make contracts that reflect their respective market power. For instance, from the sound period onwards distributors raised their

---

1 Perhaps with the exception of the first decade in movie history, 1895 to 1905.

supply price (measured as a proportion of the box-office takings) when handling 'hit' movies, leaving the exhibitor with a smaller share of a larger revenue pot (see Hanssen 2005).

The purpose of this chapter is to discuss various ways of measuring film popularity and, in particular, to explain my approach to handling datasets where audience numbers and/or box-office takings are not known. The chapter is in three sections. Section 1 develops the link between the willingness-to-pay principle and film popularity; section 2 examines the methodological problem that emerges if attendance data are not available, and discusses the practice of using the POPSTAT index of film popularity; and section 3 develops an application of POPSTAT. In places the chapter may seem overly technical. However, if at the end of it the reader is persuaded that the methodology is capable of applications from which new insights into our knowledge of film reception and audience tastes may be gathered, it will have served its purpose.

1   Willingness-to-pay

Economists treat consumers as utility seekers who are rational, in that they prefer more to less utility, but who experience diminishing amounts of extra utility as they consume increasing amounts of a commodity. In the context of filmgoing, audiences prefer Film A to Film B if the former promises higher levels of cinematic utility, but the repeated viewing of the same film reduces dramatically the additional pleasure derived, leading to the result that, as a general rule, adult audiences do not watch the same film over and over again. Economists also apply the concept of opportunity cost to consumption, maintaining that in choosing Film A ahead of Film B filmgoers understand that the cost of making this choice is the loss of utility that occurs as a consequence of not viewing Film B. However, although Film A may be viewed in preference to Film B, it might well be the case that a first viewing of Film B is then preferred to a second viewing of Film A – in this case the opportunity cost of not seeing Film B is greater than the anticipated benefit of watching Film A for a second time.

With most commodities that are scarce in supply, relative to demand for them, consumers are willing to pay more for a good that yields higher levels of utility – of course, if it were a good that is scarce in supply, but nobody wanted it, then nobody would be willing to pay a price for it at all! As examples of scarcity sensitivity, one has only to think of the prices that some football supporters are willing to pay to watch their favourite football team play in the final of a major international competition, or the prices that ballet lovers are willing to pay to watch their favourite dancer in a ballet that they adore. Film lovers would behave in exactly the same way, if they needed to, but of critical importance in understanding the nature of film as a commodity is the fact that they don't need to, and the reason for this is that the movie business is built around technological and organisational capabilities that allow it to meet the demand for a movie wherever it may emerge, with the proviso that a profit can be made by the agents involved in its supply.[2] Hence, unlike the hypothetical football match or ballet performance, although the utility promised by particular films may be extremely high for very many consumers, the industry ensures, through distribution and exhibition practices, that films that are popular with audiences are made less scarce in supply than films that are less popular. Arthur De Vany and David Walls (1996) have termed this phenomenon 'adaptive contracting'. The consequence of this is that, as a general rule, cinemas maintain a common admission price irrespective of the attractions being screened: film audiences are not required to pay a higher premium for film quality, no matter how compelling the promise of cinematic utility may be. It is interesting to note that this is not a new phenomenon. Kristin Thompson (1985) shows how well entrenched Hollywood distributors were from the late 1910s onwards, making the Hollywood product ubiquitous for audiences around the globe.

Adaptive contracting requires the exhibition side of the industry to adjust supply, in the form of the number of seats and screens and the length of playing time made available to particular films, in order to meet levels of demand for product which, when it is first released, are not fully known. In the movie business, supply adjusts to demand, but admission prices remain unchanged. The explanation for invariant cinema prices is that audiences take risks when seeing films that are new to them, because they cannot have complete knowledge of what they are going to see, and hence they know, from their past experiences of filmgoing, that their about-to-happen experience is likely to fall within a range of expected pleasures. Now, if prices were variable, so that higher prices were charged for films promising higher levels of cinematic utility, the downside risk faced by audiences would increase – a disappointing experience at a higher price is more galling for the consumer than a disappointing experience at a lower price. Thus, higher price levels would turn some consumers away from seeing films they might otherwise have seen, leaving cinema seats empty. Variable prices might turn risk adverse sections of the potential audience away from filmgoing altogether. Thus, the strategy of relatively low invariant prices has served historically to maximise attendances, given the sup-

---

2   See my discussion of the ontology of film as a commodity, in Sedgwick (2000: 7-16). A briefer exposition can be found in Sedgwick/Pokorny (2005b: 10-15).

ply of cinemas and seats and general level of cinematic demand that the strategy itself has, in part, created.

It may be objected that prior to the saturated release strategy of distributors, which emerged in the mid-1970s, considerable run-hierarchical differences in admission prices existed between first-run showcase cinemas situated in metropolitan centres and subsequent-run cinemas in the suburbs, provincial cities and small towns. In London during the mid 1930s, for instance, MGM's Empire, Leicester Square, had seating for 3,226 patrons and a top price of 72 pennies or six shillings (written 6/-).[3] Compare the revenue potential of this cinema with that of the 580-seat Belle cinema in Bolton, where the top price was just 9 pence (9d), or the 574-seat Empire in Portsmouth, whose top price was 15 pence or one shilling and threepence (1/3). Yet, all three cinemas screened the MGM society drama *Dinner At Eight* as a single feature. The film was premiered at the Empire, Leicester Square, on 17 November 1933, attracting audiences of 47,109 and 33,782, respectively, during the two weeks of its run (Eyles 1989). *Dinner At Eight* received six distinct bookings in both Bolton and Portsmouth, the final one of which in both cities was at the two above named cinemas, during the week commencing 23 July 1934. Different audiences, attending different cinemas, at different dates, paid different admission prices to see the same film. Had the patrons of the Belle, Bolton and the Empire, Portsmouth wanted to see the film earlier, they could have attended screenings of the film at its fifth-, fourth-, third-, second-, or first-run screenings in the two cities. Had they done, they would have paid higher admission prices and sat (probably) in more comfortable surroundings, thereby exercising a time and comfort preference for which they were prepared to pay a premium. However, the patrons of the Belle, Bolton and the Empire, Portsmouth were prepared to wait until *Dinner At Eight* filtered down the exhibition hierarchy; they paid less than they would have, had they seen the film earlier in its release, yet they paid no more to see it than they would have, had they seen much less popular films screened at the two cinemas. *Dinner At Eight* was not scarce in supply, and filmgoers who were content to wait, or were not willing or able to pay premium prices, could enjoy an evening's screening of *Dinner At Eight* for as little as 4 pence (4d) and 7 pence (7d) respectively.[4]

Thus, film is one of those commodities not rationed by price. Audiences do not have to pay higher prices to see the films of their choice, since the more popular they are, the greater is their availability. Further, because the relative prices of films do not vary with popularity, and audiences are willing to

---

3 See the annual Kinematograph Year Books for nationwide information about cinema addresses, ownership, seating capacity and admission prices.

4 Minimum prices given in the Kinematograph Year Books, 1932 to 1938.

pay these prices to watch the films of their choice, box-office data are an excellent measure of film popularity.

2 Measuring Film Popularity

At the present time, details of weekly box-office takings and the number of screenings are readily available for the top ranking films in the world's largest markets.[5] Hence, analysts now have first-rate data sources for investigating current film popularity patterns, at least at the macro level in those markets, a fact that partly explains the burgeoning film business orientated literature emerging from Business Schools and Economics Departments over the last decade.[6] However, with the rather important exception of the U.S., where the trade journal *Variety* has kept its readers informed about weekly box-office takings of first-run cinemas from the 1920s onwards, the availability of historic data of this type elsewhere is comparatively recent. Hence, historical studies of popular film outside of the U.S. have little hard evidence to support claims often made that particular audiences enjoyed Film X greatly, while Film Y was not to their taste. Paradoxically, historians working in the field of popular film in the U.S. have made very little use of the evidential weekly box-office data recorded in *Variety*.[7]

But in the absence of hard data about cinema attendances how can historians proceed without relying completely on anecdotal evidence? My 2006 study of the weekly attendance and box-office figures of the Regent, the largest first-run cinema in Portsmouth, England, during the 1930s, is unusual in Film Studies literature, partly owing to the fact that such sources of information are rare, and partly because quantitative approaches to analyses are not widely practiced. The Regent dataset, in the form of a ledger, is particularly rich, containing not only attendances *and* takings (which seems to be unique in surviving UK records), but also separate records of matinee takings, as well as confectionery, tobacco and ice cream sales (Sedgwick 2006).[8]

One of the questions that interested me was the extent to which films that were popular with first-run Regent audiences were similarly attractive to

---

5   See *Screen International*, and *Variety*.
6   See, for instance, the collections in De Vany (2004), and Moul and Shugan (2005).
7   See Street (2002), Sedgwick/Pokorny (2005a) and Glancy/Sedgwick (2007) as examples of work that has systematically used *Variety* box-office data.
8   My study was preceded by Sue Harper (2004). Professor Harper discovered the Regent ledger and kindly made her findings available to me. The ledger is archived at the Portsmouth City Museum and Records Office.

Portsmouth audiences in general, as those films passed through the exhibition hierarchy from box-office rich to box-office poor cinemas. The only information available about the films screened by other Portsmouth cinemas was the advertised programmes published daily in the Portsmouth *Evening News*. Clearly, an investigation of this kind required a methodology that allowed me to impute attendances/box-office revenues from those advertised programmes. Because of the onerous nature of recording these programmes in a database, data was collected for a single year (1934), during which time Portsmouth had 21 operating cinemas, screening films six days a week on weekly or twice-weekly change, single or (mostly) double-bill programmes.

Two closely related procedures were applied. The first linked the weekly box-office attendances of the Regent's 52 main film attractions screened in 1934 with the number of distinct bookings received by each of those films in the population of Portsmouth's cinemas. A correlation coefficient of 0.48 was found. So, while not a perfect fit, a positive association of some strength is evident. The fact that the correlation coefficient is not nearer in value to 1.0 might be the consequence of i) cinema exhibitors not always being able to access films of their choice, and ii) the tastes of audiences attracted to particular films screened at lower order cinemas not fully mirroring the tastes of audiences that had viewed the same films earlier, at the Regent.

Implicitly, the first procedure treats all cinemas equally. However, as is evident from the earlier discussion about the box-office potential of cinemas, it is clear that not all cinemas are of equal significance in the measurement of film popularity. The second procedure explicitly recognises this fact by assigning weights to cinemas in a population, based on their box-office potential (mid-price multiplied by seating capacity) expressed as a proportion of the mean box-office potential of all cinemas in that population. Accordingly, a cinema with a weight of 1 had a box-office potential equal to the mean box-office potential of the population of Portsmouth cinemas, a cinema with a weight of 2 had a box-office potential twice the mean and a cinema with a weight of 0.5 half the mean.

A value for each film booking is obtained by multiplying the cinema weight by the length of time (measured in a common unit such as days or weeks) that it was screened, and by its billing status (measured in this instance as 1 for a single billing, 0.8 as the leading film on a double bill programme, 0.5 as the joint attraction on a double bill programme, or 0.2 as the support film on a double bill programme). An aggregation of these values then generates a summary statistic for each film, which I call its POPSTAT score. Taken together, the POPSTAT scores of all films screened at least once in the cinemas of Portsmouth forms an index number series in which all films in the population stand in relation to one another in terms of their imputed popularity.

The major problem with the POPSTAT methodology is that it treats all films screened at each of the cinemas in the population equally: that is, it fails to reflect differences in box-office revenues generated by different films at a given cinema. Along with the two factors mentioned earlier, it is probable that this lack of sensitivity also contributes to a correlation coefficient of 0.45, describing the strength of association between the actual attendances of the 52 main weekly attractions screened at the Regent in 1934 and their subsequent POPSTAT scores, which is almost identical to that reported earlier for the association between Regent attendances and the number of separate Portsmouth bookings.[9]

3   An Application of the Methodology

A simple regression model using the ordinary least squares method suggests that attendances at the Regent explain only one fifth of subsequent POPSTAT scores.[10] Although this model is statistically significant at the 99.9 per cent confidence level, it clearly shows that other factors were at play. As mentioned earlier, one of these factors is likely to be differences in preferences among the two audience populations – the Regent audience and those attending all other cinemas in Portsmouth, captured by the POPSTAT methodology.[11] Through an analysis of the residual plot thrown up by the model, it is possible to identify those films in which tastes would appear to be distinctively different. This is depicted in Figure 1, and it represents, for each of the 52 films screened at the Regent, differences (termed 'residuals') between the predicted values of POPSTAT and actual values – values on the plot near to the horizontal axis represent films with values that are predicted closely by the model and those furthest away, films with values that are less well predicted. Two things to notice are: 1) most of the residual values are not clustered along the axis, although 36 of the 52 observations fall within a band bounded by one standard deviation above and below it, indicating the partial predictive capability of the model; and 2) expected values are equally distributed above and below actual values throughout the range.

---

9   The actual and predicted POPSTAT scores exclude the Regent.
10 It is likely that other factors, such as the weather, and local events, may all have played a part in affecting attendances, and, if built into the model they would have improved its explanatory power.
11 Sue Harper has given a colourful description of the likely social make up of the Regent audience. From this it would be strange to think that their tastes had been identical to those of audiences elsewhere in the City.

The hypothesis implicit in the model is one that is derived from the logic of the system of distribution and exhibition in which films appear first in box-office rich cinemas and then diffuse outwards in time and space through a run of lower order cinemas, namely, that films that are highly popular with the Regent audience will prove to be similarly popular with audiences attending lower order cinemas. Clearly the films represented by points in Figure 1 furthest from the horizontal axis depart markedly from this rule.

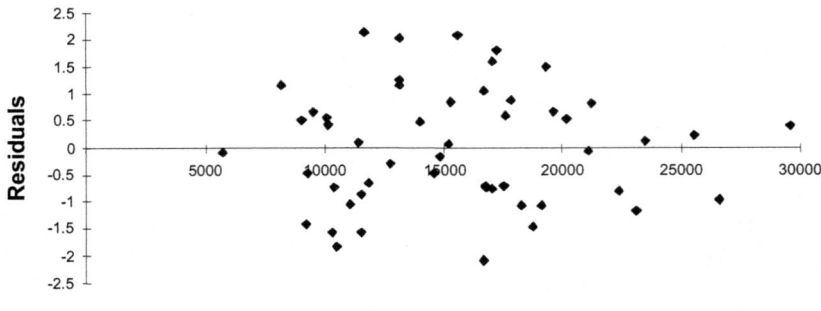

Figure 1. Plot of 'residual' values differentiating expected from actual POPSTAT values

The regression model can be used to identify those films that are at either end of the spectrum: films with high negative or positive residual values – films that the model predicts least well. These are films whose POPSTAT values are surprising, given the size of audience they attracted at the Regent. Table 1 lists them. It is divided into two sections, A and B, with Section A consisting of six films that significantly underperformed in Portsmouth cinemas, relative to their popularity at the Regent, and section B consisting of those films whose performance in the Portsmouth cinemas was surprisingly good, relative to the audience interest shown at the Regent. Organising the information in this manner makes possible a characteristics analysis (studios/genre/stars, etc.) of these films that might help to identify distinctive patterns of differences in film tastes between the two audience sets.

Although it is not the purpose of this paper to develop an analysis of these differences, some basic observations are: 1. Section A consists of films that achieved average or less than average attendances at the Regent – the mean weekly attendance for 1934 was 15,452.[12] The films came from three of the

---

[12] These films had not been especially popular in London's West End and provincial city first-run cinemas either, the highest rank of which was My Weakness, ranked 60th in 1933. See Sedgwick (2000: 266, Appendix 3).

major Hollywood studios but did not boast "A" category stars and with the exception of *Midnight Club* were very much concerned with detailed aspects of American life that did not appear to be particularly interesting for Portsmouth audiences. 2. Section B is made up of films that were on average a little more popular than those in Section A. Remarkably, Gaumont British films dominate, three of which had operetta-type musical qualities. A possible explanation for the significantly better performance of these Gaumount British films in the other cinemas of Portsmouth is connected with the quota provisions of the 1927 Cinematograph Films Act, which, in 1934, required all exhibitors to screen a not insignificant minimum of 15 per cent British films. It seems reasonable to suppose that to meet this requirement with a chance of making a profit, exhibitors preferred to screen those British films that were at least not unpopular with audiences. A more intractable problem lies with *It Happened One Night*. Given its success elsewhere in Britain – it was a national Top 10 film, and had Top 10 berths in the cinemas of Bolton and Brighton – it is not surprising that it was similarly popular with Portsmouth audiences; indeed, it was the most popular film of the year: what is surprising is its merely average performance at the Regent.[13]

Conclusion

Audience taste, its formation, and the manner in which it changes over time are important subjects in film studies and are key to understanding the reception of films at the time of their initial release. Film popularity is the most obvious manifestation of audience taste, and it is based upon the 'willingness-to-pay' principle, measured through attendance and/or box-office data. It is a concept that has both absolute and relative dimensions, in that knowing how films were received by certain sections of the audience, defined by, say, age, gender, socio-economic status and/or geography is essential in providing an evidence-based account of reception.

In the absence of attendance/box-office data, the POPSTAT methodology has been developed to give estimates of film popularity. The application of this methodology here builds upon a recent study of mine, published in *Cinema Journal*, dealing with filmgoing in Portsmouth in the 1930s. Based on a discussion of the assumptions implicit in the methodology, a simple model has been created to predict the values of the POPSTAT scores achieved by each of the 52

---

13 See Sedgwick (2000): Appendix 3 for the national charts for 1934; Table 5.7 for Bolton; and Table 6.4 for Brighton. The Portsmouth chart listings can be found in Sedgwick (2006: Appendix 1).

Film Title	Studio	Genre	Stars	Portsmouth billings	Regent attendances	Actual POPSTAT a	Predicted POPSTAT	Residuals col.7-col.8
(1)	(2)	(3)	(4)	(5)	(6)	(7)	(8)	(9)
Section A								
Midnight Club	Paramount	crime	Clive Brooks, George Raft	3	16,704	0.68	2.77	-2.09
No More Women	Paramount	drama	Edmund Lowe, Victor McLaglen	3	10,537	0.29	2.12	-1.83
Wharf Angel	Paramount	drama/ romance	Victor McLaglen, Dorothy Dell	3	11,565	0.66	2.23	-1.57
My Weakness	Fox	musical	Lillian Harvey, Lew Ayres	2	10,338	0.54	2.10	-1.55
Change Of Heart	Fox	drama/ romance	Janet Gaynor, Charles Farrell	3	18,783	1.52	2.99	-1.47
Turn Back the Clock	MGM	comedy drama	Lee Tracy, Mae Clarke	3	9,209	0.56	1.98	-1.42
Section B								
Evensong	Gaumont British	Drama/ musical/ romance	Evelyn Laye, Fritz Kortner	7	11,698	4.39	2.24	2.15
It Happened One Night	Columbia	Romance/ comedy	Clark Gable, Claudette Colbert	8	15,599	4.74	2.66	2.08
Unfinished Symphony, The	Gaumont British	biography/ drama/ musical	Mártha Eggerth, Hans Jaray	7	13,162	4.44	2.40	2.04
Jew Süss	Gaumont British	Historical drama	Conrad Veidt, Benita Hume	6	17,260	4.63	2.83	1.80
Turkey Time	Gaumont British	comedy	Tom Walls, Ralph Lynn	8	17,050	4.41	2.81	1.60
Chu Chin Chow	Gaumont British	comedy/ musical/ romance	George Robey, Fritz Kortner	7	19,284	4.52	3.05	1.48

Table 1.
Sources: The Regent Ledger; Portsmouth Evening News.
Note: a. Exhibition at the Regent is not included in the POPSTAT score.

main attractions screened at the first-run Regent cinema in 1934. The model has a low coefficient of determination, in that Regent attendance explain only one-fifth of subsequent POPSTAT scores, although it is possible to be very confident statistically about this. It suggests that, among other things, the tastes of the two audience sets (the Regent audience and the audiences of the other Portsmouth cinemas), in relation to the 52 films shown at the Regent, were far from identical. By then conducting an analysis of the differences between predicted and actual POPSTAT values it was possible to identify a series of films at either end of the range where these differences were greatest and draw some tentative conclusions.

One purpose of the chapter has been to show that economic reasoning and statistical methods have a part to play in presenting knowledge about filmgoing that is not otherwise discoverable or even expressible. They force the researcher to be explicit about assumptions behind the form of analysis conducted and to acknowledge that the methods adopted might be improved upon. Furthermore, such an approach can throw up new problems that require new scholarship, among which, in the context of this chapter, is the puzzle of the relatively poor (in relation to expectations) performance of *It Happened One Night* in Portsmouth's premier picture house.

Bibliography

De Vany, A., and W. Walls. "Bose-Einstein Dynamics and Adaptive Contracting in the Motion Picture Industry." *Economic Journal* 106 (1996): 1493-1514.

De Vany, A. *Hollywood Economics: How Extreme Uncertainty Shapes the Film Industry*. London: Routledge, 2004.

Eyles, A. "The Empire that was, 1928-61." *Picture House* 13 (1989).

Glancy, H. M., and J. Sedgwick. "Cinema Going in the United States in the mid-1930s: A Study Based on the *Variety* Dataset." *Going to the Movies: Hollywood and the Social Experience of Cinema*. Ed. M. Stokes, R. Allen, R. Maltby. Exeter: Exeter University Press, 2007.

Hanssen, F. "Revenue-sharing in movie exhibition and the arrival of sound." *An Economic History of Film*. Ed. J. Sedgwick, M. Pokorny. London: Routledge, 2005.

Harper, S. "A Lower Middle-class Taste-community in the 1930s: Admissions Figures at the Regent Cinema, Portsmouth, UK." *Historical Journal of Film, Radio and Television* 24 (2004): 565-587.

Sedgwick, J. *Popular Filmgoing in 1930s Britain: a Choice of Pleasures*. Exeter: Exeter University Press, 2000.

Sedgwick, J. "Cinemagoing in Portsmouth during the 1930s." *Cinema Journal* 46 (2006): 52-85.

Sedgwick, J., and M. Pokorny. "The film business in the U.S. and Britain during the 1930s." *Economic History Review* 58 (2005a): 79-112.

Sedgwick, J., and M. Pokorny. "The characteristics of film as a commodity." *An Economic History of Film*. Ed. J. Sedgwick, M. Pokorny. London: Routledge, 2005b.

Thompson, K. *Exporting Entertainment: America in the World Film Market 1907-1934*. London: BFI, 1985.

Jaap Boter, Clara Pafort-Overduin

Compartmentalisation and its Influence on Film Distribution and Exhibition in The Netherlands, 1934-1936

During the nineteenth and early twentieth century, Dutch society was strongly compartmentalised[1], with four major religious and ideological movements each commanding their own social infrastructure, including trade unions, schools, media and governance. Social interactions of members were supposed to be confined to their counterparts and only at the highest levels of society would representatives of these movements meet and work together. Though additional research from Blom and his co-editor Talsma has shown that this compartmentalisation was not always as strict as it was supposed to be, in general it is, as Knippenberg and Van der Wusten stated, still considered a strong explanatory model for the way Dutch society was organized during this period.

Such compartmentalisation may well have influenced the distribution of films. As its stories, characters and setting often relate to particular social groups and issues, reflecting or even challenging current status quo in a society, films likely have their appeal limited to particular compartments in a society. Holbrook and Grayson, and Kozinets provide some interesting examples from this in their work on film consumer behaviour. In our case, the Christian struggle in Nero's Rome of DeMille's *Sign of the Cross* (1932) is likely deemed more appropriate for the Catholic compartment than dancing beauty and lion tamer Mae West in Ruggles' *I'm No Angel* (1933). With Dutch regions strongly differing in the prominence of particular compartments, such influence should be evident in specific geographical distributions: films only to be shown in particular cities and/or cinemas, depending on the dominant compartment in that location. On the other hand, as suggested by Dibbets in the *Dutch Journal for Media History*, film exhibiters might try to stay away as much as possible from any ideological connotation, as this would limit financial success. In such cases, distribution patterns would reveal films being shown in any cinema, regardless of their contents. In sum, we conjecture that a historical analysis of the geographical distribution of films in The Netherlands in this period may serve as an appropriate testing ground to gain more insight into the role of compartmentalisation on film distribution and exhibition.

---

1   The Dutch word for this is 'verzuiling' and has also been referred to in English texts as 'pillarization'.

In this paper, we first discuss the nature of compartmentalisation in The Netherlands and the stance of the various compartments on films and film attendance. We then introduce our dataset of 23,674 film programmes over a three year period of 143 cinemas spread across the country and propose a method for analysing such data for patterns in distribution. While subsequent analyses indeed reveal particular patterns in the distribution of films, the interpretation of the results suggest that these are more likely attributable to general business economic motivations. We conclude with a discussion of our findings and propose avenues for further research.

Compartmentalisation in The Netherlands

From 1900 until 1930 Catholics and Protestants had emancipated and formed political parties that gained more and more power. The fear of a socialist revolution stimulated the strengthening of the own group even more. In the thirties four compartments crystallized: the Catholic, Protestant, Liberal and Socialist compartments. In hindsight, the Catholic and Protestant compartments not only were the largest compartments, each three times larger than either the Socialists or Liberals, but also are regarded as the best examples of true compartmentalisation. Both consisted of a cross section of all the different social layers in Dutch society, which was not the case with the Socialists (lower social classes) and the Liberals (higher social classes). But in terms of organization as unions, educational and cultural institutes, the Socialists were a good example of a compartment as well (Schuursma 2000: 190).

Ideally, this compartmentalisation meant that one would spend his/her life within a certain group. So if a man was a Catholic, his children went to a Catholic school, he bought bread at the Catholic baker's from the same parish and of course he would marry a girl of the same faith. But there was more to it. People wanted to spend there leisure time somewhere. To prevent that a youngster, a workman etc. would search his/her pleasures in the 'wrong' places, a dynamic club life came into being in the early teens and twenties of the twentieth century, with Catholic amateur theatre groups, Protestant camping societies, Socialist reading clubs etc. In 1924, the Socialists and the Nederlandse Verbond van Vakvereenigingen (Dutch Employee's Organisation) founded the Instituut voor Arbeiders Ontwikkeling (Institute for Labourer Education). To raise the intellectual level of its members, it offered lectures, theatrical performances and film screenings.

Since the Protestants did not want to have anything to do with cinema and even forbade cinema right from the start, one would expect to see less cinemas in heavily Protestant oriented regions (Van der Burg/Van den Heuvel 1991:

55). Catholics embraced cinema very early and tried to use the medium to convey the right moral message. When this did not work they were very active in censor committees to prevent their Catholic flock to watch the 'wrong' films. When in 1926 the law on national film censorship was finally effectuated it was still possible for local councils to have a local censor redoing the work of the national censor. Especially in Catholic councils this right was extensively used (Van der Burg and Van der Heuvel 1991: 55). Therefore we might expect different film programming in heavily Catholic oriented regions.

As shown in Figure 1, compartmentalisation had a strong geographical aspect. Especially the religious compartments of the Catholics and the Protestants were attached to certain Dutch regions. Figure 1 shows the results of the elections for the Dutch Parliament in 1933. Catholic parties (red shades), were heavily concentrated in the south. Voters of Protestant parties (overlapping blue shades), were more scattered with some strongholds in the centre, in the north and on the Zeeland Islands in the south west, with the so called 'Dutch Bible belt' stretching from the mid west through the centre to east and curving to the north. Voters of Socialist parties and voters of Liberal parties were spread in very much the same way (green dots). Both seem to mix rather well with Protestants, except for some parts in the centre. They are mostly concentrated around the large cities and to the north west of The Netherlands. Both groups were much smaller than Protestants and Catholics.

Given the strong geographical aspect of compartmentalisation in The Netherlands, one might expect particular films to be shown in particular cities or cinemas. For instance, DeMille's *The Sign of the Cross* (1932), if indeed deemed particularly appropriate for viewing by the Catholic compartment, is likely to be programmed primarily in cinemas in the south of the country.

Methodology

Dataset

The dataset used for this article was originally compiled by Pafort-Overduin for her PhD research on the popularity of three Dutch films made between 1934 and 1936: *De Jantjes* (1934, trans. *The Sailors*), *Bleeke Bet* (1934, *Pale Betty*) and *Oranje Hein* (1936, *Orange Harry*). *De Jantjes* was a huge success and beat every other movie from that period. It had 2,605 screenings, followed by *Modern Times* (1936) with 1,778 screenings. The massive success of *De Jantjes* prompted investors to have trust in a Dutch film industry, and after four years of almost no activity, the Dutch film suddenly bloomed.

The dataset contains information on 23,674 film programmes, featuring 2,402 individual films, shown between 1934 and 1936 in 143 cinemas in 18 Dutch towns. For fourteen of these towns, programme information was gathered by scrutinizing cinema advertisements in (local) newspapers between 1934 and 1936. Programme information on four further cities (Amsterdam, Rotterdam, The Hague and Groningen) was imported from the *Cinema Context Collection*. All together, the cinemas in these 18 towns cover 40% of the total number of cinemas in The Netherlands operating between 1934 and 1936. According to the *Cinema Context Collection*, 359 cinemas were operating between 1934 and 1936. The dataset used here covers 143 cinemas. Three cinemas were removed from the dataset because only a very small part of their film programmes could be reconstructed. Figure 1 shows the location of all cinemas that could be traced with the help of *Cinema Context* in yellow and the cinemas from the dataset in red. Although the selection slightly favours cinemas in the centre as compared to those in the south and north east of the country, the dataset covers most of the different parts.

The full dataset contains information on:

- the programming of fiction films: the date a film was shown, how many times a film was shown during a week, whether it was a Double bill or not;
- the film itself: year, country, production company, director and main stars;
- the exhibition place: location of the cinema in GIS code, the number of seats available;
- the advertisement of the film: was the director mentioned, was the production company mentioned and which stars were mentioned.[2]

For the present purpose, we compiled a dataset of screening incidence, with one line for each of the 2,402 films and one column (dummy variable) for each of the 143 cinemas to indicate whether the particular film was screened at this cinema or not.

---

[2] Since this information is not available in the *Cinema Context* database, it has not been used for analysis yet.

Figure 1. Distribution of compartments and cinemas across The Netherlands (1934-1936). In red areas voters voted mainly for Catholic parties, in blue areas voters voted mainly for Protestant parties, green dots show areas with voters for Socialist and Liberal parties (based on the 1933 General election; darker shades or higher density denotes greater dominance). Red dots denote the cinemas represented in our dataset; yellow dots denote other cinemas listed in *Cinema Context*.

Analysis

As outlined in our review of compartmentalisation in The Netherlands, we expect this dataset to show particular patterns, with individual films shown in specific regions and cinemas, depending on whether the compartment it was most suited for dominated in the region. Latent Class Analysis (LCA) is well suited for analysing such patterns as it simultaneously clusters both cases (films) and variables (cinemas). Also, as a form of 'fuzzy clustering' or mixture modelling, it addresses uncertainty in its output. For instance, it will assign films to clusters with a particular degree of certainty; a film may have a likelihood of 80% of belonging to cluster 1 and a likelihood of 20% to cluster 2. This is particularly apt for data with some degree of uncertainty, as historical data often can be. Finally, contrary to conventional forms of clustering (e.g., hierarchical clustering or k-means) there are straightforward statistical measures to determine the optimal number of segments and the quality of the solution.[3]

Note that our proposed methodology only looks at incidence and does not account for potential order effects. For instance, more complex models may account for the fact that film copies may travel in particular routes, with some cities or cinemas serving as typical opening night places whereas others focus on reruns of older films. In this first, exploratory research, we only look at whether a particular film has been screened at which cinema during the three year period.

Results

The proposed method results in seven clusters (Table 1), which can be divided into two categories: different types of 'filler' films (clusters 1, 2 and 3) shown in any cinema, and films screened at particular cinemas (clusters 4, 5, 6 and 7).[4]

Cluster 1 is the largest cluster with 1,147 titles and shows the most scattered collection of films, some very old films appear in this cluster that downsize the average year of production of this cluster. Almost 10% of the titles were produced in 1931. The films from cluster 1 were 'filler' films in the truest sense of the word as can be seen from the very low average number of screenings. This means that they were part of a very fast changing program; shown as a second film when a double bill was on or only screened at special children matinees. Most films came from European countries and small European production companies. Examples are *Bitter Sweet* (1933), directed and produced by Herbert Wilcox from Great Britain, or the German film company Nero Film that produced Pabst's *Die Büchse der Pandora* (1929).

---

[3] For a more in-depth introduction to mixture modeling in general of LCA in particular, see Wedel/Kamakura 2000.

[4] Further (statistical) details of the results and the choice for seven clusters are available from the authors.

	1	2	3	4	5	6	7
Size in %	47.7	17.0	15.5	7.2	5.0	4.4	3.2
Avg. year of release	1931	1933	1934	1934	1934	1934	1934
Dominant origin	EUR	US	EUR	EUR	DE	US	US
Production company	Small	Large	Small	Small	UFA	3 major US	MGM
Avg. # of screenings per film	26	114	158	510	234	268	321

Table 1 Cluster analyses of the film programming of Dutch cinemas 1934-1936

Cluster 2 resembles very much cluster 1 where age and programme schedule are concerned. The films are slightly more recent but still some very old ones appear: production years range from 1915 till 1936. Almost a third (32%) of the titles was produced in 1932. As in cluster 1 they were part of programmes that changed very often or consisted of double bills. On the other hand, these films could cover up to 73% (ABT in Alkmaar), 58 % (Olympia and Asta in Rotterdam) of a single programme. So although these were 'filler' films as well, some cinemas relied heavily on them for their programming. While cluster 1 is dominated by European productions, cluster 2 is dominated by US productions (78%). The larger US companies Paramount, Fox, Universal and Columbia take an almost equal share each. The famous Charlie Chan films (Fox) are part of this cluster. MGM is underrepresented.

Cluster 3 is Europe-oriented again, with a remarkably large portion of French films (12%; for example *Le dernier milliardair* (1934, René Clair), produced by Pathé Natan). As in cluster 1, most films are from small production companies. But the films in cluster 3 are more recent. The oldest one is from 1930 and average production year is 1934. Almost one quarter of the films was produced in 1935. As in cluster 2, the titles in cluster 3 could be the mainstay for a cinema's programme. Up to 68% (Studio 32 in Rotterdam) of a cinema's programme could consist of films from cluster 3.

Cluster 4 stands out as a special case since it holds the highest number of screenings per film. *De Jantjes* and *Modern Times* are part of this cluster. Films in this cluster are mostly from European countries and produced by small companies. Seventeen from the twenty most screened films are part of cluster 4. Interestingly, the percentage of Dutch films in the top 20 of most screened films is equal to that of the US (35% each). This is remarkable since Dutch films only make up 1% of the films offered on the Dutch market against 52% US films.

Cluster 5 is very clear-cut. It consists mainly of German films (87%), 49% of which were produced by UFA. *Die Czardasfürstin* (1934, Georg Jacoby) and *Viktor und Viktoria* (1933, Reinhold Schünzel) are examples of these. Four

UFA theatres owned by UFA relied for more than 80% on these films. The Luxor theatre in Rotterdam and the Rembrandt theatre in Amsterdam programmed 89% films from cluster 5; similar values were reached by the Asta in The Hague (85%) and the Scala in Utrecht (82%). These cinemas were very much Germany-oriented in their programming.

Clusters 6 and 7 are both dominated by US films (93% and 96% respectively). Both consist of films from major US film studios. In cluster 6 Warner Bros. has the largest share but is not clearly dominating (30%). *Front Page Woman* (1935, Michael Curtiz) is in this group. RKO Radio Pictures (18%), First National Pictures (15%) and co-productions from First National Pictures and Warner Bros (11%) have the largest other shares. No MGM films are part of cluster 6; they dominate cluster 7 (78%). Films from cluster 6 have no particularly distinguishing quality, if one looks at the highest share in programmes: 36% for the Savoy in The Hague is the highest value. 92 of the total of 143 cinemas in the dataset showed less than 10% of films from cluster 6. Seventeen cinemas did not show a single one. Cluster 7 shows the same pattern even sharper. 96 cinemas showed 10% or less from cluster 7, from which 41 did not even show a single one. MGM films were distinguishing in so far as only few cinemas could get hold of them.

The results of the clustering show no very clear pattern that can be linked to compartmentalisation. At least not if we look at the following factors: country of origin, production company, year of production, and average number of screenings. Even two films so different from each other like *I'm No Angel* and *Sign of the Cross* turn out to be part of the same cluster (4). This might be explained by their production company. Both were produced by Paramount, and it seems that Paramount worked on product differentiation. *Sign of the Cross* was shown in 20 cinemas and had 231 screenings. *I'm No Angel* had 411 screenings and was shown in 32 cinemas, 9 of which also had shown *Sign of the Cross*. For these 9 exhibitors at least, film content obviously didn't matter that much. Of course, these are still tentative observations and it is necessary to take a closer look at the films themselves, but we can safely state that business strategies seem to be a more important factor for film distribution and exhibition in The Netherlands between 1934 and 1936 than compartmentalisation.

Additional Analyses: Amsterdam 1934-1936

Although these results show that cinemas differed in the composition of their programs, these differences do not seem to be related to geographical regions where specific compartments were dominant. Instead, results suggest that programming was governed more by business economical principles of competitive positioning, with some cinemas resorting almost entirely to filler films (e.g., cluster 2: ABT Alkmaar), and others profiling themselves with a more exclusive program (e.g., the UFA cinemas in cluster 5, or the cinemas showing the latest US films of cluster 6 and 7). This echoes findings by others: Jancovich, Faire and Stubbings (2003) demonstrate how film consumption can be studied as an activity and argue with David Morley that the context of viewing is as important as the object of viewing (3). They refer to Greg Waller, who showed in his work on Lexington that "… different modes of exhibition, performance and reception came to be associated with different locations. In this way, audiences built up identifications and disidentifications with places of exhibition …" (Jancovich et al. 12). Oral history interviews conducted by our students confirm this idea.[5] Certain cinemas were known as peanut cinemas because in the first row peanuts were peeled and the peels were thrown on the ground. This was a cinema a more sophisticated lady (like the interviewee) would not visit. Newspaper advertisements, too, show the varied ways in which cinemas tried to convince cinemagoers about the respectability of a programme or the sensational character of a new film. Additionally, price differentiation and the age of the films would most likely have been distinguishing factors for cinemagoers.

Such variety in competitive positioning of cinemas is most likely to be found in larger cities where multiple cinemas are contending for the same market. To explore such differences further, we repeated our analyses for a smaller sub sample, selecting only cinemas located in Amsterdam, the city with the highest number of cinemas, and the films shown here. The resulting subset contains 1,347 films programmed at one or more of 35 Amsterdam cinemas. Again, Latent Class Analysis was used to test whether this large number of films and cinemas may be effectively summarized into a few, homogeneous segments. Results reveal three types of films, each with a different distribution pattern:

Cluster 1 (75.0%); 49% of the films from this cluster comes from the U.S., 44% from European countries. Films from the Soviet Union and East European countries like Hungary and Czechoslovakia take 2%. Another small portion (4%) of the film titles is obscure, no further information could be found on them. Almost half of the films from the U.S. (49%) is made before 1933, so there is a relatively large portion of older U.S. film in this cluster. MGM and Paramount are the largest suppliers for the U.S. part of the cluster. For the European part of the cluster Germany leads with 28% of which a quarter is produced by UFA.

---

5   This work was done by students in several courses on the history of film taught by Pafort-Overduin and is available upon request.

Cluster 2 (13.8%); this cluster is dominated by U.S. films (72%). Only 28% come from other European countries like Germany, France and Great Britain. No more than 7% of the film titles are made before 1933. Hitchcocks latest films like, T*he Man Who Knew Too Much* (1934), *The 39 Steps* (1935) and *Secret Agent* (1936) belong to cluster 2, while his slightly older films *Number Seventeen* (1932) and *Waltzes from Vienna* (1933) are part of cluster 1. This is even more pronounced with the films of Charles Chaplin. While *Modern Times* (1936) is part of cluster 2, *The Bank* (1915), *Burlesque on Carmen* (1916) and *City Lights* (1931) are part of cluster 1.

Cluster 3 (11.1%); this cluster is slightly dominated by European films (59%), especially German films (31%). Only 4% of the titles of this cluster were produced before 1933. Dutch films hits like *De Jantjes*, *Bleeke Bet* and *Het Meisje met den Blauwen Hoed* (1934) (The Girl with the Blue Hat) join this cluster.

Apparently, films were indeed likely to be shown at specific cinemas, depending on their age and country of origin. However, not all cinemas exclusively programmed just one of the three types of films. Cinema owners chose various levels of specialisation, and some offered a more diverse programme. In economics, a common ratio to describe a level of specialisation or concentration is the Hirschman-Herfendahl Index (HHI). This relatively simple formula sums the squared shares of the various options to return a score between 0 (total diversification) and 1 (total specialisation). Here, we use the shares of each of the three types of films in the total programming of a cinema to describe its programming strategy in a single value. So, a cinema's HHI score may range from 0 (all three clusters are equally present) to 1 (only one cluster is present).

Figure 2 shows the geographical position of each cinema and its level of specialisation (the HHI score), with dark green markers representing cinemas with a low HHI score (diverse programming) and red markers representing cinemas with a high HHI score (specialising in one of the three clusters). The particular pattern in the spatial distribution of HHI scores suggests that the different screening strategies may be dependent on the location of cinemas.

Cinemas marked green, with an equal share of the three clusters, are clearly situated outside the centre and at relative distance from each other. These cinemas may have been catering for their specific borough and been forced by their local monopoly to cater the tastes of a differentiated audience. Cinemas in the city centre, on the other hand, are more likely to have attracted crowds from all over Amsterdam. Closely positioned together in main entertainment districts such as the Kalverstraat and Rembrandtplein, these cinemas commanded a large enough market to afford some sort of specialisation and would have been forced to such strategies with several competitors in their direct vicinity.

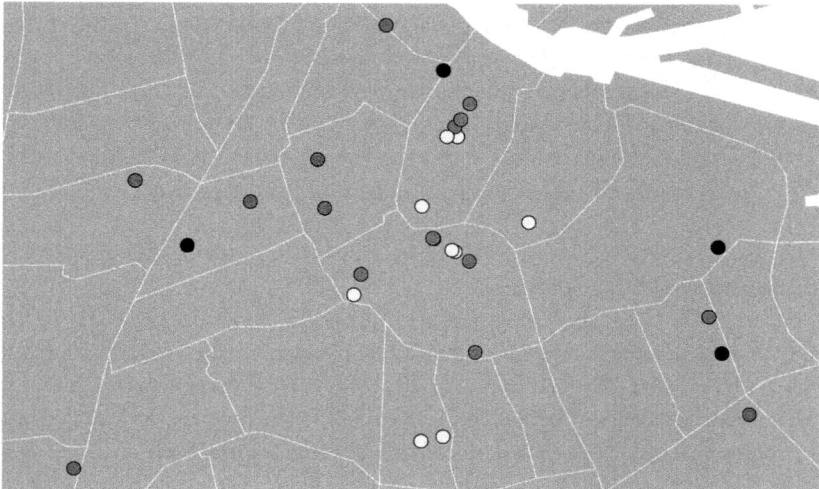

Figure 2. Level of Program Specialization in Amsterdam Cinemas 1934-1936

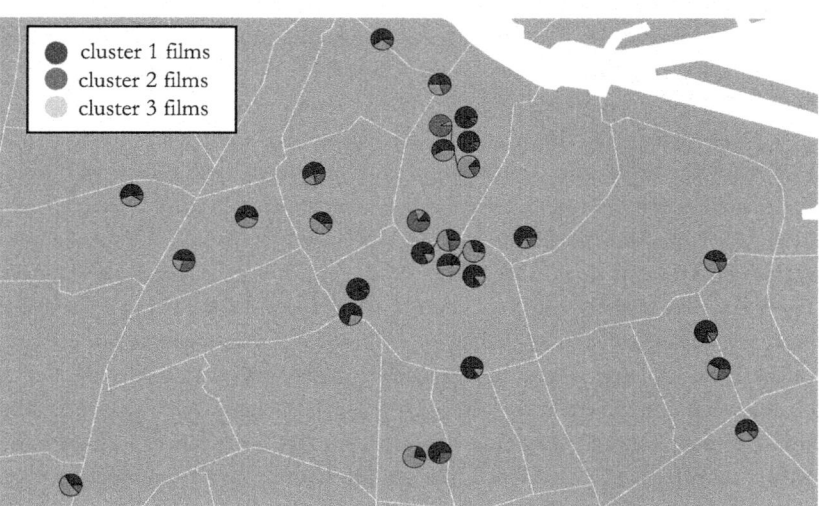

Figure 3. Program Strategies of Amsterdam Cinemas 1934-1936

Apart from choosing a particular level of specialisation, cinema owners also have to choose which type of film they wish to specialise in. E.g., while two closely situated cinemas may both opt for a specialisation strategy, this most likely would be a specialisation for different types of films. Figure 3 explores this specialisation vs. diversification strategy dimension in more detail by plotting the relative share of each cluster for each cinema.

Only two cinemas have a dominant cluster 2 programme: Cinema Royal (1,400 seats) and Corso (400 seats). Both are positioned in the centre of the city, surrounded by cinemas offering a programme with no or very few recent cluster 2 films. Cinema owners apparently often opted for a supplementary way of programming instead of direct harsh competition. Also, contracts with distributors may have had clauses with some form of exclusivity.

Conclusion and Discussion

Of the four compartments making up Dutch society in the 1930s, particularly the Catholics had clear opinions on which films were judged (un)suitable for their herds, voiced through multiple channels, such as magazines and mass. Living in specific geographical regions, one would expect films to show specific distribution patterns, based on the suitability for each compartment. However, analysing a dataset of 23,674 film programs over a three year period of 143 cinemas spread across the country, we found no indication of any influence of compartmentalisation on cinema programming in the Netherlands between 1934 and 1936. Business strategy, distributions contracts and plain economical factors seem to have been much more important.

This is not to say that compartmentalisation had no effect on the Dutch film market. For instance, there may have been an indirect effect, with compartmentalisation influencing the number of cinemas in an area, which, in turn, because of the associated business economic consequences, influenced programming strategy. A cursory glance at Figure 1 suggests there are indeed fewer cinemas in protestant regions. But is population density not of equal or more importance in the spreading of cinemas? Clearly, cinemas are concentrated in urban areas; where the population density is low, so is the number of cinemas. The one exception – the region between Hardewijk and Apeldoorn, south of Kampen and Zwolle – however, suggests that the Protestant compartment in particular may have had some influence on the number of cinemas. This populated area of potentially sufficient market size for multiple cinemas is also the largest continuous orthodox protestant area in The Netherlands. In Apeldoorn, with 65,179 inhabitants the largest city of that region, there was only one cinema for every 32,590 persons. One cinema seat had to be shared by 85 people. This is the lowest ratio in the dataset. The average rate in the dataset is 22,075 persons on one cinema or 38 people who had to share one cinema seat. This indicates that Protestants only may have been able to suppress the spreading of cinema in a homogeneous environment, and were not strong enough to do so in urban areas and areas where the population density was high enough to provide an adequate amount of customers for a cinema to make a profit. So far, the literature has not paid much attention to the role of Protestants in the development of Dutch cinema, since this compartment did not want to have anything to do with cinema. However, precisely because of their rejection of cinemas, their influence may have been more significant than presumed to date.

In sum, there may be a more complex, indirect effect of particularly Protestant dominance interacting with market size as driver for launching a cinema. Even though, as Dibbets (2006: 61) made plausible, local taxes, censorship committees and the national Cinema Union have been important determinants in the development of the Dutch cinema market. Although compartmentalisation cannot be linked directly to the screening of particular films, we believe the underexposed influence of Protestants constitutes an important avenue for further research on the role of compartmentalisation on the Dutch film market. While in-depth case studies have revealed interesting perspectives, we conjecture that quantitative analyses of preferably multiple sources, such as the present, make an indispensable contribution to the understanding of the development of a national cinema market. Such datasets can show us large patterns and make our findings comparable with that of others. However, for the explanation we also need to dig into local archives, to study individual films and collaborate internationally.

Bibliography

Blom, J. C. H., and J. Talsma, eds. *Voorbij verzuiling: religie, stand en natie in de lange negentiende eeuw.* Amsterdam: Het Spinhuis, 2000.

Burg, J. van der, and J. H. J. van den Heuvel. *Film en Overheidsbeleid. Van censuur naar zelfregulering.* 's-Gravenhage: SDU, 1991.

Dibbets, Karel. "Het taboe van de Nederlandse film cultuur: neutraliteit in een verzuild land." *Tijdschrift voor Mediageschiedenis* 9 (2006): 46-64.

Holbrook, Morris B., and Mark W. Grayson. "The Semiology of Cinematic Consumption: Symbolic Consumer Behavior in Out of Africa." *Journal of Consumer Research* 13 (1986): 374-381.

Jancovich, Mark, and Lucy Faire with Sarah Stubbings. *The Place of the Audience. Cultural Geographies of Film Consumption.* London: BFI, 2003.

Knippenberg, Hans, and Herman van der Wusten. "De zuilen, hun lokale manifestaties en hun restanten in vergelijkend perspectief." *Sociaal Nederland. Contouren van de twintigste eeuw.* Eds. Corrie van Eijl, Lex Heerma van Voss, and Piet de Rooy. Amsterdam: Aksant, 2001: 129-150.

Kozinets, Robert V. "Utopian Enterprise: Articulating the Meanings of Star Trek's Culture of Consumption." *Journal of Consumer Research* 28 (2001): 67-88.

Pafort-Overduin, Clara. "De Jordaan en haar bewoners als nationaal symbool herkend? Een onderzoek naar de representatie van de Jordaan in film, literatuur en theater en de verwerking daarvan tot een beeld van nationale herkenning in de jaren dertig." Diss. U, in progress.

Schuursma, Rolf. *Jaren van opgang. Nederland 1900-1930*. Meppel: Uitgeverij Balans, 2000.

Wedel, Michael, and Wagner A. Kamakura. *Market Segmentation: Conceptual and Methodological Foundations*. Boston, Dordrecht: Kluwer, 2000.

Deb Verhoeven, Kate Bowles, Colin Arrowsmith

Mapping the Movies

Reflections on the Use of Geospatial Technologies for Historical Cinema Audience Research

> If space is rather a simultaneity of stories-so-far, then places are collections of those stories, articulations within the wider power-geometries of space. Their character will be a product of these intersections within that wider setting, and of what is made of them. And, too, of the non-meetings-up, the disconnections and the relations not established, the exclusions. All this contributes to the specificity of place.
>
> Doreen Massey, *For Space*

The Geographies of Cinema-going: Multiple Specificities of Place and Time

This chapter offers a reflection on the practical and conceptual opportunities that arise when scholars from different disciplines collaborate on the historical investigation of cinema-going as a cultural practice. Our experience involves direct collaboration in a pilot study of Greek cinema-going in Melbourne, which we describe here in detail, as well as various shared conversations across our separate projects. What interests us is not only the practical detail about how such interdisciplinary mapping projects might best be undertaken, but also the broader scholarly implications of the application of Geographic Information Systems (GIS) software to the representation of historical data relevant to film studies. How might 'mapping the movies' for example, help us grasp the multiple cultural intersections which constitute each cinema-going experience? How might geo-spatial maps facilitate our understanding of cinema experiences in terms of the local specificities of place and time, as well as the flow of national and transnational media circulation?

Our experience suggests that when film historians turn from the investigation of film content to evaluate the wider processes of cultural learning which take place in and around the particular venues where films are screened, two interrelated shifts occur. The first is that we start to collect different kinds of data, and as we do this, we begin to imagine new shapes to conventional "film studies databases". For example, rather than pulling together all the available data on particular *films*, from their production to their plot highlights, the techno-stylistic hallmarks of their presentation, and the reviews and critical opinions occasioned by their release, we become interested in both social and physical data on the locations of *cinemas*, and in the analysis of their impact on local economies and communities. In addition, rather than assuming that each cinema reproduces similarly the general circumstances of film consumption, we now become interested in the differences between cinemas, and the connections that link them in terms of industrial patterns of distribution and exhibition. Cinema venues start to appear as key points in commercial networks, and, in a practical sense, as data fields in their own right, creating a new interrogation strategy for existing data sets which are ordinarily concerned with the properties of films and the companies which have produced them.

The second shift relates to the questions that this relatively new kind of evidence provokes: what extra-cinematic elements help us to understand why a particular movie plays to a packed house in one location and is withdrawn quickly from another? What are the cultural or economic features which differentiate one picture theatre from another situated nearby? What changes over time help us to understand why a neglected theatre can be successfully revived, or why a flourishing business can start to fail? These questions challenge the presumption that the distribution and exhibition industries are exclusively (or even primarily) engaged in selling films, and therefore that the apparent popularity or otherwise of the cinema-going occasion is driven by variations in the content of those films. Instead we can begin to imagine a more fundamental transformation of the films themselves as they move between venues, even if in a material sense we are tracking the same physical print, perhaps in slightly shabbier condition after its life on the road. Recognising the distinction between cinema venues helps us to understand that members of the audience in the packed house might experience the film quite differently than the smaller audience at another picture theatre, and it legitimates our interest in the surrounding elements that contribute to this transformation of a cultural event that has been assumed to be roughly the same wherever it occurs.

This approach enables us to think of movies not as immutable texts that construct the same fixed horizon of interpretative possibility wherever they go, but to imagine them instead as one element in a place-based cultural performance whose hallmark is not similarity, but specificity. For a cinema-goer to connect with the screening of a film print in a public venue, several specific journeys in both time and space have to be undertaken. In the first place, the venue has to exist, both physically and conceptually, as a place where films are screened, and this does not happen by chance. Whether a screening venue is a picture palace or a local hall, whether it is a sustained or faltering commercial operation, a community-run initiative, or a one-off fundraiser, there has to have been some prior evaluation of the territorial shape and social nature of the local constituency upon which it can draw. Precisely because film screenings are not impromptu gatherings, except in very unusual circumstances, consideration must have been given to the practicalities of transport options to the destination, as well as the co-location of cinemas with supporting business and cultural infrastructure. Like all buildings, therefore, cinemas come inscribed with their own journeys through time: their histories of being planned, rethought, opened, closed, sold, redeveloped, and so on.

Having first been historically positioned, the cinema venue then commences its horizontal operations as a particular point within a network of distribution territories. Films are explicitly manufactured for repeat screening, for travel from one destination to another. While digital distribution adjusts this aspect, it remains the case that historically, the transport of film cans has been as critical to the screening event as the transport of the potential film consumer. Each screening venue is interconnected within a market economy, both by the physical transport routes along which the film cans travel, as well as by commercial linkages ranging from national theatre chains to local venue co-ownership. In this way, the study of something as prosaic as train timetables becomes significant in understanding how and why films appear at particular locations (see Thorne 2007). And while the market exerts an influence on cinema programming, this influence is not one that we can simply characterise as "movies on demand". Rather, market responses at one location may influence hopeful programming choices at another. It is for this reason that the overall physical, discursive and commercial connectivity of the market is critical to understanding the context for elements which might be distinctive at one venue, or shared among localities with something in common – rural cinemas, for example.

Finally, because cinema attendance is also necessarily premeditated, we need to think carefully about the common image of the cinema audience as always already seated in the theatre, gazing up at the screen. How did they get there? How far did they travel? When and why did they decide to come, and where did they encounter the program details or advertising? How will they get home? For any audience to assemble, each individual submits to the logic of a cultural grid created out of all the pre-existing developments within an operational network of exhibition and distribution. They undertake a journey which begins with a prior decision made at another location: they travel the designated route at the preordained time; they show up at the screening at the beginning rather than the end; operate within the social conventions of the particular public assembled at the venue; and then commit a preset portion of personal time to a shared social event whose success is conceived of as much in terms of public order as personal satisfaction. This prompts us to ask new questions: how has the technological improvement in transport infrastructure over time, effectively reduced the distance between a cinema and its audience, recalling Don Janelle's concept of space-time convergence (Janelle, 1968)? Can we see an audience being drawn from further and further away, as the road network or public transport improves?

None of this is controversial, nor are these characteristics peculiar to cinema. Nevertheless, they represent methodological challenges for cinema researchers, both in terms of how to collect and represent data, and in terms of the value of this kind of data to film studies' traditional project of generating large scale generalisations about the medium and its significance.

Mapping the Meaning of Cinema-going

To move from these entanglements of quantitative and qualitative historical data to the production of maps is a seemingly straightforward matter. In one sense, of course, such maps are simply different visualisations of data collections, and no more than the next logical step from the development of major databases. This is, however, a step away from our capacity to produce generalisations from the data. A map tips the representational balance towards the particular, and restrains the scalability of results. It is for example, difficult to argue for the typicality of a map, when its representational strength (which is not without limits) lies in its precise relation to one particular place. The map therefore invokes all of the research anxieties generated by the proliferation of microhistories: what can we transfer from one local case study to a larger framework?

To begin with a very straightforward example of the way in which spatial investigations can expand our understanding of cinema-going processes at particular locations, while at the same time possibly restricting their relevance to those locations, Kate Bowles has used topographic maps in combination with historic photographs to explore the journeys undertaken by families living on farms outside a very small rural Australian town on the far south coast of New South Wales. The purpose of this exercise in thinking about locality is to assess the impact of flooding and road development on the potential audience for a picture show operating in the local hall in the late 1920s. Using maps as research tools to explore the gradient of transport routes around the district, as well as to analyse the pattern of rivers and creeks, has exposed the significant disincentive of setting out from a particular farm by foot or by bicycle without benefit of street lighting, travelling on unsealed roads, to meet up with a film arriving from a different direction, and an itinerant operator whose truck (and projection equipment) might be on the wrong side of a washed out bridge some miles away. In 1928, for example, when serious flooding occurred repeatedly throughout the district, and key bridges were not repaired for several months, the local cinema venue struggled to maintain a reliable weekly audience, and the community had to engage in a range of increasingly hectic fundraising activities to subsidise the operation of their failing picture show (Bowles, 2007). But while topography helps us to appreciate what the problem might have been – and that it might not have been primarily caused by the film programming at the venue – the opportunity to scale up and make generalisations from this case study is limited. In the same way that a map of one town cannot help you find the post office in another town, the particularity of research findings from one historical map of cinema-going practices can be difficult to transfer, and this does represent an immediate challenge to the validity and usefulness of the mapping project.

Or does it? Our argument is that in methodological terms, individual maps have the tendency to recommend questions rather than to exemplify their answers; it is the means by which a map reveals or proposes ideas in one location that can be transferred to another and which suggests the map's most significant value. This capacity for maps to recommend rather than simply exemplify is evident in Jeffrey Klenotic's detailed work on the arrival and closure of cinemas in Springfield, Massachusetts, in 1926 (see Klenotic 1998 and 2001). Klenotic has mapped the changing urban demography of individual Springfield neighbourhoods at a time when competing independents and theatre chains were seeking to establish optimum locations for new cinemas. Using GIS to house and represent residually available demographic data together with the street locations of particular cinemas, in a series of tiles that show how quickly the distribution of cinemas changed in a short timeframe, Klenotic's maps are also interpretive in the most straightforward sense, in that they are based on a survey of perceptions of Springfield neighbourhoods gathered in the early 1920s. Klenotic's specific findings therefore relate to the relationship between individual cinemas in Springfield and the neighbourhoods that surrounded them. His interest is in mapping the idiosyncracies of a discursively constituted engagement with local reputational geographies: good neighbourhoods, bad neighbourhoods, and ways of travelling through them. Whilst this is clearly of interest to other historians of Springfield, the findings themselves cannot be used to argue that this relationship between cinemas and communities was shaped exactly the same way in other American cities at that time. Rather, the usefulness of Klenotic's maps to other studies such as ours has been to model an approach to the analysis of proximal relationships, and to demonstrate the fruitful interrelation of social and spatial data with the kinds of data which cinema historians are more used to collecting: what screened, and where, and when.

While Klenotic's analysis is of particular value to Springfield, his approach also has the potential to expand our knowledge of the historic presence of the cinema industry in a distant location such as Australia. By beginning the project of mapping the Australian distribution and exhibition landscape, including the screenings of specific film titles and the opening and closing of particular cinemas, we are seeking insights into the possible interrelationships between predominantly imported films, their Australian cinema audiences, and the specificities of place which shape and are shaped by those local communities. Historical cultural mapping in this context is a research strategy specifically designed to open up new questions regarding the evident Australian cultural capacity for localisation of foreign product, and to use distribution data (the opening and run zone clearance patterns for 'significant' movies) to analyse the perceived level of cultural importance of particular geographical locations within the Australian market.

The Practical Challenge of Mapping Cinema Geographies

The collaboration between cinema researchers and geospatial researchers in achieving some of these research objectives has the practical effect of doubling our capacity to approach the task, but it also multiplies the complications. We are now confronted by conceptual hesitations both from a historical perspective unused to taking geography into account, and from geo-spatial practices facing up to the representation of history. The practical challenges emerging from the exposure of cinema history to geospatial analysis prompt us towards new data standards, and require us to develop the capacity to work with different sets of professional sensitivities and definitions of rigour.

The primary challenge in the field relates to the availability of relevant data. Today, records of cinema audience attendance are computerised for the purpose of financial reporting; pre and post war attendances were hand written on locally maintained ledgers. Many of these ledgers and logbooks have since been lost or destroyed because of their perceived ephemerality. Similarly, census data in Australia is for the most part unavailable in a digital format.[1] Related to data availability is the problem of reliance both on large data sets and the need to keep up with geospatial research and development. Census data,

---

1   According to the Australian Bureau of Statistics, only census data collected since 1996 is available in digital format (Australian Bureau of Statistics, 2007b) and electronic records before this are difficult to obtain.

information on transportation routes, and background topographic information for Australia run into gigabytes of data – this makes mapping by manual methods virtually impossible. Advances in spatial technologies, including GIS, global positioning systems and remote sensing, make available a range of tools for automating the combining, mapping and analyses of large spatial data sets. But the potential to upgrade to the sophisticated use of these technologies is not necessarily a realistic professional expectation for the cinema historian, and relies on a long-term collaboration rather than merely opportunistic consultation with the geospatial researchers who are involved in the development of new spatial technologies to obtain meaningful results.

The combination of often patchy data from cinema records with voluminous data from other sources raises particular problems in terms of the combination of data sets. Base topographic data, for example, is sourced from relevant government databases including state and federal government mapping authorities. Data will have been originally digitised from hardcopy maps ranging in scales from 1:1,000,000 for nation-wide data up to scales exceeding 1:25,000 for state derived data in and around regional and urban centres. Census data is aggregated to statistical divisions down to collector districts and from 2006 onwards at the newly derived "mesh blocks" (Australian Bureau of Statistics 2007). State government infrastructure departments have derived transportation routes, and cinema locations can be geocoded via street address or through field derived GPS locations. This variety of sources of data, which may be held on differing geographic datums in a range of geographic projections and co-ordinate systems, presents a particular challenge to film historians and geographers who intend to unify this data to facilitate spatial analyses across geographical themes.

Furthermore, consideration must be given to the quality of the data, in terms of its content and spatial accuracy, if a single spatial database is to be successfully used as a mechanism for undertaking geographical analysis for cinema audience research. The Victorian Spatial Information Strategy 2004-2007 (Victorian Spatial Council 2006) identifies four components in the consideration of data quality: positional and attribute accuracy, logical consistency, completeness and lineage. Taken together, these are measures of "nearness to the truth", the key indicators of exposure to the risk that the transfer of data either from positional readings, or from one mapping system to another (from paper-based parish maps, for example, into a digital format), may generate a complex set of spatial uncertainties which may transfer into the final analysis.

But perhaps the most interesting challenge, and the one which explicitly connects the concerns of spatial researchers to those of cultural historians, relates to the inherently static nature of spatial technologies. Whilst mapping social diversity has long been conducted by social geographers, mapping the changes in spatial patterns for micro-historical studies presents the geographer/spatial analyst with a particular challenge. GIS are inherently static and enable spatial patterns to be described at a single point in time. Space and time however, are conceptually inseparable (Massey 2005). Recent attempts have been made to address management of space and time in GIS (for example Peuquet 1994; Egenhofer and Golledge 1998; Langran 1992; Huisman and Forer 1998). Mark et al (2001) have proposed a research project that focuses on the extraction of health related information using geospatial lifelines similar to those described by Hagerstrand (1970). McBride et al (2003) describe a number of models to manage space-time data including snap-shot and animation, and mobile object simulation models. If the mapping of cinema-going practices is to be a step forward for film studies, this inherent limitation in the representation of space as always frozen in time needs careful exploration.

A Case Study in Historical Mapping: The Greek Cinema Circuit in Melbourne

Between 1949 and the early 1980s a thriving cinema circuit made up of some 30 venues, operated to service a large Greek diasporic audience in metropolitan Melbourne. In the period following WWII, hundreds of thousands of Greeks had migrated to Australia. Between 1952, when a bilateral agreement on immigration between Australia and Greece was signed, and 1974, some 220,000 Greeks came to Australia. Melbourne remains the ethnolinguistic centre of Hellenism in Australia with a concentration of approximately 215,000 Greeks and Greek Cypriots compared to approximately 160,000 in New South Wales (Tamis 2005: 63).

Deb Verhoeven and Colin Arrowsmith have collaborated on a pilot study of the spatial relationship between these migrant audiences and the cinemas which were devoted to serving them. Our initial purpose in generating maps of the locations of these venues was to look for the proximity of cinemas to the demographic location of Greek migrants and to examine the audience's facility of access (either by walking or public transport). We were looking for key factors that contributed to the success of the Greek cinema circuits in Melbourne in a period otherwise noted for cinema closures (see Verhoeven 2007). For example, of the 124 cinemas operating in Melbourne's suburbs in 1956, almost fifty percent had closed by 1961 (Catrice 2005). Brett Stokes, a geospatial science researcher using data gathered by Michelle Mantsio, a cinema studies researcher, initially presented a series of graphic maps set in the years in which census data was available (1947, 1954, 1961, 1968, 1975, 1981). As we expected, these maps indicate that the venues corresponded quite closely to demographic concentrations.

However we had not anticipated what would be revealed when the available data was animated to encompass temporal change. What the animated version of the maps illustrates, and which is not clearly evident in the static maps, is a particular relationship between demographic change and the appearance or closure of cinemas. In this case study, Greek language cinemas tend to arrive *in advance* in areas where Greek migrant community concentration develops most intensity, and they tend to close *prior* to the dispersal of that same community. There is some room for ambiguity in this analysis due to the periodisation of census data. However the location of many of the cinemas does seem to pre-empt demographic change over two or three census surveys. This leads to several interesting considerations about the anticipatory role of cinemas in relation to community congregation, while substantiating (and complicating) the link between cinemas and community formation that has to date been largely taken for granted. What arises from the animated map is a series of new questions that we had not initially thought to ask. What role does the cinema provide for diasporic communities in constructing or relocating the 'local' within a global cultural ecumene? How might cinemas participate in processes of territorialisation and re-territorialisation; in the intensities of connectivity afforded when communities live in close proximity to other community members? Did these culture-specific cinemas have a pre-emptory role, as harbingers of cultural-demographic change in a given location? Did they have a specific temporal as well as a spatial relationship to demographic clusters? Is the establishment of other local businesses servicing the community directly related to the presence of the cinemas and the establishment of the community in a particular place – in other words, what comes first: the customer, the souvlakeria, the Church or the cinema?

These are not questions about horizontal integration (an economic factor we were already researching in relation to the diasporic Greek exhibitors and distributors) but questions about the combinatory influence of specific community infrastructure. The next stage of this process for us will be to investigate the historical development of commercial and recreational services in a sample location to determine where and when the cinema 'fits in'. This will complement and draw together our more detailed research into the film businesses themselves and the audiences (for whom attending the cinema was one activity amongst many).

On this last point then, we can also observe that maps might equally be about dis-locating as locating cinemas, and cinema studies, as a site of 'pure' analysis. Historical maps have the potential to demonstrate flows of historical and spatial change and stasis; but they also demonstrate to us the interconnectedness of events and places; provoke us to see 'the cinema' as a progression of located socio-spatial events that address rather than produce historical or spatial specificity, what Ryszard Kapuscinski calls 'provincialism'. Kapuscinski cautions against provincialism as a form of both spatial and temporal solipsism:

> We normally associate the concept of provincialism with geographic space. A provincial is one whose worldview is shaped by a certain marginal area to which he ascribes an undue importance, inaptly universalising the particular... [but] there are spatial and temporal provincials. Every globe, every map of the world, shows the former how lost and blind they are in their provincialism; similarly, every history ... demonstrates to the latter that the present existed always, that history is merely an uninterrupted progression of presents, that what for us are ancient events were for those who lived them immediate and present reality. (Kapuscinski 2007: 270-271)

The challenge for film studies is therefore quite significant: if, as we are suggesting, maps shift us from the vertical claims of exemplification to the horizontal reaches of interconnectedness, then they also impel us to decentre the cinema, revealing it as one place amidst other locations, one moment in the busy context of everyday life.

Some Conclusions: Working With(in) the Limits of Maps

Combining the academic skills of the geospatial scientist with that of the film scholar helps us rethink the ways in which we have interpreted film visitation patterns in the past, by widening our scope to consider the physical, commercial and social coordinates and contours of the everyday life surrounding the cinema venue. This connects our work to earlier historical social mapping – the work of social historian Henry L. Taylor (1984), for example, who used a number of maps in addition to other sources to analyse the black ghetto-formation process in Cincinnati during the nineteenth century. For Taylor, the primary benefit of the use of maps lay in the expansion of ways to visualise research findings: "The maps not only confirm and support the descriptive data in the various historical sources but also enrich the data by providing a concrete, visual perspective that reduces complex data to simpler, more easily understandable terms modelling various types of spatial relations in the urban environment" (45). To this we would add that maps are also in themselves tools for analysis and discovery. The use of maps changes how we conceptualise historical cultural research (we need to look more widely and differently at what is before us), it challenges us to ask different questions, and it changes how we articulate our findings.

The utility of this research strategy is not only historical; at the same time as expanding our understanding of past cinema-going practices, it enables us to develop instruments to help the contemporary film production, distribution and exhibition industries analyse the decision-making behaviours of particular audiences in specific geographic locations. This connects us, however, to a conversation which has been occurring among cultural geographers for some time, about the limiting nature of the map as a means of representing the complexities of human cultural interaction. Doreen Massey's thoughtful remonstrations suggest that there is a degree of hubris in the mapping project, as conventionally conceived. In seeking to fix, pinpoint and position cultural events within a "slice through space" as she describes it, we are at risk of believing that the unmappable elements of space are those elements we can do without. One outcome of this foreclosure on surprise is the creation of maps which achieve representational fidelity in some ways, and forcefully misrepresent the nuanced, street-level and everyday nature of cultural experience in others. As Australian historian of the holocaust Inga Clendinnen (2006) writes:

> I have seen a number of two-dimensional plans of Treblinka, and tried to absorb them; examining them soberly, carefully matching the number in this square to that descriptive tag. It was a laborious business, and at the end the plan on the paper was transferred into my head and that was all that has happened. All that peering and matching had worked like a sedative upon the imagination: the image lay flat and flaccid, obstinately abstract, obstinately dead. (165)

This bracing observation is one that we need to keep at the forefront of our planning as our ongoing cinema-going research develops. It reminds us that for mapping to be a productive development for film studies, it needs to work by engaging our imagination, and challenging our assumptions. Mapping is a legitimate means of visualising the research we have already undertaken, but it offers most when it raises new questions about spatial and temporal connectivity, rather than promising closure on the question of what was going on in the past. In foregrounding the inherently limited nature of mapping, conceptually as well as practically, we hope nonetheless to demonstrate that cinema studies has something important to learn from the techniques developed by geographers. We also hope to show that we have something to contribute to the discussion, from what our research has already taught us about the always incomplete and dislocated nature of our imaginative immersion in ephemeral social history.

Bibliography

Australian Bureau of Statistics. "2006 Census: Mesh Blocks." www.abs.gov.au/websitedbs/D3310114.nsf/4a256353001af3ed4b2562bb00121564/66d7c6ca64345e1aca2572aa0080e199!OpenDocument (first published 27 March 2007a; accessed: 01/06/07).

Australian Bureau of Statistics. Personal communication with ABS enquiry line 01/06/2007b.

Catrice, D. "Cinemas." *The Encyclopedia of Melbourne*. Ed. A. Brown-May, S. Swain. Melbourne: Cambridge University Press, 2005: 135.

Clendinnen, I. "Building Treblinka." *Agamemnon's Kiss*. Melbourne: Text Publishing, 2006.

Egenhofer, M. and R. Golledge (eds.). *Spatial and Temporal Reasoning in Geographic Information Systems*. New York: Oxford University Press, 1998.

Langran, G. *Time in Geographic Information Systems*. London: Taylor & Francis, 1992.

Hägerstrand, T. "What about People in Regional Science?" *Papers of Regional Science Association* 24 (1970): 7-21.

Huisman, O. and P. Forer. "Towards a Geometric Framework for Modelling Space-Time Opportunities and Interaction Potential." *Proceedings of International Geographical Union*, Lisbon, Portugal: 1998.

Janelle, D. G. "Central Place Development in a Time-Space Framework." *The Professional Geographer* 20 (1968): 5-10.

Kapuscinski, R. *Travels with Herodotus*. Trans. Klara Glowczewska. New York: A. A. Knopf, 2007.

Klenotic, J. "Class Markers in the Mass Movie Audience: A Case Study in the Cultural Geography of Moviegoing." *The Communication Review*, 2.4 (1998): 461-495.

Klenotic, J. "'Like Nickels in a Slot': Children of the American Working Classes at the Neighborhood Movie House." *The Velvet Light Trap* 48 (2001): 20-33.

Massey, D. *For Space*. London: Sage, 2005: 130.

Mark, D., M. Egenhofer, L. Bian and J. Rogerson. "Spatiotemporal GIS analysis for environmental health: solutions using geospatial lifelines." *Geography and Medicine*. Ed. Flahault et al. Paris: Elsevier, 2001: 65-80.

McBride, S., C. Bellman and C. Arrowsmith. "Developing space-time models and representation for GIS." *Proceedings of the Spatial Sciences Coalition Conference*, Canberra, September 2003.

Peuquet, D. "It's about time: A conceptual framework for the representation of temporal dynamics in geographic information systems." *Annals of the Association of America Geographers* 84 (1994): 441-461.

Ritchie, J. *Report on Regional Cinema*. Glen Innes, *Arts North West*, 1996:8.

Smith, B. "Bringing the Movies Back to the Country: Regional Cinema in New South Wales." *Metro*, 127-128 (2001): 50-52.

Tamis, A. *The Greeks in Australia*. Melbourne: Cambridge University Press, 2005.

Taylor H. "The Use of Maps in the Study of the Black Ghetto-Formation Process: Cincinnati, 1802– 1910." *Historical Methods* 17.2 (1984): 44–58.

Thorne. "Rethinking Distribution: Developing the parameters for a microanalysis of the movement of motion pictures." *Studies in Australasian Cinema* 1.3 (2007): 315-331.

Verhoeven, D. "Twice Born – Dionysos Films and the establishment of an antipodean Greek film circuit." *Studies in Australasian Cinema*, 1.3 (2007): 275-298.

Victorian Spatial Council. "Spatial Information Data Quality Guidelines for Victoria." Available online at www.land.vic.gov.au/CA256F310024B628/0/F25DB401F08EC2F4CA25726000029E21/$File/VSIS+2004-2007+Data+Quality+Guidelines+December+2006.pdf (2006; accessed 09/05/07).

Michael Ross, Roger Sennert, Jens Wagner

Putting Itinerant Cinemas on the Map

Introduction

Itinerant cinema was the predominant form of film exhibition in the first decade of cinema culture in Europe. Information on a large number of occurrences of itinerant cinemas on fairs in Germany and neighbouring countries can be found in *Der Komet*, a contemporary trade paper. To make an analysis of the available data feasible, the source data was collected in a relational database and complemented by external data, e.g. geographical coordinates and population figures for the places visited by itinerant cinemas. A number of problems arose during this first stage, especially in respect to identifications of showmen and places. This had major consequences for the design of the final database, which can now be accessed and searched through a web-based interface. Since a major strength of the data collection is related to geographical aspects like regional distribution and routes of itinerant cinemas, in the second stage a tool for geographical visualization was developed. This not only helps to facilitate the analysis of the data, but also allows for a quicker and safer validation of the sometimes inconsistent source material. The final product is the result of a close collaboration between a film history project and an information technology project, both being part of a transdisciplinary centre for media research.

The Phenomenon of Itinerant Cinema

When the new medium of film was invented and emerged as a new form of public entertainment, it was a matter of more than ten years until stationary cinemas – i.e. fixed establishments primarily devoted to showing films to a paying audience – became the norm for film exhibition. Before the so-called "cinema boom" of 1907, the predominant form of showing films to broad audiences was the itinerant cinema.[1] Throughout Europe, itinerant showmen travelled from fair to fair to show their ever-changing audiences a varied repertoire of films.

---

[1] Other places for film exhibition were music halls, where films were only one number among many different acts, and assembly halls in hotels, public buildings etc., where travelling cinematographers performed for a limited time. For a detailed history of the emergence of cinema in Germany, see Garncarz 2008.

From today's perspective, it is easy to underestimate the phenomenon of itinerant cinema both in quantity and scope. At the beginning of the 20th century, the majority of fairs were attended by at least one itinerant cinema. Even though we lack empirical data for a representative evaluation, we know for certain that some of these cinemas were more reminiscent of huge cinema palaces with hundreds of seats than of the small shabby tents we tend to associate with fairground attractions. From the range of entrance fees one can conclude that itinerant cinemas aimed at broad audiences, from people of the lower classes to well-off citizens.

For a study of the emergence and establishment of cinema in Germany up to 1914, which is at the heart of the project "Industrialization of Perception" within the University of Siegen's Research Centre "Media Upheavals", itinerant cinemas are of particular interest. Here we have the first institutionalized form of film exhibition, which very much helped to popularize the new medium as a form of entertainment and to shape the way in which films were shown and watched for many years to come. To the film historian, information on the spreading of itinerant cinemas is of particular interest: Which regions were regularly visited by itinerant cinemas, and which were not? Does the size of a place have influence on the frequency of visits? What changes can be observed within the period in question? Who were the showmen travelling with cinemas? Did they operate in particular regions, or did they cover larger areas or even cross state boundaries?

Luckily, there is a single source that allows us to answer many of these questions. *Der Komet* was – and still is – a trade paper for itinerant showmen and other carnies. In this weekly publication, there is a column called "Fest-, Markt- und Messberichte" (Reports on festivals, markets and fairs) which reports on many, if not all the fairs and similar events in Germany, and even some of them in neighbouring countries, and gives information on the carnies present at the fair, and the attractions they presented. A typical entry for a fair roughly translates thus:

> In *Lörrach* (county of Baden) were present for the traditional shooting fair:
> Leilich, cinematograph,
> Bausch, "Planet Ride" and "chairoplane",
> Buri, "chairoplane" and shooting gallery,
> Schiefer, illusion and shooting gallery,
> Lämli, shooting gallery and high striker,
> Walter, photography,
> Surber, ball throwing gallery and high striker,
> Spindler, public player (?).
> (*Der Komet* 1168, 10 August 1907)

Digital Tools – Step 1: Digitalizing the Source

With dozens of entries like this for every week of most of the year (there were practically no fairs in winter), the task of finding and collecting all the relevant entries was enormous, not to mention the task of analyzing the information. Work on this started several years ago, when a number of MA students under supervision of Joseph Garncarz at the University of Cologne each evaluated a particular span of years, collecting all cinema-related entries from *Der Komet* and entering these into a simple Microsoft Excel table. With single columns for the carny's name, the particular name of his attraction (e.g. "Biograph" or "Kinematograph"), the type of event (e.g. parish fair or fun fair), the town visited and the pertinent issue number of *Der Komet*, all the relevant information was now available electronically for simple search routines and some statistical analysis.

However, with nearly 7,000 entries for the years of 1896 to 1926, a simple table was far too unwieldy for more complex analysis, especially if it required the introduction of additional external information: If you want to know the role of town sizes for itinerant cinemas, you need to add such data, and if a town figures more than once in the table (and most towns do), in effect you have to add this information for each occurrence of the town. To avoid this extra work, which is also a common source of errors, it was decided to turn the single table into a relational database with separate tables for different kinds of data. By the way the data is stored in a relational database and information is interconnected, changes made to a single entity are immediately effective for all occurrences of this entity throughout the database.

The mechanical conversion of the table into a relational database brought to light a typical problem of non-relational data collections: Because of typing errors and different spelling versions of names, identical persons or places could not be automatically matched. In fact, there were so many inconsistencies in the original data collections that it was decided to conduct a full revision of the material, correcting any typing errors and omissions – both of which are obviously unavoidable when working on a project of this scale.

A problem not easily resolved by proof-reading lies in the source itself. On the one hand, the source data can be ambiguous, e.g. place names which can refer to more than one place, or carnies' names which are so common that they might easily refer to more than one actual carny (especially when the first name is not stated). On the other hand, the source itself is far from free of spelling inconsistencies. From the available data one must assume that the information was passed on sometimes in writing, sometimes orally – which accounts for all sorts of reading and hearing mistakes that found their way into print. But then again, some presumable "mistakes" might be correct after all, or two variants of a name coexist without any indication which of the two is correct.

Digital Tools – Step 2: Identifications in the Database

To avoid any premature conclusions, those entering the data had been instructed to stick completely to the source, copying the information exactly as given in *Der Komet*, even if a mistake was more than likely. During the proofreading phase, this strategy was retained. As mentioned before, the inconsistencies resulting out of this make it difficult to analyze the data statistically. Therefore, a second layer of identification was introduced into the database, linking the copied source data to actual persons, places etc. The identification feature includes the possibility to make more than one identification for any element of the source data, and to grade identifications according to their probability.

For example, if the source gives the place of a fair as "Lichtenstein", this is ambiguous since there are at least eight places in Germany of that name, and that is not counting the Duchy of Liechtenstein situated between Austria and Switzerland. With the database's identification feature, it is possible to 'identify' the Lichtenstein of the source with all of these places. If other factors, especially the region in which the itinerant cinema in question usually operates, make any place more or less likely than the others, the identifications can be graded accordingly, by choosing one of five categories, in descending order of likelihood:

- Definite (100%)
- Highly probable (81-99 %)
- Probable (51-80%)
- Possible (21-50%)
- Perhaps (1-20%)

Percentage figures behind each entry serve only as an indicator for the "meaning" of each category. For example, they suggest that you usually don't have more than one identification for a single source that is "probable" or higher. If two or more identifications are on the same level of probability, they will be considered "possible". If one identification is "definite", there usually won't be any others. If there is a "highly probable" candidate, you usually won't have "possible" entries. If there is an identification which is rather unlikely but cannot be ruled out completely, it will be considered "not impossible". That said, the aim is not to get to a sum of 100% by adding the values of each identification, but to give a rough idea of the probability of each individual identification.

The identification feature and especially the grading system is the place where the film historian's expertise and intuition are needed. In many cases, there is simply no mathematical way to judge identification. Assigning the probability of an identification depends – among other things – on a knowledge of existing persons and places, on typical spelling errors and variants of the time (especially with the black-letter typeface used in the source), and on a good idea of the typical operating area of a particular carny. Especially this last aspect poses some difficulties as long as the geographical information is only available in textual form. With the visualization of the data on a dynamical map, it is much easier to recognize operating areas and other geographical patterns which are important for grading identifications as well as analyzing the complete data.

Digital Tools – Step 3: Asking the Experts

The work as described so far was realised by members of the film history project only, from the conceptualization of the task to the programming of the MySQL database (including a web-based front end, which is now open for public access via www.fk615.uni-siegen.de/earlycinema/). However, the task of geographical visualization proved too much for the film scholars turned programmers – expert help was needed. Thanks to the construction of the transdisciplinary research centre "Media Upheavals" at Siegen University, this expert help was in effect just across the corridor, where the informatics project "Methods and Tools for Computer-Based Analysis in Media Studies" is working within the same research centre.

The film history project presented the IT project with the following material to go on:

- a MySQL database containing all information from the sources and graded identifications for people (carnies) and places
- geographical coordinates for (nearly) all identified places, stored in decimal notation in two separate fields (latitude and longitude) in the place table

The following requirements were set down:

- A platform-independent, web-based solution was required, preferably without the need to install any additional programmes by the user.
- The existing MySQL database should be used as the source for the data.

- Functionality should include the possibility to select a particular carny and show the pertinent stations either completely or in a year-by-year mode.
- If possible, the route of a carny in a particular year should be visualized by lines connecting the places in the order of the carny's visit.
- An interface should allow a user of the database to visualize any search result with station lists by clicking on a button.
- If possible, the maps used should reflect the geopolitical situation of the research period (i.e. 1895-1914).

Required Technologies for the Visualisation Tool

The requirement to produce a platform-independent, web-based solution for the geographic visualisation of itinerant cinema data made it necessary to look for a web technology that is compatible with most Internet browsers while at the same time making the handling of maps (i.e. large graphic files) feasible. Apart from this, an easy-to-adapt web tool for working with maps was needed to be used in conjunction with the application technology.

AJAX

"Asynchronous JavaScript and XML" (AJAX) is a fairly recent technology, or rather a combination of technologies, for creating interactive web applications. It is of particular interest since it allows the user to change only part of a page rather than the whole page, as is usual with normal HTML websites. The handling of a web application becomes more natural, like the handling of a regular application installed locally. Thus, only small amounts of data are exchanged with the server, 'behind the scenes' as it were. This has impact on interactivity, speed, functionality and usability.

Technically, AJAX is based on open standards like JavaScript and XML. Via the Java Script XMLHttpRequest object of the browser, an 'asynchronous call' is made to the server. It is asynchronous in the sense that it does not interfere with normal page loading but loads only parts of the page at a time. The retrieved data is commonly formatted in XML again. Since JavaScript and XML are standards in most recent web browsers, AJAX is suited to cross-platform web applications that do not need additional software on the client side.²

Web GIS

There are a number of terms to describe geographic information systems which are based on the Internet or an intranet, including GIS online, NetGIS, Distributed GIS, Internet Mapping, or Web GIS, which is the term we use here.³ In contrast to a desktop GIS, where the complete functionality und data are supplied on the client, a Web GIS provides the data and functionality via a server. The client simply uses an ordinary web browser to access and display the data. Simple functions like zoom or movement of the map can be handled by the client.

Three major products currently dominate the market of presenting personalized maps on the Internet: Yahoo Maps, Google Maps, and Google Earth. Google Earth is different from the other two products by being able to show 3-dimensional objects; the user also needs to install a special programme or, since June 2008, at least a browser plugin to be able to use it. Programming with Google Earth requires KML, a special XML variant, whereas Google Maps und Yahoo Maps can be controlled via JavaScript and offer a wider range of possible interactions with other applications. At the time of realising this project in 2007, and perhaps even today, Google Maps was superior to the Yahoo product in terms of speed of processing and displaying data, especially with large amounts of data. Another point in favour of Google Maps was the fact that its API was much better documented than that of Yahoo Maps.

Realisation

The realised application is based on a standard LAMP system (Linux Apache MySQL PHP). The user interface of the application makes use of AJAX and includes the API of Google Maps. The film historical data is imported into our own Mediana database system. Its object data layer allows to access the data on object level without the limitations of a particular database.

---

2   On the other hand, there are still great differences in the way that browsers interpret 'standards'. Therefore an AJAX framework was used that takes care of the application-dependent aspects.
3   For an early classification of different types of web-based GIS see Plewe (1997).

The user interface of the application consists of a single page which contains all relevant controls. On the left side the Google Maps plugin shows the currently selected data. On the right side, all search parameters can be modified to manipulate the map immediately.

The first parameter is the year to display data from. After choosing a year, all places visited by any carny in that year are displayed on the map. This function can be used to create animations to show the spread of itinerant cinemas within a particular time.

The second parameter is the selection of a single carny. After choosing one, you have the option to view only the stations visited in a specific year or all stations. The first option allows to display the route of a carny in the year chosen. This can be enhanced by an animation function, where a line is drawn from station to station in the order in which the places were visited originally. A list of stations provides further details like dates of a visit, and makes it possible for the user to choose between different places in case the identification of a particular place was ambiguous: by checking or unchecking the check boxes in question, different possible routes can be tested. The other option, to show all stations of a carny throughout the years covered by the database, is helpful for ascertaining a particular area in which the carny typically operated.

Further amenities like an AutoCentre function for centring the map around the calculated centre of the stations currently displayed, or an AutoZoom function that adjusts the zoom level so that all stations from the current search are within the visible section of the map, help the user to get a good visual idea of the data. Clicking on a station icon in the map provides further information on the particular place, including population figures from contemporary censuses. A search field for place names is also included which by default is limited to those places within the currently visible section of the map.

Finally, a small web service was added. This allows users of the original web interface of the database to submit any search result to the map application and view the result geographically.

Digital Tools – The Benefits

The successful geographical visualization of the stations of itinerant cinemas is of great importance for the ongoing research on itinerant cinema, within the Siegen project and beyond. First of all, the availability of visualization had the desired result of being a great aid in determining the probability of many of the identifications in the original data. In many cases, it was possible to rule out places to far off the regular region of business of a particular carny, or to establish with some certainty the identity of two similarly-named carnies. Thus, the data which is available for further research has much gained in quality.

Apart form that, the analysis itself is made much easier with the visualization tool. It is now possible to easily recognize patterns of distribution, typical carnies' routes, dominant areas of film exhibition and developments of all these in time. Thanks to the web-based construction of both the database and the visualization tool, all historians of itinerant cinema will benefit from these advantages.

Future Work

From the perspective of the film history project, it would be worthwhile to work on a solution that makes use of contemporary (historical) maps. Even though it may sound more like a gimmick or toy than a necessity, we believe that the use of historical maps may well deepen our understanding of the phenomenon of itinerant cinema. For example, the international scope of itinerant cinema can only be correctly judged if we work with the national boundaries of the time. Furthermore, if we had access to historical railroad maps within our system, these would enhance our understanding of the travelling routes and the dependence (or independence) on railroads at the time (as opposed to the modern motorways we find in Google Maps). The main obstacle to realise this is the lack of available historical maps in digitised format. A series of test runs with self-digitised maps failed, since the projection of the historical maps was either erroneous or not compatible with the Google Maps projection.

Acknowledgements

This work is financially supported by the Deutsche Forschungsgemeinschaft (SFB/FK 615, Projects A5 and MT).

Bibliography

Alameh, N. "Chaining geographic information Web services in Internet Computing." *IEEE* 7.5 (2003): 22-29.

Bernhardsen, Tor. *Geographic Information Systems: An Introduction.* Hoboken, NJ: Wiley, 2002.

Cha, Seung-Jun, Yun-Young Hwang, Yoon-Seop Chang, Kyung-Ok Kim and Kyu-Chul Lee. "Integrating Ajax into GIS Web Services for Performance Enhancement." *Lecture Notes in Computer Science* 4488 (2007): 562-568.

Garncarz, Joseph. *Maßlose Unterhaltung: Die Etablierung des Kinos in Deutschland, 1896-1914*. Frankfurt a.M./Basel: Stroemfeld, 2008 (in preparation).

Gottipati, Hari. *Hacking Maps with the Google Maps API*. 2005. www.xml.com/pub/a/2005/08/10/google-maps.html

Miller, Christopher C. "A Beast in the Field: The Google Maps Mashup as GIS/2." *Cartographica: The International Journal for Geographic Information and Geovisualization*. 41.3 (2006): 187-199.

Nod, Tom and Shawn Helwig. *Rich Internet Applications. Technical Comparison and Case Studies of AJAX, Flash, and Java based RIA*. Madison, WI: UW E-Business Institute, 2005. www.uwebi.org/docs/final_1.pdf

Paulson, Linda Dailey. "Building Rich Web Applications with Ajax." *Computer* 38.10 (2005): 14-17.

Plewe, Brandon. *GIS Online. Information retrieval, mapping and the Internet*. Santa Fe, NM: OnWord Press, 1997.

Sayar, Ahmet, Marlon Pierce, and Geoffrey Fox. "Integrating AJAX Approach into GIS Visualization Web Services." *Advanced International Conference on Telecommunications and International Conference on Internet and Web Applications and Services* 2006: 169.

Yuri Tsivian

Cinemetrics, Part of the Humanities' Cyberinfrastructure

The subject of this paper, an online application called *Cinemetrics* (see www.cinemetrics.lv), is intended for further study and analysis of cinema. Cinemetrics is an open-access interactive website designed to collect, store, and process scholarly data about films. Its ultimate goal is to create an extensive multi-faceted collection of digital data related to film editing. At the moment Cinemetrics is programmed to handle the aspect of editing known in film studies as *cutting rates*.

1 What are Cutting Rates?

A peculiar thing about the film medium, noticed by many, is that it bridges the gap between spatial and temporal arts. On the one hand, filmmakers, like painters or architects, deal with recognizable spatial shapes; on the other, films unfold in time, as do poems or musical compositions. Though we tend to perceive their unfolding as continuous, most films consist of segments called *shots* separated by instant breaks called *cuts*.

With rare exceptions, films contain a number of different shots. Shots differ in terms of space and in terms of time. We know enough about space-related distinctions between shots, which are easy to name ("shot 1: baby playing; shot 2: man looking") and categorize ("shot 1: medium long high angle shot; shot 2: facial close up"). Time-related differences between shots are more elusive and harder to talk about, for, unlike in music or poetry with their scaled feet and measures, variations in shot length are not ones of distinction, but of degree. The only distinction a critic is safe to make when discussing shot lengths is between *brief* and *lengthy*.

Shot lengths are sometimes convenient to present as the frequency of shot changes, or cuts, hence the term *cutting rates*. The shorter the shots, the higher the cutting rate. Unsurprisingly, cutting rates are linked to the story and its space-time articulations: car chases are cut faster than park rambles, conversations shot in close-ups faster than ones presented in medium shots; likewise, montage sequences meant to cover larger spaces of story time will have higher cutting rates than will sequences shown in real time.

Less evident, but as important, is the relationship between cutting rates and the history of film.

2 What Factors Make Cutting Rates Change Across Film History?

We still do not know enough about this, and it is this gap in our knowledge that Cinemetrics is designed to fill up. What we already know, however, allows us to link changes in cutting rates to various aspects of film history, including the history of film style, the history of film industry, film's cultural history, and the history of cinema as technology.

It was due to technology, for instance, that the first films/shots produced by cinema's French inventors Lumière brothers were all around 50 seconds each (for such was the capacity of their 1895 camera/projector), or that cutting rates jumped each time a new editing device was introduced in the more recent era – Scotch-tape splicing in the 1960s, editing on videotape in the 1980s or digital editing in 1994 (see Bordwell 2006: 155). But to explain why it was in the United States that the fast-paced "American cutting" was born in the 1910s, or how it happened that some ten years later French and Soviet films managed to outstrip American cutting rates, one needs to address, as has been done, the state of the film industry: the specific mode of production then dominant in Hollywood (see Staiger 1985), and, counter-intuitively, the non-dominance of this mode in post-WWI Europe (see Thompson 2004).

Factors of style and culture further complicate the picture. Looking, for instance, at pre-revolutionary Russia with its taste for slow languorous film melodramas, we find Russian film trade papers campaigning against "American cutting," for here it was felt that "psychological" or pictorial acting styles – the main asset of Russian film divas – called for "full scenes" which must not be cut up (see Tsivian 2000, 2004). The 1917 Revolution turned the tables. Young Soviet directors like Sergei Eisenstein took over, declaring that the cinema of the future will need no actors at all – since anything an actor can convey will be much better communicated by means of cutting, or "montage." It was this idea that fueled some of the fastest-cut pictures in the entire history of film, as well as well-known Soviet "montage theories" which claimed that the true constituent of the film is not the shot, but the cut.

3 Average Shot Lengths

While debates about fast *vs.* slow cutting rates are central to the history of film, the notions of fast and slow will be of little use unless we have an idea of the normal. Distinct from the film critic, the student of film history cannot afford to rely on intuition, for as I have just shown the sense of cutting speed changed depending on when, where and by whom this or that film was made –

saying nothing of different norms intrinsic to different genres. It is for this reason that an increasing number of film scholars resort to numeric data about cutting.

The method which film scholars interested in the history of cutting have been using for more than 30 years is based on calculating the Average Shot Length (ASL) of a film – an index obtained by dividing the length of the film in seconds by the number of shots in it.[1] The result can be used in two ways. If we calculate ASLs for all the films made by the same director or edited by the same editor, and plot the results onto a timeline (diachronic statistics), we will get a better sense of their range of experimentation and creative evolution. Or we may choose to inspect cross-sections of film history (synchronic statistics) and, by comparing their prevailing ASLs, get a sense of how cutting rates changed over the last hundred years.

It was the latter approach adopted by Barry Salt prior to 1992 and by David Bordwell prior to 2006 that yielded an overview of the way cutting rates fluctuate across film history. Having divided the span of film history into 5-year thick "splices" and calculated the mean ASL for each, Salt has shown the growth of cutting rates between 1912 and 1926, their decrease between 1928 and 1939, their relative stability during the forties and fifties, and their upsurge from the 1960s to the 1980s.[2] And Bordwell's more recent numbers show that between 1990 and now Hollywood films continue to pick up pace, the fastest of them reaching an ASL of less than 2 seconds (see Bordwell 2006: 121-124).

I, too, once applied the ASL method in order to compare the last film made by the pre-Revolutionary Russian director Evgenii Bauer with the first film made by his Soviet successor Lev Kuleshov, and when I put the obtained ASLs side by side with the international data collected by others I felt my heart beat faster, for it turned out that between 1917 and 1918 the cutting tempo in Russia had jumped from being the slowest to being the fastest in the world (see Tsivian 1992). Not that the difference could not be sensed without counting, but I felt excited that now we could not only assume but also demonstrate this.

ASL data work, but we need to keep in mind that these data are relational. It is useful to know how long the average shot of a film is compared to figures obtained for other films, but ASL can become misleading if you treat it as an index of the film's dynamic quality. Take *Dragnet Girl* (1933) by Yasujiro Ozu

---

1 For more details see Barry Salt's and David Bordwell's articles on www.cinemetrics.lv.
2 See Salt 1992: 147, 174, 214, 249, 266, 283, 296; Bordwell 2006: 88-106. Salt and O'Brien group their data by countries, which makes his picture more complex than a brief summary can render.

and *Rashomon* (1950) by Akira Kurosawa. The former has an ASL of 4 seconds,[3] the latter of 13 seconds. Though it may seem tempting to conclude that Ozu's film is more dynamic, those who know *Rashomon* will rightly disagree. The reason why *Rashomon's* ASL is so much longer than *Dragnet Girl's* is because Kurosawa alternates very brief shots with lengthy ones. It is this contrast between activity and stillness in *Rashomon* that its ASL figure fails to convey.

Yes, average numbers round off edges, but this does not put film statistics out of court. The new method I created and made available to film scholars through the Cinemetrics website in November 2005, enables us to obtain and present cutting-related data in a more flexible way than we were able to earlier on.

4   What Cinemetrics Brings to the Study of Cutting Rates

Rather than calculate average shot lengths arithmetically, Cinemetrics does so by taking and storing the time-span of each separate shot. Distinct from the arithmetical ASL, which is a single datum, Cinemetrics treats each film as a database of shots highlighting its individual features. Specifically, it tells us about the film's *cutting swing* (standard deviations of shorter and longer shots from ASL), its *cutting range* (difference in seconds between the shortest and the longest shot of the film) and its *dynamic profiles* (polynomial trendlines which reflect fluctuations of shot lengths within the duration of the film).

Take, once again, *Dragnet Girl* and *Rashomon* as measured, processed and represented by Cinemetrics (Figures 1 and 2). We can tell at a glance from the ups and downs of these wavy trendlines that the cutting swing in *Rashomon* (numeric value 13.6 seconds) is more considerable than it is in *Dragnet Girl* (3 seconds) and that its dynamic profile shows a marked tendency towards deceleration, while in *Dragnet Girl* changes in cutting rate through the course of the film are barely perceptible.

Let me add that *Rashomon* has a higher contrast of shots scales (Big Close-ups *vs.* Extreme Long Shots) and includes more shots with mobile framing than we find in *Dragnet Girl*. This is not something Cinemetrics accounts for yet, but we are moving there. When the Cinemetrics database grows larger, its client tools become more multi-purpose, and its statistics more wide-ranging, my hope is we may be able to deduce a complex formula, or coefficient, of film dynamics.

---

3   I use the figure given in Bordwell (1988: 377). The figure I obtained with Cinemetrics is slightly less (3.8 seconds): www.cinemetrics.lv/movie.php?movie_ID=49

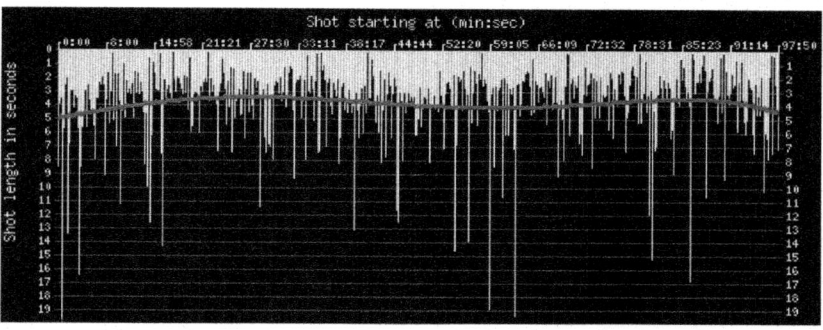

Figure 1. *Dragnet Girl*

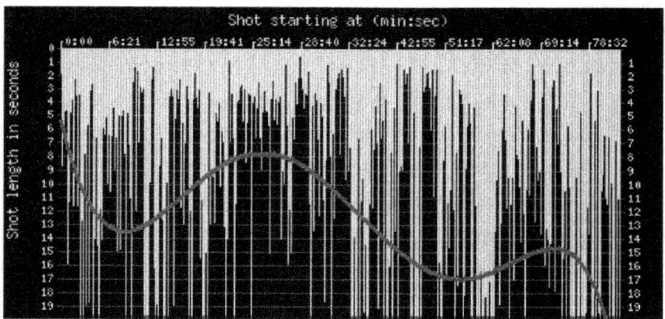

Figure 2. *Rashomon*

5   Inventory

In its present form, Cinemetrics includes: a) a software toolkit used for data collecting (the "client tool") and data processing (the "statistics tool"); b) a database for storing the obtained data; c) accessories: a discussion board, news board, supplementary database, and a library of essays pertaining to its subject.

6   How Cinemetrics Works

The way in which Cinemetrics interacts with its website users can be called a "tools for data" policy. This interaction takes 5 steps. The user (1) downloads the client tool free of charge; (2) uses the tool to measure the cutting rates of a film of his or her choice; (3) submits the measurements to the site; (4) upon submission, Cinemetrics processes these data using its statistics tools, and (5) stores them as part of the Cinemetrics database making the data available to other users.

7 The Client Tool

Technically speaking, the tool is designed to register cuts, not to measure shots. In simple mode, this frequency is established by a mouse-or-keyboard stroke on the "shot change" button each time the user detects a cut. The advanced mode offers 8 buttons instead of one, 7 of them marked with a specific shot scale from BCU to LS. The user can also customize these 8 buttons. As Cinemetrics is designed to measure frequencies, this can be the frequency of anything that recurs: certain words, faces, locations or tunes.

8 Statistics Tools

After the film has been measured and its data submitted, Cinemetrics automatically processes them, displaying the resulting information as a) statistical figures and b) statistical graphs. The figures are: average shot length; number of shots; minimum and maximum shot lengths and the range between them; and standard deviation. The graphs show: the distribution of shorter and longer shots (calibrated in seconds) within the duration of the film calibrated in minutes (see the white "icicles" against the green-barred "night" on Figures 1 and 2). The straight red line that runs across the "icicles" (go to the *Sunrise* entry on www.cinemetrics.lv/movie.php?movie_ID=1955 to see how the line works) is a trendline which shows whether the film in question gathers speed as its story unfolds (in *Sunrise,* it does). Underneath, a box named "Degree of the trendline" is found. When you change the degree and click on "Redraw" the trendline turns into a curve that reflects fluctuations in shot lengths with closer approximation (at degree 6, *Sunrise* looks like a hill, at 12, like a mountain ridge). In order not to succumb to the illusion of smoothness which trendlines tend to provoke, it is important to read your trendline against the more chaotic "icicles" whose behavior the trendline summarizes.

If the advanced mode of the client tool has been used, as is the case with *Sunrise,* you can color-code the "icicles," and, by checking and un-checking the "Display?" boxes, select and isolate the feature you are interested in (in the *Sunrise* analysis this is the distribution of dialogue and expository titles).

9 Cinemetrics Database

The Cinemetrics database is a shared-use open-submission collection of data collected by people that use the client tool and processed by the statistics tools. Its default sorting is alphabetic by film titles, but it can also be sorted by other parameters, such as year, submitter's name, submission date, simple *vs.* advanced mode of measuring, and by the film's average shot length. By clicking on a film title the user gets access to the page that provides basic statistics and interactive graphs related to this film.

As counted on September 20, 2006, the database contains information on 150 film titles dating from 1915 to 2005, submitted by 17 contributors from 8 countries. Every new submission is announced on the "News" board – go to it to get a sense of the growing rate of submissions. Film scholars and teachers, such as Charles O'Brien of Carleton University, Canada, Casper Tybjerg of the University of Copenhagen, or me, submit films along the lines of their research interests. A unique feature of Cinemetrics is that by submitting your film measurement data you receive their analytical picture in return.

The majority of Cinemetrics contributors, however, are students from American campuses – University of Chicago, NYU, Pittsburgh University, and University of Madison, Wisconsin. Indeed, Cinemetrics has proven a good educational device. There is a "Comments" box on each page of the database that can be used to communicate with contributors – go to *Citizen Kane*, for instance, to see the way these boxes can be used in a teacher-student interaction. Cinemetrics' "Discussion board" with its 13 topics opened within 10 months is another place where the educational process takes place.

10   What Cinemetrics Adds to What We Know

It may sound a truism, but it is one worth repeating: in science as in scholarship, progress is measured not by new answers given to old questions, but by new questions put to old answers. What narrative factors make cutting rates change within the duration of a film? What correlations are there between staging and editing, between the scale of a shot and its duration? These are just two questions out of the many to come.

I only developed the method in 2005, but it has already caused a notable response. My Cinemetrics analysis of Griffith's famous *Intolerance* that yields telling variations in cutting rates between the four epochs pictured in the film (Tsivian 2005a/b) moved prominent French film theorist Raymond Bellour (2006) to connect the dynamic profile(s) of this film to the concept of "the present moment" by the acclaimed psychologist Daniel N. Stern, and to the *time-image* concept propounded by philosopher Gilles Deleuze. It does seem that Cinemetrics helps to generate questions that are of use not only to the history, but also to the theory of film.

Bibliography

Bellour, Raymond. "Daniel Stern, encore." *Trafic* 57 (printemps 2006): 55-62.

Bordwell, David. *The Way Hollywood Tells It. Story and Style in Modern Movies.* Berkeley, Los Angeles, London: University of California Press, 2006.

Bordwell, David. *Ozu and the Poetics of Cinema.* Princeton: University Press, 1988.

O'Brien, Charles. *Cinema's Conversion to Sound. Technology and Film Style in France and the U.S.* Bloomington and Indianapolis: Indiana University Press, 2005.

Salt, Barry. *Film Style and Technology. History and Analysis.* London: Starword, 1992.

Staiger, Janet. "The Central Producer System: Centralized Management after 1914" and "The Division and Order of Production: the Subdivision of the Work from the First Years through the 1920s." *The Classical Hollywood Cinema: Film Style and Mode of Production to 1960.* By David Bordwell, Janet Staiger, Kristin Thompson. London: Routledge, 1985: 128-153.

Thompson, Kristin. "Early Alternatives to the Hollywood Mode of Production: Implications for Europe's Avant-gardes." *The Silent Cinema Reader.* Ed. Lee Grieveson, Peter Kramer. London: Routledge, 2004: 339-367.

Tsivian, Yuri. "'What is cinema?' An agnostic answer." (In French.) *Trafic* 55 (2005a): 108-122.

Tsivian, Yuri. "Editing in *Intolerance.*" *The Griffith Project 9 (1916-18).* Ed. Paolo Cherchi Usai. London: BFI Publishing, 2005b: 52-57.

Tsivian, Yuri. "New Notes on Russian Film Culture Between 1908 and 1919". *The Silent Cinema Reader.* Ed Lee Grieveson, Peter Kramer. London: Routledge, 2004: 339-348.

Tsivian, Yuri. *Immaterial Bodies: Cultural Anatomy of Early Russian Films.* CD-ROM. Produced by Barry Schneider. Ed. Marsha Kinder. Los Angeles: Annenberg Center of Communication; University of Southern California, 2000.

Tsivian, Yuri. "Cutting and Framing in Bauer's and Kuleshov's Films." *Kintop: Jahrbuch zur Erforschung des frühen Films* 1 (1992): 103-113.

Ralph Ewerth, Markus Mühling, Thilo Stadelmann,
Julinda Gllavata, Manfred Grauer, Bernd Freisleben

Videana: A Software Toolkit for Scientific Film Studies

Abstract

Within the research project "Methods and Tools for Computer-Assisted Media Analysis" funded by Deutsche Forschungsgemeinschaft, we have developed the software toolkit *Videana* to relieve media scholars from the time-consuming task of annotating videos and films manually. In this paper, we present the automatic analysis tools and the graphical user interface (GUI) of *Videana*. The following automatic video content analysis approaches are part of *Videana*: shot boundary detection, camera motion estimation, detection and recognition of superimposed text, detection and recognition of faces in a video, and audio segmentation. The GUI of *Videana* allows the user to subsequently correct erroneous detection results and to insert user-defined comments or keywords at the shot level. Furthermore, several research applications of *Videana* are discussed. Finally, experimental results are presented for the content analysis approaches and compared to the quality of human annotations.

Introduction

The research project "Methods and Tools for Computer-Assisted Media Analysis" (MT) of the collaborative research center "Media Upheavals" develops (a) the database system *Mediana* to allow media scholars to manage arbitrary textual and audio-visual data objects and supports related research work flows, and (b) the software toolkit *Videana* as part of *Mediana* which includes computer-assisted methods to support the scholarly analysis of audio-visual material, in particular images and videos.

In this paper, we will discuss how far academic film studies can be supported by *Videana* in a quantitative manner. Clearly, the interpretation of audio-visual scenes will be reserved exclusively to humans for a conceivable time. Nonetheless, computers can disburden media scholars from typically very time-consuming manual annotation tasks. In particular, the quantitative analysis of the following elements of film and video composition can be supported: montage of shots (e.g., cut frequency), camera motion, a description of displayed scene content, mainly with respect to faces and superimposed text, and audio information.

Korte (2001) describes several elements of cinematic composition, some basic elements of shot and sequence protocols as well as several types of visualization, such as graphics displaying shot composition, shot and sequence protocols and cut frequency diagrams. Some years ago, researchers have developed computer systems which support the task of creating shot protocols and simplify the generation of visualizations (e.g. scene and sequence diagrams, cut frequency diagrams). For example, the system *filmprot* was developed at the University of Marburg (Institute for Media, Giesenfeld 1991), while Korte developed *CNfA* ("Computergestützte Notation filmischer Abläufe", i.e. "Computer-based notation of cinematic episodes"; Korte 1992, 1994) at the University for Visual Arts of Braunschweig. However, these systems worked only in conjunction with particular analog video recorders which are not available anymore. The software *Akira (University of Mannheim,* Kloepfer*)*, the software *VideoAS* (University of Jena, Olbrecht/Woelke), and the website *CineMetrics.lv* belong to the more recent developments for the purpose of annotating (digital) videos but they do not include tools for automatic video content analysis.[1]

Finally, it should be mentioned that media content analysis is not only of interest for purposes of media studies. The proliferation of media data is rapidly increasing, e.g. if one considers the popularity of MP3 music files, digital photo collections of home users, digital videos, web-based video databases (e.g. youTube.com) and IPTV (Internet Protocol Television, e.g. *Joost:* www.joost.com). Hence, it is obvious that the need for efficient search operations in large media databases is growing accordingly. Anticipating these recent developments, efficient content-based search in media databases has been a field of extensive research since the middle of the 1990s.

Videana: A Software Toolkit for Video Analysis

As mentioned above, the big advantage of computer assistance is the automation of formal and compute-intensive analysis tasks. For example, these are tasks such as the temporal segmentation of a video into shots, identification of the kind of montage of subsequent shots (cut, dissolve, fade, etc.), finding and recognizing superimposed text, recognition of camera and object motion, recognition of camera distance, information about the presence of actors, recognition of audio events etc.

---

[1] See the papers by Tsivian and Kloepfer in this volume for a description of their applications.

Figure 1: The main window of *Videana*. On the left side, there is a window for playing a video. There are two timelines at the bottom which visualize the analysis results for the temporal segmentation of the video into shots as well as for face detections. The vertical lines in the *Cuts* timeline represent cuts (abrupt shot changes), the colored (here: grayish) areas in the timeline *Faces* mark the sequences where a frontal face appears. Two timelines are presented for each kind of event: the upper one represents the total duration of a video, whereas the lower one zooms into a certain time period which can be selected in the upper timeline and is surrounded by a rectangle. Further timelines are displayed in case that the corresponding analysis results or user annotations are available for the related events of camera motion, superimposed text or audio events. On the right side, the temporal segmentation is presented in another way. Single shots are represented by three frames (beginning, middle, and end frame of a shot). By a mouse click on an icon, the related video frame is accessible directly, while a double click starts playing the video from this position.

Up to now, the following automatic video content analysis algorithms are integrated in *Videana*: Shot boundary detection, text detection and recognition (video OCR: optical character recognition), estimation of camera motion, face detection, and audio segmentation which segments the video into sequences of silence, speech, music and background noise. Based on a plug-in approach, any type of analysis algorithm can be updated, exchanged or removed easily. The graphical user interface (GUI) of *Videana* allows users to play videos and to access particular video frames. Furthermore, the GUI allows users to manually correct erroneous analysis results.

As soon as a temporal segmentation of a video has been obtained, an icon is created for the first, the middle and the last frame of each shot. These icons are displayed to the user in the shot list view (see Figure 1). Such a view is also possible for scene segmentation but currently this segmentation has to be provided by the user manually. *Videana* offers functions to automatically generate diagrams with respect to brightness changes and cut frequencies for a video. Figure 2 shows a cut frequency diagram for a 30-minute movie sequence. The results of the different analysis algorithms are visualized in separate timelines: *cuts*, *text*, *camera*, *face*, and *audio*. The user can insert arbitrary comments and keywords for particular events and shots. All these metadata, generated either automatically or manually, can be saved in an MPEG-7 ("Multimedia Data Description Interface", Martinez 2002) XML file. The MPEG-7 standard formalizes the representation of metadata for audio-visual objects and establishes a basis for data exchange between different multimedia applications.

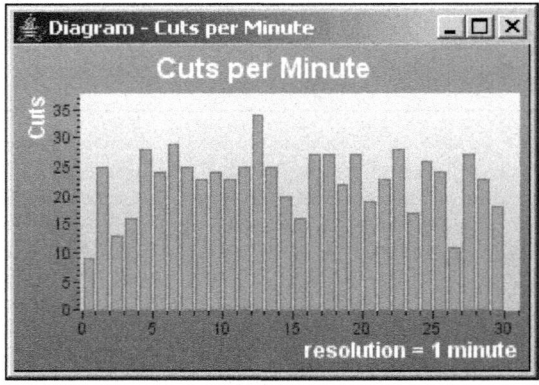

Figure 2. A cut frequency diagram generated by *Videana* for a 30-minute film sequence.

Shot Boundary Detection

One of the most important tasks in digital video analysis is the segmentation of a video sequence into its fundamental units, the shots. A shot is generally understood as an audio-visual sequence recorded continuously without any interruption. The transitions between shots can be abrupt or gradual; abrupt transitions are called cuts, gradual transitions are the results of chromatic or spatial editing effects, such as fade in/out, dissolves or wipes.

Since the beginning of the 1990s, a huge number of segmentation approaches have been suggested. Widely known approaches were suggested by Yeo/Liu (1995), Hanjalic (2002), or Bescos (2004), particularly for cut detection. To detect gradual transitions, general approaches as well as specialized detectors for certain effects have been developed (e.g. Hanjalic 2002 for dissolves, Truong et al 2000 for fade in/out). Many approaches for cut detection are based on the comparison of two consecutive frames. More recent approaches (Tahaghoghi et al 2005, Yuan et al 2005) compare all images within a short time window with each other to get more robust results. In the TRECVID evaluation series[2] such approaches could achieve the best recognition rates in 2005: 95% of the cuts were found (recognition rate, "recall"), and 95% of all positions reported by these detectors were indeed cuts ("precision" of the result). The approach developed by the authors (Ewerth/Freisleben 2004) belonged to the top five approaches, which achieved a recognition rate as well as a precision of at least 90%. Twenty-one institutes from all over the world participated in this study. The detection of gradual transitions has not yet reached this quality. Here, the recognition rate and the precision of the best approaches (Amir et al 2005; Yuan et al 2005) achieve approximately 80%.

Camera Motion Recognition

From an aesthetical point of view, camera motion is often used as an expressive element in film production. Video compression formats like MPEG-1 or MPEG-2 exploit the large temporal redundancy in videos for data compression and thus support motion estimation based on pixel blocks for consecutive video frames. The runtime for the extraction of such motion vectors is very low compared to the decoding of a whole image and the calculation of the optical flow field (calculation of motion for each pixel). Although the use of MPEG motion vectors improves runtime performance, a big part of these vectors is often "noisy" and thus not optimal in the sense of a motion description. Based on these observations, we have developed an approach (Ewerth/Schwalb/Tessmann/Freisleben 2004) which uses MPEG motion vectors for calculating the camera parameters. The "unreliable" motion vectors of a vector field are removed by an effective method in a preprocessing step, called "outlier removal". The parameters of a 3D camera model are estimated by means of these remaining motion vectors using the Nelder-Mead algorithm for solving the minimization problem. The used model has the advantage that it basically allows the distinction between camera translation and camera rotation in the corresponding direction. Experiments with synthetic video sequences

---

2   TREC, the Text Retrieval Conference, conducted a video retrieval evaluation for the first time in 2001. Since 2003, there is a separate annual Video Retrieval Evaluation Workshop called TRECVID; see also: www-nlpir.nist.gov/projects/ t01v.

showed that outlier removal leads to clearly better results. For zoom-in and zoom-out, a recognition rate and a precision of 99% (98% and 94% without outlier removal) could be achieved and the results for rotation around the z-axis could be improved from 86% to 95% (recognition rate) and from 75% to 89% (precision). We participated in the TRECVID evaluation 2005 using the described system. Overall, twelve institutes participated in this "low-level-feature detection task" concerning camera motion. The evaluation required the analysis of 140 news videos in total with a respective duration of 30 to 60 minutes. The submitted results should include all camera shots which contain horizontal, vertical camera movement or zoom (in/out). For the purpose of evaluation, the organizers finally selected approximately 2000 shots from the 140 videos obviously containing (or obviously not containing, respectively) camera motion or zoom. Besides achieving good results for the recognition of horizontal camera movement ("pan": 76% recognition rate, 92% precision), our system reached the second-best result regarding vertical movement ("tilt": 72% recognition rate, 96% precision) and the best result with respect to zoom recognition (89% recognition rate, 93% precision).

Detection and Recognition of Superimposed Text

Superimposed text often hints at the content of an image. In news broadcasts, for example, the text is closely related to the current report, and in silent movies it is used to complement the screen action with intertitles. Involved algorithms can be distinguished by their objective, whether it is text detection, localization or tracking (in videos), text segmentation (also called text extraction) or text recognition (Jung et al 2004). A text detector answers the question whether there is any text in an image or shot, and where it is. Then, text segmentation crops localized text out of the image to yield black letters on a white background. This step is necessary to feed the result into an OCR program, which transforms the image into machine-readable text. A non-uniform background would impair this process. Exemplary results of these three stages are depicted in Figure 3.

Automatic optical character recognition (OCR, normally on scanned text pages) has been a research topic since decades, and text detection, segmentation and finally recognition in images and videos has been investigated for more than 10 years now. This led to a plethora of methods that are surveyed by Jung et al (2004). The work conducted in the authors' workgroup includes proposals for text detection (Gllavata/Ewerth/Freisleben 2004a) and text segmentation (Gllavata/Ewerth/Stefi/Freisleben 2004; Gllavata/Freisleben 2005) as well as a method for tracking moving text across several video frames

(Gllavata/Ewerth/Freisleben 2004b). The proposed text segmentation method was able to boost the word (character) recognition rate from 62% to 79% (76% to 91%) on a set of test images (Gllavata/Freisleben 2005). Recently, the Tesseract OCR engine (Vincent 2006) has been integrated into *Videana*, such that the software is now able to annotate shots with localized and recognized words automatically.

Figure 3: The images on the top row show the result of text localization. The middle row depicts the results of the text segmentation process, in which the background has been removed and the text has been marked black. In the last row, the result of the recognition software (OCR) is shown.

Detection and Recognition of Faces

Face processing in images and videos is composed of face detection and face recognition. Yang et al (2002) give a comprehensive survey on the detection problem, while face recognition is surveyed by Zhao et al (2003). Face detection can be viewed similar to text detection: The detector decides whether there are faces in an image or shot, and typically solves the localization problem, too. *Videana* applies the method of Viola and Jones (2004) from the Intel Open Computer Vision Library (OpenCV) to detect frontal faces. It yields a detection rate of 92.1% on relevant standard test sets (containing 130 images with 507 faces overall) with 50 false positives (Viola and Jones 2004). In face recognition, two different scenarios can be distinguished:

- Identification: the system has to recognize the identity of a given face image by comparing it to known faces in its database, or to reject it as unknown.
- Verification: the system judges whether a given face image fits a given identity claim based on its database.

The 2002 Face Recognition Vendor Test (FRVT) has shown (Phillips et al 2002) that current face recognition technologies are able to achieve recognition rates higher than 90% under certain conditions. The identification (or recognition) rate is the percentage of faces that could be matched correctly with a known face in the database. If a face could not be recognized, two kinds of errors are possible: False alarms (or false accept), meaning that a face was falsely recognized as a wrong (known) face; and false rejects, meaning that a known face was not recognized as known at all (Phillips et al 2007). Summarizing, the study of Phillips et al (2002) drew the following conclusions:

- Best systems reached identification rates of 90% (false alarm rate 1%) for indoor images. For only 0.1% false alarms, the identification rate was 80%.
- The better systems were not sensitive to illumination for normal indoor images.
- 3D models improved the results, by morphing the head's pose to a frontal view.
- The identification of faces in outdoor images did not work satisfactorily: 50% identification rate at a false alarm rate of 1%.
- There was no difference in recognition rate whether single still images or video sequences were used as source material.
- It was more difficult to recognize younger faces than older faces.
- The recognition rate for male faces was higher than that for female faces.
- The recognition rate dropped linearly with the logarithm of the database size (number of persons).

The 2006 FRVT study (Phillips et al 2007) assessed the development of industry-strength face recognition technology since 2002. It also covered iris recognition (Iris Challenge Evaluation 2006) and investigated 3D face data and high resolution images in addition to the previous test. Several improvements over the older results are reported:

- The identification rate was improved considerably, lowering the false rejection rate (having 0.1% false alarms) by a factor of 4 to 6, depending on the actual algorithm.

- Under improved illumination conditions and using very high resolution images, the identification rate reached 99% (at 0.1% false alarms), corresponding to a reduction of false rejections by a factor of 20.

- Handling of uncontrolled conditions was improved, reaching the controlled identification rates of 80% (at 0.1% false alarms) of the 2002 candidates.

- Interestingly, the top algorithms were able to match or even do better than human face recognition performance on unfamiliar faces under illumination changes.

These results show the state of the art in face recognition technology when one can control the circumstances under which face images are taken. Taking into account the lower resolution of videos and that the recording environment might be arbitrary in videos, these results also suggest that it is difficult to index a video by appearing faces. This and the better exploitation of the large amount of single still images in a video sequence is an area for future research.

Although a specific face identification system may be useful for media research purposes (i.e. to answer questions like "in which shots did a given person appear?"), *Videana* currently contains a *general* person recognition system yielding an index of appearing persons over time for any video (Ewerth/Mühling/Freisleben 2006). Its single prerequisite is just a given segmentation of the video into shots or, optionally, scenes. The result is a set of appearing persons, and for each a list of shots in which he or she appeared. In principle, this system is able to detect and recognize both frontal and profile faces, but the currently employed OpenCV detector is not technically mature enough to detect profile faces reliably (and will be replaced for this reason in the near future). Frontal faces are precisely detected, which is mainly due to a good recognition of the eye region. This fact enables us to correct in-plane rotations of the head resulting from leaning the head to either shoulder (see Figure 4 for examples).

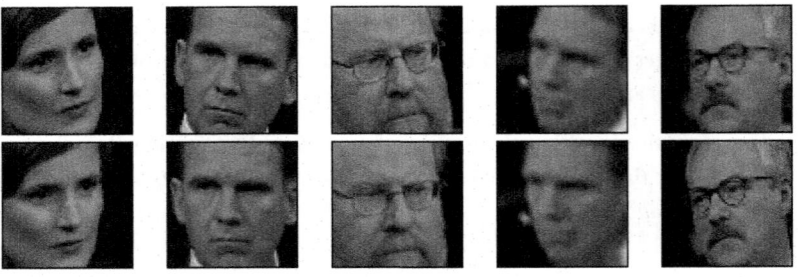

Figure 4, upper row: Examples of leant heads, leading to in-plane rotation of the face. The lower row shows the same faces after they have been rotated back to an upright position by *Videana's* face recognition system using the detected position of the eye region. This step is important for a later comparison of two faces.

After a first grouping phase, a further analysis is applied to persons who appeared in more than a predefined minimum number of shots. This analysis aims at finding face features that best discriminate this face group from the other groups. Finally, the classification is re-run using these group specific features. Preliminary results for the recognition of frontal faces are very promising. In particular, the correction of in-plane rotation and facial feature selection significantly improve the results: Based on a TV discussion sample, sufficiently large clusters could be built for 5 of the 6 appearing persons that could be used to represent a person and learn the specific facial features. The recall rate was 84% at 94% precision for the clustering (i.e. only 6% of the persons associated with a group did not conform to the group's main identity). The baseline system reached only a recall rate of 71% for the same precision score.

Applications of *Videana*

There are many applications to employ *Videana* for film studies. For example, we have conducted a case study in conjuction with the research project "Industrialization of Perception", which is also part of the Siegen research center. *Videana's* batch mode for shot segmentation allows users to analyze a number of videos automatically. This batch mode has been utilized to exemplarily analyze the cut frequencies of seven short films from the period of 1907-1913 from the USA and France. For example, it can be easily seen that the average cut frequency (ACF) of the American films is higher than that of the French films, and the ACF of the films of the 1911-1913 period is nearly twice as high as the ACF of the period 1907-1909. Of course, a larger number of videos is needed to obtain empirical evidence about such data. However, a tool such as *Videana* allows researchers to analyze a large number of videos with respect to related research questions – annotating all these video manually would be a very time-consuming task.

Another project that applies *Videana* is "Media narrations and media games", also part of the Siegen research center. This project investigates hybrid forms of game and narration, which are observable in computer games and feature films since the 1990s. The aim is a formal-aesthetical and function-logical analysis of these sequences and a summarization into a typology. Besides supporting these research activities by means of the basic functionality provided by *Videana*, an extension is currently being developed which is able to learn certain sequence types or semantic concepts. For example, the underlying audio-visual data characteristics of narrative and playing sequences in computer games and feature films can be learned automatically. A possible application would be to let the software classify shots in such hybrid videos into narrative or interactive shots. In a next step, it could be analyzed which features allow to distinguish between these sequences and the others at the level of signal processing and machine learning. Of course, it would be left to media scientists to interpret these results.

Finally, the software toolkit *Videana* has been utilized for psychological research in an external cooperation, conducted together with Klaus Mathiak (RWTH University Aachen, Germany) and Rene Weber (University of California, Santa Barbara). An automatic semantic video analysis system was developed (Mühling et al 2007) to support interdisciplinary research efforts in the field of psychology and media science. The psychological research question studied is whether and how playing violent content in computer games may induce aggression. To investigate this question, the extraction of meaningful content from computer games is required to gain insights into the interrelationship of violent game events and the underlying neurophysiologic basis (brain activity) of a player. Previously, human annotators had to index game content according to the current game state, which is a very time-consuming task. The automatic annotation of a large number of computer game recordings (i.e. videos) speeds up the experimentation process and allows researchers to analyze more experimental data on an objective basis. The proposed computer game video content analysis system for computer games extracts several audiovisual low-level as well as mid-level features and deduces semantic content via a machine learning approach. This system requires manual annotations only for a single video to facilitate a semi-supervised learning process. Experimental results demonstrated the usefulness of the proposed approach for such research: 91% of the game events of inactive, preparation, search and violence could be recognized correctly.

Planned Extensions for *Videana*

There are several areas for future work. It is expected that exchanging the current face detector improves the results of face detection (and also recognition) of non-frontal faces. Furthermore, it is planned to combine face recognition with speaker recognition technology to exploit the audio stream of videos, in order to obtain a multimodal person recognition system. This way, the robustness of *Videana's* person indexing module will hopefully be improved.

On the other hand, we are further planning to investigate the detection of semantic concepts (for example, "indoor/outdoor" via exploitation of depth-information extracted from the video-stream, "war", "politician" etc.). This could be, together with the already implemented segmentation algorithms (shots, persons, audio), the basis of automatic storyline extraction, although this will probably not work in a fully automated manner in the near future.

Automatic Analysis versus Human Annotation

In this section, we briefly summarize the capabilities of state-of-the-art video analysis algorithms and compare the analysis performance of automatic computer systems with the quality of human annotations. In the field of shot boundary detection, state-of-the-art cut detection algorithms achieve recall and precision values of about 90% to 97%, whereas the detection of gradual transitions does not reach this quality and lies at approximately 80%. Similar results are achieved by camera motion estimation algorithms (80% to 90% recall at a precision of 95%). The research in the field of face detection is as good as described above, while recent algorithms demonstrate impressive recall and precision values of almost 100%. Up to date results in face recognition exhibit reasonable performance (90% recognition rate at a false alarm rate of 1%), whereas the recognition of persons in arbitrary video sequences is a clearly more challenging task. The performance of general semantic concept detection algorithms varies strongly depending on the type of the concept. The following examples show average precision values for some selected concepts, as they were obtained by the best systems at TRECVID's high-level feature detection task in 2005: map 53%, sports 52%, mountain 45%, car 37%, people walking/running 35%, US-flag 25%, explosion/fire 12%, and prisoner 5%.

Intuitively, one might think that humans always achieve a recognition rate of nearly 100%, but subjectivity and diminishing attention seem to be limiting factors. The comparison of manual annotations against each other shows the performance of automatic software systems in a more favourable light. Concerning some features, automatic analysis algorithms even outperform human annotations. For example, the correlation of two manual annotations concerning camera motion revealed 66% recall at 100% precision for pan, respectively 34% recall at 94% precision for tilt (Bailer et al 2005), while automatic camera motion algorithms achieved 89% recall at 96% precision respectively 80% recall at 100% precision against another human annotation. Similar results can be observed in the field of shot boundary detection: in our experiments, the consensus of our (human) annotations lies between 80% and 97% with respect to the official (human) TRECVID annotation. Interestingly, these results are comparable to the best automatic systems evaluated at TRECVID.

A similar result can be observed in the psychological study of Weber et al (2006), which was later supplemented with our video analysis system. To be able to investigate interrelationships with the player's brain activity, the following game states of game sessions had to be annotated manually: inactive, preparation, search/exploration and violence. Weber et al (2006) report an inter-coder reliability of 0.85 for human annotators. Our automatic system demonstrates an excellent performance achieving an accuracy of up to 91% with respect to a human annotation.

Overall, it can be concluded that particular computer-based analysis approaches have reached a sufficient level of maturity and hence it is obvious that software tools can significantly aid scientific media analysis. In particular, they allow researchers to analyze larger data sets on an objective basis. Of course, humans still can do many things better, for example object/background separation, person recognition in arbitrary videos or generic object recognition, and last but not least, the qualitative interpretation of scene content will be reserved exclusively to humans for a conceivable period of time.

Acknowledgements

This work is financially supported by the Deutsche Forschungsgemeinschaft (SFB/FK 615, Project MT).

Bibliography

Amir, A., G. Iyengar, J. Argillander, M. Campbell, A. Haubold, S. Ebadollahi, F. Kang, M. R. Naphade, A. Natsev, J. R. Smith, J. Tešić, and T. Volkmer. "IBM Research TRECVID-2005 Video Retrieval System." *TRECVID Online Proceedings* 2005. 31.08.2007. www-nlpir.nist.gov/projects/tvpubs/tv.pubs.org.html.

Bailer, W., P. Schallauer, and G. Thallinger. "Joanneum Research at TRECVID 2005 – Camera Motion Detection." *TRECVID Online Proceedings* 2005. 31.08.2007. www-nlpir.nist.gov/projects/tvpubs/tv.pubs.org.html.

Bescos, J. "Real Time Shot Change Detection Over Online MPEG-2 Video." *IEEE Transactions on Circuits and Systems for Video Technology* 1.4 (2004): 475-484.

Ewerth, R. and B. Freisleben. "Video Cut Detection without Thresholds." *Proceedings of the 11th International Workshop on Systems, Signals and Image Processing*. Poznan, Poland, 2004: 227-230.

Ewerth, R. and B. Freisleben. "Improving Cut Detection in MPEG Videos by GOP-Oriented Frame Difference Normalization." *Proceedings of the 17th International Conference on Pattern Recognition. Vol. 2*. Cambridge (UK) 2004: 807-810.

Ewerth, R., M. Mühling, and B. Freisleben. "Self-Supervised Learning of Face Appearances in TV Casts and Movies." *International Journal on Semantic Computing, Special Issue on ISM* (2006): 78-85.

Ewerth, R., M. Mühling, T. Stadelmann, E. Qeli, B. Agel, D. Seiler, and B. Freisleben. "University of Marburg at TRECVID 2006: Shot Boundary Detection and Rushes Task Results." *TRECVID Online Proceedings* 2006. 31.08.2007. www-nlpir.nist.gov/projects/tvpubs/tv.pubs.org.html.

Ewerth, R., M. Schwalb, P. Tessmann, and B. Freisleben. "Estimation of Arbitrary Camera Motion in MPEG Videos." *Proceedings of the 17th International Conference on Pattern Recognition. Vol. 1*. Cambridge (UK) 2004: 512-515.

Giesenfeld, G., and P. Sanke. "Ein komfortabler Schreibstift für spezielle Aufgaben: Vorstellung des Filmprotokollierungssystems 'Filmprot' (Vers. 1.01)." *Filmanalyse interdisziplinär*. Ed. H. Korte, W. Faulstich. Second Edition. Göttingen: Vandenhoeck & Ruprecht, 1991: 135-146.

Gllavata, J., R. Ewerth, and B. Freisleben. "Text Detection in Images Based on Unsupervised Classification of High-Frequency Wavelet Coefficients." *Proceedings of 17th International Conference on Pattern Recognition. Vol. 1*. Cambridge (UK), 2004: 425-428.

Gllavata, J., R. Ewerth, and B. Freisleben. "Tracking Text in MPEG Videos." *Proceedings of ACM Multimedia*. New York, 2004: 240-243.

Gllavata, J., R. Ewerth, and B. Freisleben. "A Text Detection, Localization and Segmentation System for OCR in Images." *Proceedings of the 6th IEEE Int. Symposium on Multimedia Software Engineering*. Miami 2004: 310-317.

Gllavata, J., R. Ewerth, T. Stefi, and B. Freisleben. "Unsupervised Text Segmentation Using Color and Wavelet Features." *Lecture Notes on Computer Science: Proceedings of the 3rd International Conference on Image and Video Retrieval.* Dublin, 2004:216-224.

Hanjalic, A. "Shot Boundary Detection: Unraveled and Resolved?" *IEEE Transactions on Circuits and Systems for Video Technology* 12.2 (2002): 90-105.

OpenCV. Intel's Open Source Computer Vision Library. 31.08.2007. www.intel.com/technology/computing/opencv/

Jung, K., K. I. Kim, and A. K. Jain. "Text Information Extraction in Images and Video: A Survey." *Pattern Recognition* 37 (2004): 977-997.

Korte, H. "Projektbericht CNfA – Computergestützte Notation filmischer Abläufe – Erweiterte und aktualisierte Fassung." *IMF-Schriften* 1 (1992).

Korte, H. *Handbuch CNfA, Prototyp 3, Computergestützte Notation filmischer Abläufe.* Braunschweig: 1994.

Korte, H. "Einführung in die Systematische Filmanalyse." Berlin: Erich Schmidt, 2001.

Martinez, J. M. "MPEG–7 Overview." *Technical Report N4980, ISO/IEC JTC1/SC29/WG11.* Klagenfurt 2002.

Mühling, M., R. Ewerth, T. Stadelmann, B. Freisleben, R. Weber, and K. Mathiak. "Semantic Video Analysis for Psychological Research on Violence in Computer Games. *Proceedings of ACM International Conference on Image and Video Retrieval 2007 (CIVR 07).* 2007: 611-618.

Phillips, P. J., P. Grother, R. J. Micheals, D. M. Blackburn, E. Tabassi, and J. M. Bone. "FRVT 2002: Overview and Summary." 31.08.2007. www.frvt.org/FRVT2002/documents.htm.

Phillips, P. J., W. T. Scruggs, A. J. O'Toole, P. J. Flynn, K. W. Bowyer, C. L. Schott, and M. Sharpe. "FRVT 2006 and ICE 2006 Large-Scale Results." March 2007. 31.08.2007. www.frvt.org/FRVT2006/Results.aspx.

Tahaghoghi, S. M. M., Thom, J. A., Williams, H. E., and Volkmer, T. "Video Cut Detection Using Frame Windows." *Proceedings of the Twenty-Eighth Australasian Computer Science Conference.* 38 (2005): 193-199.

Tsivian, Y., and G. Civjans. "CineMetrics.lv: Movie measurement and study tool database", 31.08.2007. www.cinemetrics.lv

TREC Video Retrieval Evaluation. 31.08.2007. www-nlpir.nist.gov/projects/trecvid/.

Truong, B. T., C. Dorai, and S. Venkatesh. "New Enhancements to Cut, Fade, and Dissolve Detection Processes in Video Segmentation." *Proceedings of the 8th ACM International Conference on Multimedia.* Marina del Rey, 2000: 219-227.

Vincent, L. "Announcing Tesseract OCR." *Google Code Blog, August 2006.* 31.08.2007. code.google.com/p/tesseract-ocr/.

Viola, P., and M. Jones. "Robust Real-Time Face Detection." *International Journal of Computer Vision.* 57.2 (2004): 137-154.

Weber, R., U. Ritterfeld, and K. Mathiak. "Does Playing Violent Video Games Induce Aggression? Empirical Evidence of a Functional Magnetic Resonance Imaging Study." *Media Psychology.* 8 (2006): 39-60.

Yang, M.-H., D. J. Kriegman, and N. Ahuja. "Detecting Faces in Images: A Survey." *IEEE Transactions on Pattern Analysis and Machine Intelligence* 24.1 (2002): 34-58.

Yeo, B., and Liu, B. "Rapid Scene Analysis on Compressed Video." *IEEE Transactions on Circuits and Systems for Video Technology* 5.6 (1995): 533-544.

Yuan, J., L. Xiao, D. Wang, D. Ding, Y. Zuo, Z. Tong, X. Liu, S. Xu, W. Zheng, X. Li, Z. Si, J. Li, F. Lin, and B. Zhang. "Tsinghua University at TRECVID 2005." *Online Proceedings of TRECVID Conference Series 2005.* 31.08.2007. www-nlpir.nist.gov/projects/tvpubs/tv.pubs.org.html

Zhao, W., R. Chellappa, P. J. Phillips, and A. Rosenfeld. "Face Recognition: A Literature Survey." *ACM Computing Surveys* 35.4 (2003): 399-458.

Vera Kropf, Matthias Zeppelzauer,
Stefan Hahn, Dalibor Mitrovic

First Steps Towards Digital Formalism: The Vienna Vertov Collection[1]

"Digital Formalism: The Vienna Vertov Collection" aims at a computer-aided analysis of the films of Soviet avant-garde filmmaker Dziga Vertov (1896-1954). Besides the development of tools for the digital analysis of films by Vertov, the project focuses on describing the function of cinematic elements in Vertov's work in relation to film form and the perception of the cinematic: what specific cinematic elements affect the audio, visual, haptic, and synaesthetic aspects of perception and how can innovative, high-level media analysis help identify, describe, and analyse (contextualise) these. The collaboration between science (media engineers) and the arts (media researchers) produces an interdisciplinary approach exploring the integration of film theory, advanced digital technology, and conservational/museological principles. The participating institutions include the University of Vienna's Department for Theatre, Film, and Media Studies, the Austrian Film Museum, and the Interactive Media Systems Group at the Vienna University of Technology. The Vertov Collection preserved at the Austrian Film Museum forms the material for analysis.

In the following we will present a few of the more significant theoretical and technical aspects of the project.[2] After an introduction to the goals and prospects of "Digital Formalism" from the perspective of the project partners, we delve deeper into the fundamental questions of our research. What common ground do formalism and digital technology share? How can the formalist method be defined in the age of digital media? What is meant by identifying Vertov as an "ancestor of Digital Formalism"? What specific challenges does this project pose for automatic film analysis? What kinds of tools must be designed to deal with archived material? And what is needed in order to implement them in uncovering hitherto hidden formal patterns in Vertov's films?

---

1   This paper was composed in 2007 and is now partly outdated. An overview on the current state of affairs at the Digital Formalism project can be found in the forthcoming publication *Digitaler Formalismus* (*Maske und Kothurn* 4.2008).

2   We would especially like to thank Barbara Wurm (Humboldt University, Berlin), Andrea Braidt, Klemens Gruber (Vienna University), Michael Loebenstein (Austrian Film Museum), Christian Breiteneder (Vienna University of Technology) and all other participants of the project for contributing their ideas, knowledge and advice.

Goals and Prospects of "Digital Formalism"

We aim to establish Digital Formalism as a theory *and* as a method. We advance the concept of formalism for film and media theory as a way to make comprehensible contemporary digital media and digital art. Our intentions are not only to contribute a formalist position to the discussion of new media, but also to propose a certain set of theoretical and analytical tools. The formalist method is to be translated into a digital framework.

The history of digital technology forms another important area of research. Assuming that theory and technology interact culturally and inspire each other, we conjecture that there is a significant historical connection between formalism and the digital. In this sense we want to trace the development of digital technology against the backdrop of the history of twentieth-century formalist thought.

The film historical focus is on analysis of selected films by Dziga Vertov. The exceptionally complex structure dominant in his œuvre makes providing a detailed analysis an equally complex task. Our computer-aided analysis tools can help to uncover currently hidden formal structures in Vertov's work. Since we argue that Vertov's highly elaborate techniques of filmmaking anticipate digital media, the digital tools developed in this project form a method that is contained implicitly in the material itself.

The digitization of the Vertov Collection preserved at the Austrian Film Museum offers the possibility to conduct a large-scale and in-depth analysis of the formal construction in Dziga Vertov's filmic work and makes the collection accessible as a resource for investigating the aesthetics and politics of film production in the Soviet Union of the 1920s. In addition to the benefits that this brings for Vertov research in general, and the benefit of public accessibility of the collection, we also aim to utilize digital tools for film archival purposes. Digital analysis excels in terms of speed and the volume of data to be processed. Thus, tools that allow an automated comparison of multiple versions of one film as well as automated surveys can facilitate restoration work and provide restorers as well as educators with the means for the visualization of an otherwise "invisible" field of work.

The complex structures contained in Vertov's films, such as accelerated montage and multiple exposures, pose major challenges to automatic film analysis. The core of the project is the development of tools for the computational understanding of media aesthetics; in other words, the automated extraction of high-level film elements such as rhythm, types of dialogue sequences, and use of black film, etc.

Within the computer science part of the project several key areas for research have been identified. Content-based retrieval techniques will be used to identify specific structures in Vertov's films, such as shot cuts, shot rhythm, and camera motion. These techniques will help generate annotations from the films, a very time consuming and error prone task when performed manually.

Data mining techniques will help reveal patterns and correlations in the films that have not yet been analyzed by film experts, e.g. the use of black frames, patterns of black and white contrasts, and patterns of montage. Additionally, data mining is a powerful approach for revealing hitherto unobserved structures in the films. Data mining allows the creation of new perspectives on the material.

Finally, we will develop interactive visualization techniques for presenting the results of the analyses. Visualization techniques allow the user to study sophisticated spatio-temporal patterns and create and verify hypotheses. The combination of interactive data mining and visualization techniques enables the creation of a powerful set of film analysis tools.

The Formalist Method in the Digital Age

In our definition, Digital Formalism becomes a platform for interdisciplinary exchange. The intertwining of technical and theoretical approaches to film demands a concept that is capable of combining both. The formalist tenet – *that art is defined by form* – serves as an interface. Keeping in mind that formalization can be seen as a theoretical method *and also* as a technical method it can be understood both ways – as the basis for an analytical approach in the humanities and as the heart of digital technology. This is why we assume that there is a strong coherence between the digital and the formalist that can be summed up in the principle of film analysis. The double meaning of the word "formalization" is also the starting point for our research on the historical interaction between the emergence of computer technology and that of formalism in the twentieth century.

What role does the formalist method have in the age of digital media? Around 1915 formalism began as a movement in literary criticism by the OPOJAZ in St. Petersburg and the Linguistic Circle in Moscow.[3] In the 1920s, the Russian formalists also applied their method to the "new" medium of film in a series of essays published in 1927 by Boris Ejchenbaum under the title *Poetika Kino*.[4] Despite being practically eliminated in the Soviet Union after 1930, formalism became a major intellectual influence in the twentieth century –

---

3   For an overview of the history of Russian Formalism see Erlich (1955), Hansen-Löve (1978) and Grübel (1996).
4   Recently reprinted in Beilenhoff (2005).

amongst others, the formalist ideas were fundamental to French structuralism. In the 1970s formalism was prominently revitalized for film theory by neo-formalism (the so called "Wisconsin Project"[5]), which emerged to become one of the major tendencies in film studies through to the present day. Digital Formalism is our answer to the current changes in the perception and production of media due to digital technology, which demand a further rethinking of the formalist tenets and method.

Formalism is not a rigid theory but rather a theoretical *approach* and a set of analytical tools that have to be adapted to the material that will be analyzed. While the notion that form is the "particular something without which art is impossible" (Boris Ejchenbaum, 1927) could be read as a very general statement, it in fact points to a very specific method of precise examination. In formalist terms *form* is not an abstract idea but must be understood as a set of artificial devices (*priem*), which comprise a given artwork. Formalism thus turns against narrow and arbitrary interpretations of so-called "content" by arguing that it is necessary to examine the specific structures of an artwork *before* one can talk about its meaning.

Victor Šklovskij's influential text "Art as Procedure" (1916)[6] defines an artwork as a composition of artificial procedures. While some of them are familiar to the recipient's perception there are others that defamiliarize conventional structures known by the recipient. This process of defamiliarization (*ostranenie*) marks the purpose of art: the sharpening of senses by breaking down the habits of everyday perception. Choosing specific artificial procedures enables the artist to establish a new view of formerly unknown structures and of new meanings. Based on the idea of human perception attuning to widely-used artificial procedures, film history can be seen as a chain of alternating links of familiarization and defamiliarization.

Just as digital technology opened the field of formal possibilities for the film medium and lead to an explosion of new artificial devices, it has also altered habits of perception. The criteria of artificial conventions have changed so greatly that it is difficult to trace and estimate the degree of their familiarity. For this reason the age of digital media makes it necessary to reconsider the ideas of Russian formalism.

Even in the digital age the films of Dziga Vertov are alienating. They contain procedures that reach and breach the neurological limits of human perception and thus give the whole artwork the tendency to defamiliarize. For that reason Dziga Vertov can be considered a formalist filmmaker, interested in

---

5   See Bordwell/Thompson/Staiger (1985) and Thompson (1988). For an overview see also Hartmann/Wulff (2003) and Hahn (2006).

6   Reprinted in German in Striedter (1971: 4-35).

exploring the formal possibilities of the new medium, and using them to create a cinematic experience that goes beyond everyday perception, uncovering the procedures of filmmaking within the artwork itself.

"Digital Vertov" and the Formalist Approach to Filmmaking

The Vertov Collection of the Austrian Film Museum includes numerous film copies and related material such as sketches, manuscripts, and diaries, which reveal new insight into Vertov's working methods. The Austrian Film Museum will digitize the film copies frame by frame in the course of this project. Of special interest for our analysis are the *Kinopravdas* (a series of newsreels, 1922-1925), Vertov's "opus magnum" *Celovek s kinoapparatom* (*Man With A Movie Camera*, 1929), *Kinoglaz* (1924), his first sound film *Entuziasm* (1930), *Odinnadcayji* (*The Eleventh Year*, 1928) and *Šestaja čast' mira* (*A Sixth Part of the World*, 1926), as well as all other feature films he produced between 1926 and 1931.

What is striking about this project is that – for the first time in more than 40 years – it is possible to actually compare all existing versions of Vertov's films by using the international network provided by the Film Archive Federation FIAF and through the use of digital technology. For decades this was virtually impossible due to export restrictions from the USSR. The fact that the tradition of Soviet films is often fragmentary, that films are impaired by censors' interventions or due to the natural decomposition of master materials poses a considerable challenge to researchers. In this regard, "Digital Formalism" is the first truly "philological" project focusing on Vertov's film work.

But what does Vertov have to do with Digital Formalism? Our line of argument is based on the assumption that Vertov must be considered a formalist filmmaker at the same time as an ancestor of digital working techniques from an "analogue era".[7] Vertov does not use the moving pictures recorded by the camera to tell a story, but rather treats them like bricks to construct films on the montage table. He thus creates a distinct kind of formalist film-language, a purely cinematic means of expression through associative montage, playful experimentation with formal elements and rapid visual rhythms, a film-language in many ways anticipating the aesthetics of today's art and popular culture, like video clips. Vertov's invention – film as a composition of visual patterns – is the result of highly experimental and unconventional working techniques. Today, comparable effects are easily accomplished with the aid of digital produc-

---

7   Parallels between Vertov and the Digital are also addressed by Lev Manovich (2002: xv-xxix) in "Prologue: Vertov's Dataset".

tion tools. Since Vertov realized the aesthetics of New Media way ahead of their time, we call him a "digital artist" *avant la lettre*.

Vertov's innovative working techniques correspond with his "holistic approach" to film. As an investigator of the aesthetical, theoretical *and* technical dimensions of cinema he calls for a deliberate integration of these aspects. The constructivist Vertov sees himself as a kind of film engineer who experiences the world through his Camera-Eye (*Kino-Glaz*). Thus, his formal experiments not only aim at aesthetic innovations but also explore the specific quality of the medium film from a technical point of view.

Numeric Transcription

Figure 1. "Numeric Transcription of a montage piece of a film by Dziga Vertov – the moment of the flying of the flag on the day of the opening of a pioneer camp".

The drawings, schedules, diagrams and sketches shed the most light on Vertov's unconventional working methods. The schedule in Figure 1 is an outstanding example that vividly illustrates what we call Vertov's "formalist approach" to filmmaking.[8]

---

8   We would like to thank the Austrian Film Museum and Barbara Wurm for providing the photograph reproduced here. The schedule was first published in Aleksandr Belenson's *Kino-segodnja [Film Today]: Ocerki sovetskogo kinoiskusstva* (Moskva 1925) – a book dedicated to Kuleschov, Vertov and Eisenstein. It is part of the

It is, as the title says, a "Numeric Transcription" of a montage sequence from *Kinoglaz*. The recorded scene takes place at the opening of a pioneer camp and shows the moment of the flying of the flag. The numbers on top of the schedule (from 1 to 52) refer to the "succession of the parts" or the *shots* in the order in which they are edited in the film. The left column contains a list of the "acting persons and objects" – the head of the pioneer leader (1), a female pioneer at the pole (2), pole and flag (3), Intertitle: "Fly the flag!" (4), a trumpet player (5), Face No 1 (6), Face No 2 (7), et cetera. These are what we call the *motifs*. The numbers inside the schedule display the *number of frames* or the length of each shot. The column on the right side contains the *total number of frames* for each motif.

The schedule that was first published in 1925 was very likely drawn up after the finishing of the film. We don't know whether Vertov actually made a transcription of his own movie or if he used notes or editing lists compiled earlier. For our line of argument it is insubstantial if this transcription is 'correct' in comparison with the film itself or if Vertov actually used this kind of diagram in the working process. The crucial point is that he *made* this schedule – which must have been a lot of work as it is handmade – as this reveals a strong interest in film as a systematic technical construction. The process of montage is literally translated into a numeric system. In this regard one could even argue that Vertov treats the filmstrips digitally – although the schedule is perfectly 'analogue' in the common usage of the word.[9]

A close look at the schedule reveals enough to give a clear idea of the recorded scene even without actually seeing it in the film. Regarding the rhythm of montage in general, one can see that the changes from one shot to the next are edited in rapid succession. Most of the shots last only a couple of frames (respectively fractions of a second) – a kind of accelerated montage, which is typical for Vertov. The plot of the scene – the flying of the flag – is thus organized in a complex assembly of fragments. A look at the right column reveals that motif no 3 "pole and flag" has the most frames (208) followed by motif no 2 "female pioneer at the pole" (183) – this fact alone shows that – unsurprisingly – the flag itself is the dominant motif in this scene containing 905 frames in total (which is less than a minute, as the film is projected with 18 frames per second). Moreover, it suggests that it is the pioneer from motif no 2 who is actually flying the flag since she is the person with the most frames.

---

collection of the Austrian Film Museum [V 39] and was recently reprinted along with other formerly unpublished work sketches in: Tode/Wurm (2006: 105).

9   The discussion of the terms 'digital' and 'analogue' forms a fundamental research issue in our project. For different aspects of the topic see Schröter (2004).

A number of different rhythmic patterns can be gathered from the schedule: in the beginning of the scene the montage alternates between shots of the pioneer leader, the pioneer, and the flag with varying shot lengths. In the next sequence different shots of faces (motifs 6 to 9, the spectators) are alternated with shots of flag (3) and pioneer (2), all of these shots having a length of 10 frames. This periodic 10-frame-rhythm is repeated again later on and dominates much of the scene. Towards the end of the flag-scene there is a sequence of longer shots showing the pioneer (motif no 2, 93 frames), the shadow of the flag (motif no 15, 65 frames) and the legs of the pioneer (motif no 16, 60 frames), suggesting that the flag is finally being raised. The scene is concluded by a succession of short shots of faces followed by a longer shot of the flag (motif no 3, 48 frames).

A detailed analysis of the schedule reveals that it contains a considerable amount of information about the film in the form of numeric data. The fact that Vertov made such an elaborate transcription of a scene from one of his own films shows his efforts to advance techniques of filmmaking in a very radical way. With perfectly analogue methods he thus anticipates a digital view of film.

Automatic Film Analysis

Vertov is a filmmaker who stresses formalistic principles in his work. His films can be considered an assemblage of numerous visual patterns, with particular importance given to rhythmic patterns of montage. The high degree of structure in Vertov's films makes them well suited for automatic content-based analysis.

The Material

The Austrian Film Museum supplies the films on 35mm triacetate film. The films are several decades old and multiple-generation copies (mainly backup copies) of the master material. The films are black and white and mostly do not contain sound. Only a few of Dziga Vertov's more recent films contain sound (e.g. *Enthuziasm*). The frame rate for playback of the films is not clearly specified. Usually, a frame rate of 18 frames per second is used for playback.

Prior to working with the material it needs to be digitized. High quality frame by frame digitization will be carried out by scanning each frame separately. The result is one grayscale image for each frame in standard definition or higher. This approach avoids the production of interpolated frames. Interpolated frames are introduced during digitization when the material is converted from one frame rate to another frame rate. Digital videos usually have a frame rate of 25 or 30 fps. If the material originally had 18 fps, the process of digitization would insert interpolated frames in order to convert the film to the higher frame rate. However, interpolated frames represent information that is not present in the original film. Consequently, this information is not suitable for analysis and would falsify the results of the automatic analysis.

After digitization each film is represented by an image sequence. This format is well suited for further processing and the generation of digital videos.

Challenges in the Context of the Material

The films provided are all black-and-white films. Furthermore, most of the films are silent. This makes the automatic analysis much more difficult since neither colour nor sound information may be used in the analysis. Colour is important information for recognition tasks, such as face recognition and shot-cut detection. Audio is a modality complementary to video that contains orthogonal information. The audio track of a film contains speech, music, and environmental sounds that provide important semantic information. For example, music reflects excitement and the temper of a scene and speech allows the identification of distinct people.

Another important issue is the quality of the provided films. The available filmstrips are multiple-generation copies of the master material and are several decades old. There are numerous artefacts that result from copying, storing, and playback of the films.

The material of the films is organic. That means that the material changes its structure over time. The most important artefact that is generated in this context is the evidence of the filmstrip's vertical shrinking. When a shrunken filmstrip is copied, the frames in the old film do not match with the frames in the new filmstrip. This results in misaligned frames in the new filmstrip, as shown in Figure 2. Another artefact introduced by misaligned frames is the displacement of the frame line. For example in Figure 2, the frame line is not positioned between the current and the next frame. Due to the shrinking of the material the frame line is positioned inside the visible area of the frame and produces a dark horizontal bar. Another artefact resulting from storage is caused by the horizontal shrinking of the filmstrip. Horizontal shrinkage is usually not as strong as vertical shrinkage. However, it may result in frames where the perforations become visible at the left and right side of the frame.

Figure 2. A misaligned frame in a filmstrip of Vertov's *Kinopravda 21*. The top of the next frame is visible on the bottom edge of the frame. Consequently, the frame line becomes visible inside the frame.

The misaligned frames produce an unstable image. When the film is played back we observe that the frames move especially in vertical direction. The reason for this is that shrinking influences the aspect ratio of the frames and distorts the proportions. The displacement of frames is not very disturbing for the human observer because we are able to compensate for it. However, a computer system is highly disturbed by such displacements. Prior to working with the material, we need to correct the distortions and register the frames in order to enable frame by frame comparisons, which are an important part of digital film analysis.

Another issue is that the process of copying introduces dirt when the film is copied under suboptimal conditions. Dirt highly disturbs the observer and occludes information in the film that is important for film analysis.

Further artefacts are scratches, especially vertical line scratches, which are mechanical defects introduced during the play-back of the films. The amount of dirt and scratches increases with each generation of a copy. Figure 3 shows two frames that illustrate different types of artefacts.

Figure 3. Two frames with a number of different artefacts (shadows, scratches, etc.)

Finally, the process of copying degrades the contrast of the film. With each copy the frames become more saturated. That means that intermediate gray values are lost while the portion of saturated (totally black and totally white) areas increases.

In addition to the numerous artefacts we have thus far identified, the material provides us with information that may be helpful in automatic analysis. The filmstrips contain labels inserted by cutters and archivists, that indicate shot cuts. The labels represent numbers that are references to entries in a montage list (shot list). The labels have been inserted in the intermediate area between two successive frames (the border line). Figure 4 shows an example of such a label.

The labels help to enhance shot cut detection, since each shot cut is labelled consistently by number. The labels are not positioned directly at the cuts but in most cases two or three frames after a shot cut (see Figure 4 for illustration). The labels can be useful for two purposes. We can integrate a label detection algorithm into the shot cut detection in order to improve the quality of shot cut detection. Another possibility is to use the labels as a ground truth that forms the basis for the evaluation the quality of a shot cut detection algorithm. In this case, the labels are not incorporated into shot cut detection, instead, we compare the positions of the detected shots with the positions of the labels in the filmstrip.

Figure 4: A manually inserted label two frames after a shot cut. The magnification reveals that the label represents a number (the number of the shot).

Requirements for Automatic Film Analysis

There have been a number of challenging requirements identified for the analysis of Vertov's films. In a first step, shot cut detection will be carried out in order to temporally segment the films. A shot cut is the most important basic entity of a film. Hard cuts and transitions will be detected, such as wipes and (cross-)fades. Shot cut detection is the basis for the computation of shot frequency, which is an important measure for the rhythm of the film and the progression of tension.

After shot cut detection, each shot can be further analyzed and classified. In this step, we distinguish between different types of shots. Intertitles, very common in silent films, are also detected. They contain text that is related to the content of a film. We can perform text recognition to gain semantic information from the titles. Likewise detected are shots with "multiple image" or split-screen montage. Vertov often employs split-screen montage to illustrate concurrency and to accelerate the rhythm of the film. The frequency of split-screen shots in a film and the number of splits in the shots is important information for film theorists.

The identification of symmetries will be another focus of the automatic film analysis occurring in the context of this project. Symmetries play an important role in Vertov's films. He often employs symmetric compositions in his shots.

In addition to temporal segmentation and the classification of different types of shots, motion in the films will be analyzed. This incorporates camera motion estimation and detection of object motion. Camera motion estimation focuses on the detection of basic camera movements, such as rotations (pan, tilt, and roll), translational movements (track, boom, and dolly) and zoom. The annotation of the camera movements in a film is a crucial but time consuming task in manual film analysis. Automatic techniques can speed up this process significantly. The detection of object motion is much more difficult, especially when concurrent camera motions exist or motion occurs in the background. In general, it is not possible to separate the motion of objects and the camera. Object motion may be computed only under certain assumptions, for example when no camera movements exists or the background is static.

Vertov often reused material in several film productions. Consequently, his later films contain shots and motifs that have already been used in earlier films. Furthermore, there are compilations where material from different filmmakers (including Vertov) has been merged. A goal of this project is to develop techniques to compare different films and identify reused material. This is a non-trivial task, since the reused material is not an identical copy of the original material. The reused material may have been copied several times and may contain scratches, dirt, and other artefacts that are not present in the source material. The comparison of different films will be one of the main focuses of the project. The development of automatic film comparison algorithms is beneficial, since manual comparison by a human user would be much too time consuming.

The strong foundation of the project in media theory offers a perspective that is currently not represented in debates regarding digitization of cultural heritage. Digital Formalist Analysis will enable scholars, students of film/media studies, and actors in creative industries to study, discuss, and scrutinize audio-visual artefacts and their specific artistic and historical-cultural acquaintance with the senses.

Bibliography

Beilenhoff, Wolfgang (ed.): *Poetika Kino. Theorie und Praxis des Films im Russischen Formalismus*. Frankfurt a.M.: Suhrkamp, 2005.

Bordwell, David, Kristin Thompson, and Janet Staiger: *The Classical Hollywood Cinema. Film Style and Mode of Production to 1960*. London: Routledge, 1985.

Drubek-Meyer, Natascha (ed.): *Apparatur und Rhapsodie. Zu den Filmen des Dziga Vertov*. Frankfurt a.M., Wien: Lang, 2000.

Erlich, Victor: *Russian Formalism. History, doctrine*. s-Gravenhage: Mouton, 1955.

Gruber, Klemens (ed.): *Verschiedenes über denselben. Dziga Vertov 1896-1954*. Wien: Böhlau, 2006.

Gruber, Klemens (ed.): *Maske und Kothurn* 1.1996: *Dziga Vertov zum 100. Geburtstag*.

Gruber, Klemens and Aki Beckmann (eds.): *Maske und Kothurn* 2.1996: *Der kreiselnde Kurbler. Dziga Vertov zum 100. Geburtstag (2)*.

Grübel, Rainer: "Formalismus und Strukturalismus" *Grundzüge der Literaturwissenschaft*. Ed. Heinz Ludwig Arnold, Heinrich Detering. München: Deutscher Taschenbuchverlag, 1996: 386-408.

Hahn, Stefan: *Narrativer Film als kognitiver Prozess: Neoformalistische Forschung und Verstehen nonlinearer Erzählstrukturen in* Amores Perros. Dipl. Wien 2006.

Hansen-Löve, Aage A.: *Der russische Formalismus. Methodologische Rekonstruktion seiner Entwicklung aus dem Prinzip der Verfremdung*. Wien: Verlag der Österreichischen Akademie der Wissenschaften, 1978.

Hartmann, Britta and Hans J. Wulff: "Neoformalismus, Kognitivismus, Historische Poetik des Kinos" *Moderne Filmtheorie*. Ed. Jürgen Felix. Mainz: Bender, 2003: 191-216.

Jakobson, Roman: *Poetik. Ausgewählte Aufsätze 1921-1971*. Ed. Elmar Holenstein. Frankfurt a.M.: Suhrkamp, 1979.

Jakobson, Roman: *Semiotik. Ausgewählte Texte 1919-1982*. Ed. Elmar Holenstein. Frankfurt a.M.: Suhrkamp, 1992.

Kjeldsen, R. and J. Kender: "Finding Skin in Color Images." *Proceedings of the Second International Conference on Automatic Face and Gesture Recognition*, Killington, VT, 1996: 312-317.

Kropf, Vera: *Der Zackenzauber auf dem Zelluloid. Die optische Tonspur von den Anfängen der Tonaufzeichnung bis zum gezeichneten Ton um 1930*. Dipl. Wien 2006.

Manovich, Lev: *The Language of New Media*. Cambridge/MA: MIT, 2001.

Michelson, Annette: "From Magician To Epistemologist: The Man With the Movie Camera". *Artforum* 10.7 (1972): 60-72. Reprinted in: Gruber (1996).

Petric, Vlada: *Constructivism in Film. The Man With The Movie Camera. A Cinematic Analysis*. Cambridge: University Press, 1987.

Schröter, Jens (ed.): *Digital/Analaog – Opposition oder Kontinuum? Zur Theorie und Geschichte einer Unterscheidung*. Bielefeld: Transcript, 2004.

Sklovskij, Viktor: "Kunst als Verfahren" (1916). Reprinted in: Striedter (1971).

Striedter, Jurij (ed.): *Russischer Formalismus. Texte zur allgemeinen Literaturtheorie und zur Theorie der Prosa*. München: Fink, 1971.

Tode, Thomas and Barbara Wurm (ed.): *Dziga Vertov. Die Vertov-Sammlung im Österreichischen Filmmuseum / The Vertov Collection at the Austrian Film Museum*. Wien: Synema, 2006.

Thompson, Kristin: *Breaking the Glass Armor. Neoformalist Film Analysis*. Princeton: University Press, 1988.

Tsivian, Yuri: *Lines of Resistance: Dziga Vertov and the Twenties*. Pordenone: Le Giornate del Cinema Muto, 2004.

Vertov, Dziga: *Tagebücher, Arbeitshefte*. Ed. Thomas Tode. Konstanz: Universitätsverlag, 2000.

Vertov, Dziga: *Schriften zum Film*. Ed. Wolfgang Beilenhoff. München: Hanser, 1973.

Vertov, Dziga: *Kino-Eye: The Writings of Dziga Vertov*. Ed. Annette Michelson. Berkeley, CA: University of California Press, 1995.

Zhang, H. J., A. Kankanhalli, and S. W. Smoliar: "Automatic partitioning of full-motion video." *Multimedia Systems* 1.1 (1993): 10-28.

Warren Buckland

Ghost Director

Did Hooper or Spielberg Direct *Poltergeist*?

Spielberg released two films in 1982 – *E.T.*, which he directed but did not write; and *Poltergeist*, which he wrote and produced but did not direct (he hired Tobe Hooper). But controversy surrounds Spielberg's actual role on *Poltergeist*. Before the film's release, Dale Pollock noted that "Spielberg will ... be pacing the list of horror films with 'Poltergeist', which he produced (and according to reports, largely directed)" (1982a: H1). In his biography of Spielberg, Joseph McBride (1987) argues that "[Spielberg's] involvement on *Poltergeist* was unusually intense for a producer and writer. ... It was generally believed in Hollywood that Spielberg simply moved in and took over the film creatively" (336). And in *The Guardian* a few years ago, David Thomson (2002) chipped in: "it is pretty well agreed now that [*Poltergeist*] deserves to be read as a Spielberg work". The language of these critics is equivocal: "according to reports"; "It was generally believed"; "it is pretty well agreed"; and their aesthetic evaluations of the film are vague and impressionistic.

Spielberg spelled out the nature of his collaboration with Hooper: "[Tobe Hooper is] just not a strong presence on a movie set. If a question was asked and an answer wasn't immediately forthcoming, I'd jump up and say what we *could* do. Tobe would nod in agreement, and that became the process of the collaboration. I did *not* want to direct the movie – I had to do 'E.T.' five weeks after principal photography on 'Poltergeist'" (quoted in Pollock 1982b: G2; emphases in the original).

Hooper, for his part, simply noted that "I directed the film and I did fully half of the story boards" (quoted in Pollock 1982b: G1). He maintains that no problem exists concerning his and Spielberg's creative input into the film. Spielberg attempted to quell the intense media interest in the controversy by writing an open letter to Hooper in the form of a full-page ad in the June 9 1982 issue of *Variety*. It began: "Regrettably, some of the press has misunderstood the rather unique, creative relationship, which you and I shared throughout the making of *Poltergeist*" (quoted in McBride 1987: 339). I shall attempt to distinguish legend from fact in regards to *Poltergeist*'s disputed authorship.

Using Statistics to Analyse Style

I decided to analyse *Poltergeist* for my book *Directed by Steven Spielberg* (2006; the following is an abbreviated version of my analysis in that book). In matters of "authorship attribution," I discovered that statistics is frequently used to quantify style and credit an author. Don Foster's (2001) headline-grabbing statistical style analyses of the anonymous novel *Primary Colors* (which he correctly attributed to Joe Klein), the Unabomber's manifesto (whose author he identified), and the anonymous "Funeral Elegy," which he attributed to Shakespeare (his most problematic attribution), are only the most visible versions of the use of statistics to determine authorship. Through a shot-by-shot analysis, I use statistical methods to compare and contrast *Poltergeist* to a selection of Hooper's and Spielberg's other films. From this analysis I determine how *Poltergeist*'s style conforms to and deviates from Spielberg's and Hooper's filmmaking strategies. Such an analysis contains a lot of number crunching and statistical testing, which are necessary if we want to go beyond impressionistic criticism and make an informed judgement on the creative force behind *Poltergeist*. The results of my analysis may surprise you.

Counting Shots

To place *Poltergeist* into context, I examined the stylistic elements of films whose authorship is undisputed: Spielberg's *E.T.* (1982) and *Jurassic Park* (1993), Hooper's *Salem's Lot* (1979) and *The Funhouse* (1981). I then compare these films of undisputed authorship with *Poltergeist*, to determine whose style it matches. Of course, the result of such a speculative analysis is never 100% certain, but can only be stated with a degree of probability.

Statistical analysis explores style numerically by quantifying – that is, measuring and counting – a film's stylistic features, especially those relating to the shot. It is more credible and valid than the standard *Cahiers* and *Movie* schools of stylistic analysis – *mise-en-scène* and auteur criticism – because it downplays the critic's subjective impressions of a film in favour of a more detached and accurate analysis.

Privileging the director has always created controversy in what is an inherently collaborative medium. But we need to remember some of the more level-headed claims filmmakers and critics have made in its defence. For Karel Reisz (1968), the director "is responsible for planning the visual continuity during shooting, and he [sic] is therefore in the best position to exercise a unifying control over the whole production" (58). For V. F. Perkins (1972), "The director is there to ensure that the details of performance and recording are related to the total design" (179). And Anthony Asquith (1950) suggested the film director can be compared to an orchestra conductor, for both control a large creative team. The film director does not need to write the script or light the set, just as an orchestra conductor does not need to compose the music or play an instrument. Each instrument in an orchestra is not just playing solo, but is subordinate to the whole orchestra, which creates a unique sound not existent in any one instrument. The conductor is in control of generating this unique sound from the various instruments. The film director, like the conductor, is the only member of the creative team who bears the whole work in mind, controlling the way each instrument contributes to the work's total design.

Guided by Barry Salt's research (1974, 1992, 2004), I quantify the individual styles of Spielberg and Tobe Hooper by measuring and counting the formal elements of a selection of each directors' films – elements that are typically under the director's control, including: duration of the shot; shot scale; camera movement; angle of the shot; low camera height; use of shot/reverse shot; length and number of shots in a typical scene. I then compare the style of *Poltergeist* to that of Spielberg's and Hooper's films, to see whose style it matches.

Shot duration is simply measured in seconds. The average length of each shot in a film is calculated by dividing the number of shots into the film's length to produce the film's average shot length (ASL).

The following scale of shot are identified and counted: Very Long Shot (VLS): human subject is small in the frame; Long Shot (LS): full shot of the human body; Medium Long Shot (MLS): the human subject filmed from the knees up; Medium Shot (MS): the human subject filmed from the waist up; Medium Close-Up (MCU): the head and shoulders; Close-Up (CU): the head only; Big Close-Up (BCU): part of the face or fragment of the body. I count the number of shot scales used in each film, and determine low long each one is on screen.

I also count the camera movements in each film, which I note down in two stages: type of movement (still, pan, track, crane, pan and track), and direction (sideways, up, down, back, forward).

The angle of shot is also quantified: is the camera at eye level? Or is it a low camera angle or high camera angle? I distinguish low camera *angle* from low camera *height*. In a low camera angle, the camera is pointing upwards; in a high camera angle, the camera is pointing downwards. When a shot is classified as low camera *height*, the camera is close to the ground. Low camera angle and low camera height are therefore not the same. Camera angle is defined in terms of the subject being filmed (whether the camera is pointing up to or down on the subject). Camera height is defined in terms of the camera's relation to the ground. A camera can be low on the ground, but not pointing upward (as is typical in Yasujiro Ozu's films). This would be low camera height but not low camera angle. Sometimes, of course, the camera is low on the ground and pointing upward. This is low camera height plus low camera angle.

Shot/reverse shot (or reverse angles) refers to a pair of shots in which the camera changes direction by more than 90° in the horizontal plane (Salt 1992: 146). It is commonly used when filming two people facing one another. Salt distinguishes "in front of the shoulder reverse angles" (what Steven D. Katz [1991] calls internal reverse angles, in which the camera is placed inside the circle of action), and "behind the shoulder reverse angles" (what Katz calls external reverse angles). An optical point-of-view shot (shot of character looking/ shot of what they see from their vantage point) is a subset of reverse angle cutting. When counting reverse angles I did not feel the need to distinguish between these different types.

I define a scene using John Ellis's (1982) criteria: a scene displays a marked unity of space, time, characters, and events: "The segment is a relatively self-contained scene which conveys an incident, a mood or a particular meaning. Coherence is provided by a continuity of character through the segment, or, more occasionally, a continuity of place" (148). I mark a change in scene if at least two of the following take place: the film changed location; a temporal break occurs; the film cuts to a different set of characters and events.

Following Salt, I collected this data by going through each film shot-by-shot – or at least the first 30 minutes of each film, because this constitutes a representative sample and generates sufficient data for comparison. I entered the data into the statistical software package SPSS (an elaborate spreadsheet), and applied a few very simple statistical tests that summarize the data.

Reasons for Classifying *Poltergeist* as a Tobe Hooper Film

The data for all five films can be found in Appendices 1 to 5 at the end of this essay. The following comments offer a partial interpretation of those Tables.

Camera movement: Both *Salem's Lot* and *The Funhouse* have less than 20% moving camera, whereas *E.T.* and *Jurassic Park* have over 20%. Only 15% of shots in *Poltergeist* involve a moving camera, which is closer to Hooper's films than to Spielberg's.

Shot scale: Hooper chooses more medium close-ups (MCU) than Spielberg, but fewer long shots (LS). Hooper uses over 30% medium close-ups, whereas Spielberg averages out at 27%. *Poltergeist* is closer to Hooper's average because it contains 34% medium close-ups. Conversely, the amount of long shots Hooper uses is around 5-6% whereas Spielberg's is 14%. *Poltergeist* contains only 7% long shots, very close to *Salem's Lot* and *The Funhouse*. In general, Spielberg's shot scales vary more than Hooper's, and the relatively limited variation of shot scale in *Poltergeist* is closer to Hooper than to Spielberg. On average, 58% of Hooper's shot scales fall within the "big close-up to medium close-up" range; for Spielberg, the figure is only 45%. In *Poltergeist*, 55% of the shot scales fall within this range, significantly closer to Hooper than Spielberg.

Shot duration: Hooper uses a higher number of shots in the 1-3 second range than Spielberg, who typically spreads out his shot lengths. *Salem's Lot* and *The Funhouse* are almost identical – 45% and 46% of shots fall within the 1-3 second range. Conversely, in *E.T.* only 41% of all shots fall within the 1-3 second range. *Jurassic Park* is even lower, at 35%. In *Poltergeist*, 54% of all shots fall within the 1-3 second range, much closer to Hooper. In more technical terms, the values for shot length are more positively skewed in Hooper than they are in Spielberg – that is, more slanted away from the average shot length towards the lower values. A film in which shot lengths are perfectly distributed around the average has a skew value of 0. The skewness values for shot duration in Hooper's films are: *Salem's Lot*: 5.6; *The Funhouse*: 4.1; in Spielberg's films the value is 2.7 for both *E.T.* and *Jurassic Park*. *Poltergeist*'s skewness value is 5.5, very close to Hooper's values and significantly higher than Spielberg's.

Reasons for Classifying *Poltergeist* as a Steven Spielberg Film

Despite the strong evidence that Hooper exercised control over camera movement, shot scale and shot duration (in the 1-3 second range) in *Poltergeist*, information exists pointing to Spielberg's influence.

Low camera height: 53% of all shots in *Poltergeist* were filmed at a low camera height, where the camera is 3 feet or lower from the ground. Compare this with *Salem's Lot*'s 29%, *The Funhouse*'s 33%, *E.T.*'s 49% and *Jurassic Park*'s 42%. The decision to use low camera height is of course motivated by the story material – the two young children in *Poltergeist*, the 3 foot E.T. and two young children in *E.T.*, and the two young children in *Jurassic Park*. However, the director always has a choice, and can film children or aliens at higher heights or adults at lower heights. In *Jurassic Park*, for example, the two young children do not even appear in the first 30 minutes of the film, the length of the sample, yet 42% of the shots were still filmed at low camera height. We can infer that the decision to use so many low camera heights in *Poltergeist* was Spielberg's suggestion, which constitutes one of the pieces of advice he offered to Hooper on the set.

Shot duration: Hooper tends to allow his larger shot scales (in the "medium to very long shot" range) run for long periods of time. (This has the effect of compensating for and balancing out the short duration of his smaller shot scales, making Hooper's overall average shot length close to Spielberg's.)

In *Salem's Lot*, the average length of each medium shot (MS) is 9.3 seconds; in *The Funhouse* each medium shot averages out at 9.5 seconds. By contrast, in *E.T.* the medium shot averages out at only 5.2 seconds, and in *Jurassic Park* it is 6 seconds. In *Poltergeist*, the average length of a medium shot is 6 seconds, the same as *Jurassic Park* and close to *E.T.*, and significantly shorter than the duration of Hooper's medium shots. The evidence for the medium long shot (MLS) is almost the same: *Salem's Lot*: 14.4 seconds; *The Funhouse*: 9.8 seconds; *E.T.*: 6.9 seconds; *Jurassic Park*: 9 seconds; *Poltergeist*: 9 seconds. In other words, the average length of a medium long shot in *Poltergeist* is closer to the two Spielberg films, and is shorter than both of Hooper's films. The medium long shots in the two Hooper films average out at 12.1 seconds, and at 8 seconds in the two Spielberg films. *Poltergeist*'s 9 seconds is closer to Spielberg's average and clearly shorter than Hooper's average, suggesting that his average length for the medium long shot, as for the medium shot, was influenced by Spielberg. It seems that Spielberg wasn't as successful at trimming the length of the long shots in *Poltergeist*, for they average out at 17 seconds. We have already seen that Hooper uses far fewer long shots than Spielberg, making the small number of long shots a Hooper trait. Perhaps Spielberg recognized that Hooper used so few long shots that he (Spielberg) was reluctant to trim them in the editing room. He was not, however, reluctant to trim Hooper's medium and medium long shots.

Conclusion: Did Spielberg Ghost Direct *Poltergeist*?

On the basis of evidence extracted from the film, and contrary to widespread industry and press rumour, Hooper *did* demonstrate a sufficient amount of control over the style of *Poltergeist*, at least in the pre-production and production stages. Spielberg no doubt made specific suggestions (in addition to much of the content, he surely recommended filming at a low camera height; to film some scenes in a long take, such as the parents watching television in their bedroom at night – a shot that lasts 96 seconds; use an analytic cut-in on Robbie's clown to make it more scary). However, in the film's *overall* style, *Poltergeist* shares several traits with Hooper's other films (except low camera height). *Poltergeist* deviates from Hooper's style primarily in the post-production stage of editing, where large scale shots have been trimmed to fit Spielberg's style, except for the long shot, whose number are so few that they were not trimmed in the editing room. Hooper's claim that he designed fully half the shots in *Poltergeist* may even be an understatement, and the observation that Hooper did not supervise the film's editing, but that Spielberg did, rings true.

My conclusions run counter to the widely-held belief – one I also held before analysing the film – that *Poltergeist* should be added to the list of films directed by Spielberg. On the strength of my statistical style analysis, *Poltergeist* is a film directed by Tobe Hooper.

References

Asquith, Anthony. "The Tenth Muse takes Stock." *The Cinema 1950*. Ed. Roger Manvell. Harmondsworth: Penguin Books, 1950: 30-45.

Buckland, Warren. *Directed by Steven Spielberg: Poetics of the Contemporary Hollywood Blockbuster*. New York: Continuum, 2006.

Ellis, John. *Visible Fictions: Cinema, Television, Video*. London: Routledge, 1982.

Foster, Don. *Author Unknown: On the Trail of Anonymous*. London: MacMillan, 2001.

Katz, Steven D. *Film Directing: Shot by Shot*. Studio City, CA: Michael Wiese, 1991.

McBride, Joseph. *Steven Spielberg: A Biography*. London: Faber and Faber, 1987.

Perkins, V. F. *Film as Film: Understanding and Judging Movies*. Harmondsworth: Penguin Books, 1972.

Pollock, Dale. "Film '82: A New Beginning." *Los Angeles Times*, January 1, 1982a: H1; H10-11.

Pollock, Dale. "'Poltergeist': Just Whose Film is It?" *Los Angeles Times*, May 24, 1982b: G1-2.

Reisz, Karel (with Gavin Millar). *The Technique of Film Editing*. Second edition. London: Focal Press, 1968.

Salt, Barry. "Statistical Style Analysis of Motion Pictures." *Film Quarterly*, 28.1 (1974): 13-22.

Salt, Barry. *Film Style and Technology: History and Analysis*. Second edition. London: Starword, 1992.

Salt, Barry. "The Shape of 1999: The Stylistics of American Movies at the End of the Century." *New Review of Film and Television Studies*. 2.1 (2004): 61-85.

Thomson, David. "Alien Resurrection." *The Guardian*, Friday March 15, 2002: http://www.guardian.co.uk/Archive/Article/0,4273,4374066,00.html (accessed August 14 2007)

Appendix 1: The Statistical Style of *Poltergeist*

270 shots (first 30 minutes); ASL: 6.7 seconds
41% of the shots are reverse angles
5% are low camera angle
12% are high camera angle
53% are at low camera height (at or below a child's eye level)
85% of the shots are still, 15% are moving
Out of the 15% of moving shots, 8% use panning, 7% use tracking, and 1% craning. In terms of the direction of the camera movement, 8% involve sideways movement, 2% upward, 3% backwards, and 2% forwards.

Shot Scale

BCU: 2% of all shots; Average length of each BCU shot: 2.5 seconds
CU: 19%; 3.3 seconds
MCU: 34%; 5 seconds
MS: 20%; 6 seconds
MLS: 10%; 9 seconds
LS: 7%; 17 seconds
VLS: 8%; 7.6 seconds

Shot Duration

53% of all shots fall within the 1-3 second range;
69% within the 1-5 second range;
85% within the 1-10 second range.
Shot duration skewness value: 5.5

Correlation of Shot Scale and Duration

When we correlate shot scale with shot length, we end up with the following figures for the amount of time each type of shot remains on screen during the first 30 minutes:
BCU: on screen for a total of 15 seconds (1% of the time)
CU: 2 minutes 53 seconds (10%)
MCU: 7 minutes 36 seconds (25%)
MS: 5 minutes 27 seconds (19%)
MLS: 4 minutes 16 seconds (14%)
LS: 5 minutes 20 seconds (18%)
VLS: 2 minutes 40 seconds (9%)

Appendix 2: The Statistical Style of *Salem's Lot*

254 shots (first 30 minutes); ASL: 7 seconds
68% of the shots are reverse angles
14% of the shots are at a low camera angle
10% of the shots are at a high camera angle
29% of shots are at a low camera height
83.5% of the shots are still/16.5% are moving
Out of the 16.5% of moving shots, 7.5% use panning, 9% use tracking, and 0.5% crane. In terms of the direction of the camera movement, 11% move sideways, 0.5% move down, 3% backwards, and 2% forwards.

Shot Scale

BCU: 2%; Average length of each BCU shot: 3.1 seconds
CU: 24%; 3.6 seconds
MCU: 33%; 5.3 seconds
MS: 17%; 9.3 seconds
MLS: 7%; 14.4 seconds
LS: 6%; 8.7 seconds
VLS: 11%; 8.7 seconds

Shot Duration

46% of shots fall within the 1-3 second range;
64% within the 1-5 second range;
84% within the 1-10 second range.
Shot duration skewness value: 5.6

Correlation of Shot Scale and Duration

BCU: on screen for a total of 19 seconds (1% of the time)
CU: on screen for 3 minutes 40 seconds (12 % of the time)
MCU: 7 minutes 32 seconds (25% of the time)
MS: 6 minutes 50 seconds (23% of the time)
MLS: 4 minutes 6 seconds (14% of the time)
LS: 2 minutes 11 seconds (7% of the time)
VLS: 3 minutes 54 seconds (13% of the time)

Appendix 3: The Statistical Style of *The Funhouse*

240 shots (first 30 minutes); ASL: 7.5 seconds
38% reverse angle shots
9% low camera angle
8% high camera angle
33% low camera height
81% of shots are still, 19% are moving.
Out of the 19% of moving shots, 7% use panning, 10% tracking, and 1% crane. In terms of direction of camera movement, 9% involve sideways movement, 2% upwards movement, 1% downwards, 2% backwards, and 5% forwards.

Shot Scale

BCU: 8%; Average length of each BCU shot: 3 seconds
CU: 13%; 3 seconds
MCU: 36%; 4.8 seconds
MS: 20%; 9.5 seconds
MLS: 11%; 9.8 seconds
LS: 5%; 20 seconds
VLS: 7%; 8.8 seconds

Shot Duration

45% of all shots fall within the 1-3 second range;
63% within the 1-5 second range;
83% within the 1-10 second range.
Shot duration skewness value: 4.1

Correlation of Shot Scale and Shot Duration

BCU: on screen for a total of 56 seconds (3% of the time)
CU: on screen for 1 minutes 40 seconds (6% of the time)
MCU: 7 minutes (23% of the time)
MS: 7 minutes 27 seconds (25% of the time)
MLS: 4 minutes 16 seconds (14% of the time)
LS: 4 minutes 26 seconds (15% of the time)
VLS: 2 minutes 30 seconds (8% of the time)

Appendix 4: The Statistical Style of *E.T.*

288 shots (first 30 minutes); ASL: 6.25 seconds
35 % of the shots are reverse angles
9% of shots at a low camera angle
18% of shots at a high camera angle
49% of shots at a low camera height
74% of shots are still/26% are moving
Out of the 26% of moving shots, 9% use panning, 15% use tracking, and 3% crane. In terms of the direction of the camera movement, 15% involve sideways movement, 3% upward movement, 1% downward, 2% backwards, and 5% forwards.

Shot Scale

BCU: 6% of all shots; Average length of each BCU shot: 2.7 seconds
CU: 16%; 3.6 seconds
MCU: 26%; 5.1 seconds
MS: 17%; 5.2 seconds
MLS: 10%; 6.9 seconds
LS: 15%; 9 seconds
VLS: 9%; 9 seconds

Shot Duration

41% of all shots fall within the 1-3 second range;
66% fall within the 1-5 second range,
86% within the 1-10 second range.
Shot duration skewness value: 2.7

Correlation of Shot Scale and Shot Duration

BCU: on screen for a total of 50 seconds (3% of the time)
CU: on screen for 2 minutes 45 seconds (9% of the time)
MCU: 6 minutes 38 seconds (22% of the time)
MS: 4 minutes 10 seconds (14% of the time)
MLS: 3 minutes 28 seconds (12% of the time)
LS: 6 minutes 39 seconds (22 % of the time)
VLS: 4 minutes 11 seconds (14% of the time)

Appendix 5: The Statistical Style of *Jurassic Park*

252 shots (first 30 minutes); ASL: 7.1 seconds
36% of shots are reverse angles
11.5% low camera angle
7.5% high camera angle
42% low camera height
74% are still/26% are moving
Out of the 26% of moving shots, 13% use panning, 10% tracking, and 2% crane. In terms of the direction of the camera movement, 17% move sideways, 3% move upwards, 3% move downwards, 1% move backwards, and 3% forward.

Shot Scale

BCU: 4%; Average length of each BCU shot: 4 seconds
CU: 9.5%; 5.6 seconds
MCU: 28%; 4.5 seconds
MS: 21%; 6 seconds
MLS: 14%; 9 seconds
LS: 13%; 11.6 seconds
VLS: 11.5%; 8.5 seconds

Shot Duration

35% of all shots fall within the 1-3 second range;
54% within the 1-5 second range;
80% within the 1-10 second range.
Shot duration skewness value: 2.68

Correlation of Shot Scale and Duration

BCU: on screen for a total of 36 seconds (2% of the time)
CU: 2 minutes 15 seconds (7.5%)
MCU: 5 minutes 20 seconds (18%)
MS: 5 minutes 9 seconds (17%)
MLS: 5 minutes 16 seconds (17.5%)
LS: 6 minutes 23 seconds (21%)
VLS: 4 minutes 7 seconds (14%)

Christoph Brachmann, Hashim Iqbal Chunpir, Silke Gennies,
Benjamin Haller, Philipp Kehl, Astrid Paramita Mochtarram,
Daniel Möhlmann, Christian Schrumpf, Christopher Schultz,
Björn Stolper, Benjamin Walther-Franks, Arne Jacobs,
Thorsten Hermes, Otthein Herzog

Automatic Movie Trailer Generation Based on Semantic Video Patterns

Abstract

Automatic video summarization has become an important field of research with the advances in digital audio and video analysis and much effort has been put into movie abstracting for large media databases. However, in the movie industry content summarization for advertising trailers has been perfected to a form of art. In this paper we introduce the approach of automatically generating entertaining Hollywood-like trailers based on a trailer grammar. The extraction of features from movies using state-of-the-art image and audio processing techniques builds the foundation for the selection of meaningful and usable material which is re-assembled according to defined grammar rules. We present a system for generating trailers for contemporary Hollywood action movies. User testing of our automatically produced trailers for this movie genre shows promising results that suggest further research in this field.

1 Introduction

Beside the original intention of a trailer or a teaser – advertising a particular movie – the short preview of a movie has become an attractive movie genre in itself (Kernan 2004), especially since many trailers are available on the Internet. With the development of current digital technology the question arises if and to what extent it is feasible to automate the process of trailer production based solely on extracted movie features. Such a system could provide improvements in different movie-related fields. For example, it could (a) suggest innovative ways of video browsing in digital movie databases, (b) help developing and testing experiments to formalize existing movie editing methods (film theory), and (c) simplify or even extend the work of editors.

In this paper, we present our approach of an automatic trailer generation system that we implemented and tested for action movies, and which can also be extended for use with other genres. In section 2, a short overview of previous work related to automatic trailer generation is given. Section 3 describes the ontology-based formalism we developed and now use as a basis for our system. Section 4 illustrates our system, which is capable of analyzing a movie and generating an action movie trailer for it. In section 5 we discuss experimental results of our system. Finally, section 6 draws a conclusion and addresses possible aspects of future work.

2   Related Work

The specific field of generating movie trailers automatically has only little related work so far. The more general task of summarizing video content has been explored in detail. Works that come close to our aim are Chen et al (2004) and Lienhart et al (1997), where the possibility of generating a movie trailer is mentioned explicitly. Both claim to do the composition of footage according to rules derived from film theory and present ways to retrieve crucial information for trailer generation. They do not focus on how to compose trailers.

Other works within the field of video summarization rather focus on the task of pure summarizing in order to provide means to handle the increasing amount of video data. Three basic approaches have evolved. The first one is video skimming as in Christel et al (1999) and Smith/Kanade (1998), where video material is analyzed and condensed to important scenes. Typically the linearity of the input video is preserved here. The second one is summarizing contents in a pictorial way (Uchihashi et al 1999, Yeung/Yeo 1997). In Uchihashi et al (1999), salient single frames of video sequences are captured, sized according to their importance, and arranged in a linear comic-strip-like way of telling a story. The third video-browsing approach is closely related to the pictorial summarization but focuses on a hierarchical, not necessarily linear way of presenting the video content (Ponceleon/Dieberger 2001, Zhang et al 1993). The degree of automation varies. There are completely automatic works (Lienhart et al 1997, Smith/Kanade 1998, Uchihashi et al 1999) and semi-automatic works (Zhu et al 2003). Typically automatic summaries highly depend on low level analysis of image and audio, while the semi-automatic summary tools provide some manual annotation framework enabling high-level analysis to conclude what is happening in a scene. This approach even uses a hierarchy for video summarization quite similar to that defined by our trailer grammar; however, it does not discuss video summarization for the movie trailer format.

Another interesting work is Ma et al (2002), focusing on the question of how a video is perceived by a user.

3 Trailer Grammar

In order to successfully re-assemble movie footage in a short video which can be called a *trailer*, first of all the meaning of this label must be understood. According to Arijon (2000), films are created based on an underlying *film grammar* to successfully communicate with the audience. Kernan (2004) argues that a trailer is not only a video of a defined length consisting of a random assembly of shots and scenes, but also a movie genre in its own right. Therefore we assume that trailers, as a special kind of film, can be described by syntactic elements and semantic rules which constitute a *trailer grammar*. After giving a definition of the term trailer we will examine how this grammar can be modeled via syntactic and semantic elements.

3.1 The Definition of a Trailer

In order to define a trailer with respect to an automatic generation, the term *trailer* refers to the fact that these short movies were originally shown at the end of a film program in movie theaters (Kernan 2004). During the 20th century, trailers evolved from pure advertisement to a movie genre with its own unique conventions, based on the demand to combine an artistic form with the highly commercial need of attracting the biggest possible audience. Since movies and trailers exist in many different forms in different cultural environments, we focus our automatic approach on the Western culture's most dominant trailer and movie industry: Hollywood blockbuster cinema. Trailers from this domain have developed a general formula that pays as little attention to genre or specific target groups as possible (Kernan 2004). Our aim is to produce short videos that resemble rather conventional *theatrical trailers* by having a length of more than one minute and featuring footage from the original movie. These are opposed to so-called *teaser trailers* which are typically produced before primary shooting is finished. Teasers consist mostly of texts, voice-overs, graphic elements, and which have a maximum running length of one minute. In the following the term *trailer* therefore refers to a theatrical trailer for a contemporary Hollywood movie.

3.2 The Syntactic Elements of a Trailer

Shots and *transitions* are usually the basic elements of any edited movie. Within these elements we presume that certain types can be identified by a shot-by-shot analysis of original movie trailers. In order to determine these types, an appropriate set of descriptions, i.e. an appropriate vocabulary, has to be defined. These descriptions inevitably involve a trade-off regarding level of detail. We developed the following guidelines to clarify this issue. Shot types must: (a) be able to cover all shots of a trailer, (b) be clearly distinguishable from each other (no redundancy), (c) have a well-defined meaning, (d) apply to as many existing trailers as possible, and (e) be defined based on the movie features that can be extracted by our analysis tools (technical feasibility). In order to distinguish between the original movie/trailer shots and the shots we produce for our trailers we refer to the latter as *clips*. In order to fulfill the requirements listed above we define the types of *clips* by the following *properties:*

- a category (reflecting the shot's formal features),
- the playback speed (to model effects like slow-motion or acceleration),
- the volume of the original footage sound (so that clips can be muted or amplified),
- and location, corresponding to the footage location in the source movie.

3.3 The Semantic Elements

In order to assemble these syntactic elements in a trailer-like way, semantic rules are needed. We propose to represent these rules as a hierarchy of super- and sub-patterns as shown in Figure 1. Each super-pattern consists of a number of sub-patterns either in a specific or random order. The highest level of patterns is the *trailer pattern*. Since there is not only one universal pattern which can describe all trailers at once, this pattern can be used to distinguish between different types of trailers. A trailer pattern consists of at least one *phase pattern*. The phase patterns again are composed of *sequence patterns*, which in turn consist of a number of *clip/transition pairs*. These pairs are the lowest level of the hierarchy.

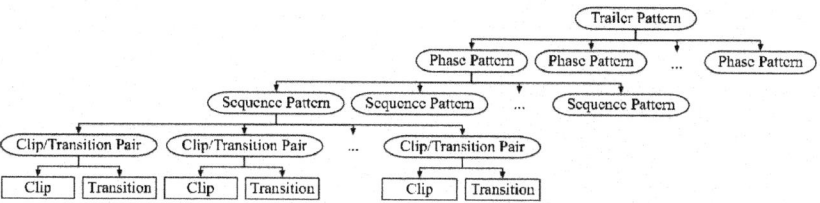

Figure 1. A branch of the hierarchical view of a generic trailer structure.

4 Trailer Generation System

Our system consists of two major components. The first one is a collection of various image and audio processing modules that provides a set of features extracted from the movie. The second component provides an implementation of the proposed trailer grammar. This component is able to categorize the annotated information of the first component and to use that data to automatically assemble a full trailer.

Most trailers try to summarize the plot and setting of the announced movie and to introduce the relations between the main characters. Presently, the automatic extraction as well as the generation of a narrative, or at least some kind of dramatic arc, seems hardly feasible. Therefore, our approach focuses on a genre which relies significantly more on visual sensation, speed and effects than on narrative: the action movie. We performed a shot-by-shot analysis of various action movie trailers from the last 15 years. Thereby we identified specific grammar elements and selected appropriate image and audio processing modules that are able to provide the corresponding footage for generating an action movie trailer.

4.1 Extracting and Annotating Movie Features

In order to extract features of a given action movie we not only use methods of image and audio analysis on different levels of abstraction, but also derive data from Internet resources. By combining the output of several modules with each other we enhance the value and reliability of the annotated data. In order to have a basis for evaluating the output we manually annotated the action movie *The Transporter (2002)*. In our system features from a movie are extracted by the following modules:

- shot boundary detection based on gray-level histogram changes
- motion-based segmentation which divides a movie into frame ranges with homogeneous optical flow intensities
- face detection along with a k-means clustering of the detected faces based on Principal Component Analysis
- text detection which detects frame ranges with disturbing overlaid text, e.g. credits, subtitles etc.
- a tool which extracts movie data such as title, director, actors, genre, famous quotes, awards won and production company from the Internet Movie Database (www.imdb.com)
- audio-based segmentation which divides a movie into frame ranges with homogeneous sound volume intensities
- detection of sudden volume change in a movie
- detection of frame ranges comprising speech using a phoneme-based speech recognition
- speech recognition which detects frame ranges containing famous quotes of the movie (given by the IMDb) by using each quote as one entity in the language model
- detection of frame ranges with music along with a level of disturbance, based on image-based spectral analysis
- detection of sound events (explosion, crash, gunshot, scream) based on spectral feature extraction and Support Vector Machine classification

4.2 A Framework for Generating Trailers of an Annotated Movie

The second component of our system is provided with the annotation from the automatic feature extraction. This annotation is used in combination with our semantic patterns in order to generate a trailer of the particular movie. In addition to original movie footage we include automatically produced animations and add music and sound effects from a separate audio archive. The process of generating trailers from annotated movies is split into the following sub-components (see also Figure 2):

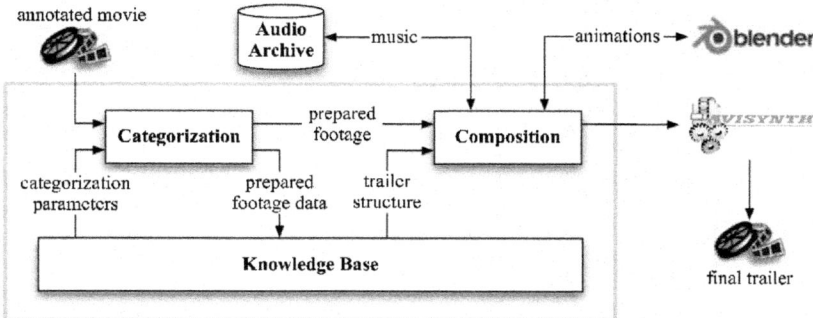

Figure 2: Diagram of the trailer generation process.

(1) In order to build a trailer we define a knowledge base that contains models for trailer structure elements and defines parameters for categories of video footage frame ranges. The movie annotation is filtered into the syntactic elements *clips* which then are classified into *categories* using these parameters. Next, the trailer model is created based on rules in the knowledge base and influenced by the availability of footage. In this way, the system generates a unique trailer model that is built to fit the available footage.

(2) The composition framework translates the established trailer structure into specific trailer elements: Apart from video footage we incorporate runtime-created text animations for movie title, credits etc., as well as pre-produced music and sound effects content from our own audio archive. Footage, text animations and audio are finally composed to a unique, fully automatically generated trailer based on trailer semantics.

Knowledge Base Functionality

In order to incorporate trailer semantics, we implement a knowledge base that is designed to hold the knowledge for trailer construction using the public domain software CLIPS (www.ghg.net/clips/CLIPS.html). The trailer grammar concepts are represented in an ontology. We cast specific knowledge about action trailer syntax and semantics. As instances of these classes, using has-a relations to model our hierarchical view of the trailer structure. The properties of clips (category, speed, volume, location) are implemented as slots and among these the category is implemented as a class of several slots again, specifying a list of video analysis attributes for its classification. The combination of several annotation attributes to a category leads to semantic higher-level knowledge about the footage.

Categorization

Given a set of category definitions the categorization module processes the annotation data in order to build clips for each category. We build the clips based on frame ranges as opposed to a shot-based approach, allowing the categorization process to be independent from scene/shot information. Let A be a set of video frames and A_{movie} the set containing all original movie frames, then the frame set of an analyzed movie feature $A_{featurex}$ (e.g. all frames showing a face) is a subset of A_{movie}. The first step of the categorization process is to filter out the desired frames by corresponding thresholds (e.g. only get big faces indicating a close-up shot). This results in a new set which we refer to as an *attribute frame set* $A_{attributex}$ with $A_{attributex} \subseteq A_{featurex} \subseteq A_{movie}$. We process these attribute frame sets as tracks and perform an intersection as illustrated in Figure 3. Furthermore, for each clip we calculate a probability value based on weighting factors assigned to the attributes.

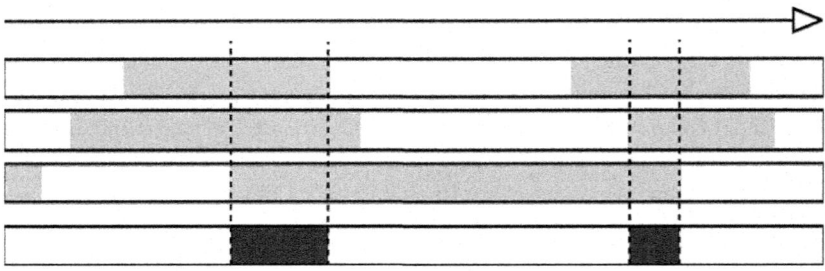

Figure 3: The intersection approach of the categorizer for a sample footage.

Trailer Structure

Once the movie footage has been segmented and categorized, information about the amount of clips within each category is stored in the knowledge base. The system then builds the trailer structure on an abstract level. In order to introduce variety into the trailer models, each semantic element in our hierarchy has a selection choice of lower level elements assigned to it. While offering multiple choices at each node in the trailer structure tree, the sequence of patterns can still be controlled to ensure consistency with the given trailer grammar. This approach grants easy and fast altering of the structure by linking more sub-patterns to a super-pattern or by deleting links. To avoid a purely random selection of a linked sub-pattern and to emphasize certain patterns, a weighting system is attached to the selection logic. Based on the trailer ontology and availability of categories, the knowledge base reasons which parts of the trailer structure fulfill all requirements. In case of certain parts failing due to lack of footage, fallback structures are considered first. If no such fallback exists, clip attributes are loosened: clips can then be chosen from random categories rather than specific ones. The result is a finished model of a trailer structure giving detailed information about which transitions to use, which background music to play, which clips of which category to show, what position within the movie they should come from, at what speed they should be played, and how high the volume of the original footage should be.

Selection of Clips

The clips in the trailer model come with properties regarding clip category, footage volume, speed, and location for footage selection. Given these parameters for the designated clips of the original movie, our system has three methods for clip selection: (1) Preferred location selection, based purely on the requested location and clip location in the movie, so the clip chosen is the one closest to the requested location. (2) Best clip from preferred location, which is similar to the preferred location selection, but additionally taking into consideration the quality of the clip so the clip chosen is the best clip available starting from the requested location. (3) A random clip of a given category is selected.

3D Text Animations and Audio

Text animations displaying information on movie title, release date, actor names, movie company as well as legal disclaimers are one distinctive feature of movie trailers and an essential component of a trailer structure. The composition system dynamically creates a script from which the 3D software Blender (blender.org) produces one digital video file per animation ready to be used for final composition, using predefined animation templates. For additional music soundtrack and sound effects, we provide the possibility to incorporate pre-produced sound files.

Final Composition

Selected footage, animation clips and audio soundtrack are composed into a final video using Avisynth (www.avisynth.org) scripts. True to the methods used in standard movie trailers, sound effects are added to text animations to make them more effective. Changes in trailer soundtrack are masked by special transition sound effects. Fade/flash shot transitions (as determined by the trailer structure model) are implemented. The result is the finished trailer modeled according to a trailer structure created using our trailer ontology.

4.3 Automatically Generating Action Movie Trailers

We define 26 clip categories, such as *CharacterSpeaking, PersonSilent, Quote, FastAction, Explosion, Setting, Gunshot, Scream* etc., and 3 transition categories, namely *HardCut, FadeBlack, FlashWhite*. The definition of each category includes a set of attributes along with specific value ranges for the annotated features and weighting factors. An extension of our set of categories is possible and would be necessary to model more complex trailers or trailers of other movie genres.

As the basic structure of our action movie trailer pattern we identified five different phase patterns representing typical stages of action trailers. These phase patterns are again made up of sequence patterns corresponding to typical action trailer shot sequences. The phases are:

- *Intro* (slow and moody shots of locations and people together with speech establishing a conflict or introducing the main characters). Sequence patterns usually involve clips such as *Setting, CharacterSilent* or *CompanyName*.

- *Story* (medium fast shots of action and people together with dialogue to wrap up the task the main characters have to face). Sequence patterns use Intro clips but also add action with clips such as *SlowAction, Shout,* or *Fire*.

- *Break* (a long and very significant or dramatic comment by one of the main characters – typically without background music). Clips used in sequence patterns are *Quote* and *QuoteLong*.

- *Action* (a fast montage with loud sound of the fastest action scenes together with close-ups of the main characters). Sequence patterns use *ActorName, FastAction, Explosion, Gunshot* and clips of other similar categories.

- *Outro* (typically very calm or without any music and shows – sometimes mixed with close-ups or a short shot of one of the main characters uttering an extremely comic or tough comment – the title and credits of the movie together with a release date). Sequence patterns use clips such as *Quote, Title, Credits* or *Spectacular*.

With the defined elements (clips, transitions and patterns), as well as their relations to each other we can describe an action movie trailer in a formal way. This description can be used by our system to generate an action trailer from any movie (as long as the automatic analysis provides enough footage for the different categories).

In order to include text animations we provide four animation templates which all have a different artistic style, each matched to the action movie genre. Our audio archive is a collection of pre-produced sound files and consists currently of 37 music files and 22 sound effect files. Currently we use four categories of music files according to the mood of our trailer phases (Intro, Story, Action, Outro) and three sound effect types that are mostly used in professional trailers ("boom", "woosh" and "wooshbang").

5   Experimental Results

For several action movies, we let our system generate five test trailers per movie, each being unique due to the random choices built into the system architecture.[1] Many of the generated trailers give a quite good impression of the story and its characters. Although the framework makes no attempt to understand the storyline, important elements of the story are often contained in the selected shots. A good selection of quotes from the main characters seems to create an implicit storytelling, so the quotes have probably the greatest overall impact on the perceived quality of our trailers. We also tested a comedy, *Groundhog Day* (1993), and an old action movie, *James Bond: From Russia With Love* (1963). As expected, the results were unsatisfactory – for different reasons. The detection modules mostly failed for the James Bond movie due to the very different image and audio qualities, whereas for the comedy the action trailer pattern was clearly not fitting.

In addition to our own evaluation, we performed a test viewing with a group audience of 59 people. Since producing movie trailers is a creative process, a purely statistical analysis, like a shot-by-shot comparison of generated and official trailers, would not help much. Official trailers merely present the trailer artist's choice out of millions of other possible approaches. Using them as a ground truth would unnecessarily restrict the scope of possible best solutions.

We showed two trailers generated by our software, for *Transporter 2* and *Terminator 2*. As a reference, we showed two professionally produced trailers with different aesthetic appearances, for *War Of The Worlds* and *Miami Vice*, and three pseudo-trailers that each used a different level of randomness for the selection and ordering of shots or frame ranges, combined with music. One of these was generated by the commercial software Muvee Autoproducer

---

1   Trailers produced by our system can be downloaded from www.tzi.de/svp.

(www.muvee.com). The test viewers were asked to rate the same six aspects for each trailer. The detailed scores of all trailers are shown in Table 1.

As expected, the overall rating of the random trailers is significantly lower than any of the others, while *War Of The Worlds* performed best. Our automatically generated trailers received high ratings for good composition and "cuts & effects", and lower ratings for "narrative aspects". The *Terminator 2* trailer received its highest rating (7.66) in the category "cuts & effects". This shows that our system succeeds in timing the cuts and adding animation screens with emphasizing audio effects to enhance the genre-typical powerful appearance. The categories "character introduction" and "plot introduction", which depend highly on sophisticated high-level analysis, received the lowest scores (6.36, 6.88). The results are still surprisingly good considering the fact that the system makes no attempt to analyze the movie's storyline, but instead tries to imitate that behavior by showing faces and inserting pieces of dialogues. As a consequence, the quotes in the generated *Terminator 2* trailer reveal some important clues about the characters and the plot (e.g. the Terminator's role as a protector from the future), but other important aspects, especially of the background story, are missing.

The results show that our attempts of automatic categorization and composition appear to be generally successful. They suggest that our automatic trailers are a clear improvement over random shot selection methods. Furthermore, it seems that wrongly chosen shots, resulting from inaccuracies of the analysis modules, typically do not disturb the flow of the trailer. Also, our results show no noticeable difference between the judgment of people who had seen the movies and of those who had not. For further evaluation, it may be interesting to perform viewer tests on trailer variations from only one movie to make the results more comparable between the different types of test trailers.

	scene selection	composition	cuts & effects	character introduction	plot introduction	advertisement value	total score
War of the Worlds, 2005 (official trailer)	8.41	7.91	7.79	7.47	7.40	8.16	7.86
Miami Vice, 2006 (official teaser)	4.97	6.27	6.27	3.27	3.59	4.95	4.89
The Transporter, 2002 (Muvee Autoprod.)	5.05	4.03	4.22	2.97	3.59	3.95	3.97
Bad Boys, 1995 (random frame ranges)	4.64	3.67	3.41	3.19	3.22	3.52	3.61
Blade, 1998 (random order of selected clips)	4.16	3.24	3.24	4.07	4.07	3.43	3.70
Transporter 2, 2005 (generated)	7.47	7.54	7.90	6.80	6.80	7.37	7.31
Terminator 2, 2001 (generated)	7.58	7.63	7.66	6.36	6.88	7.46	7.26

Table 1. Detailed average ratings from the user testing (max. score: 10).

6 Conclusion and Future Work

This paper presents a novel approach of intensively using a trailer grammar in combination with data automatically extracted out of a movie by different image and audio analysis techniques for generating a Hollywood-like action movie trailer. First, a trailer grammar was defined that can be applied to various movie genres. Second, a system was implemented, which provides means for using extracted features to build a trailer according to any defined trailer pattern based on our trailer grammar. One such trailer pattern was created by manually analyzing several action movie trailers. Using our system we generated trailers for some action movies according to this pattern, and these have shown that automatic trailer generation is not only possible, but can even achieve good results. Still, our trailers lack some elements a manually edited trailer comprises, e.g. telling a coherent story or voice-over narration.

Testing our system with further action movies should form the basis for refining current analysis modules, categorization and composition components, and our action trailer model. Also, many expansions are conceivable. The classification of movie footage into semantic categories could be expanded by adding more categories (e.g. *Kissing, Fight*) based on more sophisticated image and audio processing techniques. Concerning the composition framework, more animation styles as templates and a way of matching styles to movie content could be added. We also believe that the effect of a generated trailer could be vastly improved by adding pre-produced generic voice-overs to the soundtrack.

To enable our system to handle movie genres besides the action genre some significant expansions are necessary. First, further analysis modules need to be added and existing ones need to be improved to provide a richer annotation usable across movie genres. Second, trailer patterns for comedy, romance, drama, horror etc. need to be developed and incorporated into the generation knowledge base. Finally, the composition system would have to include animation and audio templates to render these models. A possible extension and a slightly complementary approach of our system is described by Kehl (2007). The author uses 14 dramatic trailer units and 33 narrative units in order to generate a trailer. Based on these units, the narrative content may be covered by this approach.

While in this work we have provided a basis for automatic trailer generation, a major aspect of future work remains the trade-off between technical feasibility and the semantic and aesthetic requirements the movie trailer must live up to.

Bibliography

Arijon, D. *Grammatik der Filmsprache*. Frankfurt a.M.: Zweitausendeins, 2000.

Christel, M. G., A. G. Hauptmann, A. Warmack, and S. A. Crosby. "Adjustable filmstrips and skims as abstractions for a digital video library." *ADL* (1999): 98-104.

Chen, H.-W., J.-H. Kuo, W.-T. Chu, and J.-L. Wu. "Action movies segmentation and summarization based on tempo analysis." *MIR '04: Proceedings of the 6th ACM SIGMM international workshop on Multimedia information retrieval.* New York, NY: ACM, 2004: 251–258.

Kehl, P. *Structures of Narrative: A Formal Description of Movie Trailers*. Master Thesis, University of Bremen, 2007.

Kernan, L. *Coming Attractions – Reading American Movie Trailers*. Austin, TX: University of Texas Press, 2004.

Lienhart, R., S. Pfeiffer, and W. Effelsberg. "Video abstracting." *Communications of the ACM*. 40.12 (1997): 54-62.

Ma, Y., L. Lu, H. Zhang, and M. Li. "A user attention model for video summarization." *Proceedings of ACM Multimedia* 2002: 533-542.

Ponceleon, D. and A. Dieberger. "Hierarchical brushing in a collection of video data." *Proceedings of the 34th Hawaii International Conference on System Sciences.* 2001: 1654-1661.

Smith, M. A. and T. Kanade. "Video skimming and characterization through the combination of image and language understanding." *IEEE International Workshop on Content-Based Access of Image and Video Database*. 1998: 61-70.

Uchihashi, S., J. Foote, A. Girhensohn, and J. Boreczky. "Video manga: Generating semantically meaningful video summaries." *Proceedings of ACM Multimedia*. 1999: 383-392.

Yeung, M. and B. Yeo. "Video visualization for compact presentation and fast browsing of pictorial content." *IEEE Trans CSVT*. 7 (August 1997): 771-785.

Zhu, X., J. Fan, A. K. Elmagarmid, and X. Wu. "Hierarchical video content description and summarization using unified semantic and visual similarity." *Multimedia Systems*, 9.1 (2003): 31-53.

Zhang, H. J., A. Kankanhalli, and S. W. Smoliar. "Automatic partitioning of full-motion video." *Multimedia Systems*, 1.1 (1993): 10-28.

Leonardo Boccia, Peter Ludes

Key Measures and Key Visuals in Brazilian and German TV Annual Reviews

Préludes

In order to highlight the mutual enforcement of auditive and visual components, we focus on the interplay between Key Measures and Key Visuals: Hardly any offering on TV relies on visual stimuli alone. More and more, sounds and music do not only play in the background, but become professionally produced in exact linkage to the visualizations shown. The digitization of both sound and visuals, as well as ever faster computations, enhance the complementary presentation of what may be called the professional audio-visualization of the public spheres. In the composition and sonorous manipulation of programs and reviews of TV stations, collective memories and neglects, chances and also pastiches or collages emerge in some cultures with global and trans-cultural elements. However, to weave a plot of musical intersections that involve the virtual images of the most controversial contemporary events, it is necessary to have adequate technical support and a vast pool of national and global musical archives. Not all TV networks are equipped to edit soundtracks and to manipulate the standardized and transnational images with musical narratives that transmit from the background to the stage front in the diverse sensorial levels of the screen media. We analyze these *"key" melodies or measures, which encompasses sounds, melodies and stereotypes*. Our model of combined "Key Measure Visuals" is based on analyses of TV annual reviews from Brazil and Germany, from 2003 to 2006. It aims to show how sound strategies, visual conventions and visual strategies complement each other.

The concept of Key Visuals was developed by Peter Ludes for his research projects on TV news in the United States, the Federal Republic of Germany, and the GDR (1989-1997) and Media Information Upheavals (1998 and 1999) in Siegen University's Collaborative Research Program on Screen Media. It necessitated the development and implementation of digital tools of content analyses, which are documented in Ludes (2001, on the CD-ROM, with 86 minutes examples for Key Visuals from TV news and WWW information offerings). A further DVD-ROM production on European media symbols (Ludes 2002) as well as the cooperation with computer scientists and scholars from the humanities and social sciences from Brazil, China, Germany, the UK, and the United States, partially coordinated via a common website (www.

keyvisuals.org) with many analyses and examples (Ludes 2005) turned the formerly Western-limited research into a truly international one.

However, one major insufficiency remained, namely the adequate analysis of the complementarities and tensions between the audio- and visual components of "Tele-Audio-Visions". Since 2004, Leonardo Boccia, a composer and musicologist, and Peter Ludes, a scholar in media and communication as well as social theory, have cooperated to enlighten this multi-modal sphere. Due to the so far better state of research into visuals, we focus here first on music and sounds and then on the complementarities and tensions between them and visual elements (see Zielinski 1989, Segeberg 2005, Wyatt 2005, Huber 2007, and Werner/Lankau 2007) in TV annual reviews. The concept of Key Measures therefore has been developed in analogy to the much earlier concept of Key Visuals and is put here into the forefront.

1 Introduction: The Concepts of Key Measures and Key Visuals

New post-production technology improves the audio dimension of the television programs. "The rapid evolution of post-production technology over the last few years is virtually unprecedented. As it steps into the digital domain, the advances in digital editing and sound design equipment have expanded the producer's horizons. From prime time broadcast to art gallery installation, from educational teaching tools to high-end commercials, today's digital tools are limitless" (Kellison 2006: 150). Music and sounds accompany visual equivalents of print media headlines; in this sense the term Key Measures encompasses key elements of the most publicized visual narratives with music and sound effects. Television Year End Reviews or Annual Reports "re-view and re-sound" the most important events of a year. They are based on journalistic professional selections, repeatedly shown and form a basis for further selections for Reviews of the Decade, etc, with (media) culture specific audio-visual narratives.

However, television annual reviews, elaborated through post-production technologies allow widening the dimension of audio-visual events. The composition, edition and transmission of the audio-visual manipulation of programs and reviews of the largest TV stations in the world excite collective culture-specific, trans-cultural and in a few instances (e.g. major wars, terrorist attacks or sport events, especially the Olympic Games) collective audio-visual memories, which usually are generation- and strata-specific, transform over time and can be formally sketched as shown in Figure 1. These new types of mass mediated collective audio-visual memories, only for certain, definitely not all topics, partially have converged from formerly distinguished collective memories of music (and sounds) vs. collective visual memories (from first-eyes experiences over paintings, photos, movies, TV programs, to streaming videos), as shown in Figure 1.

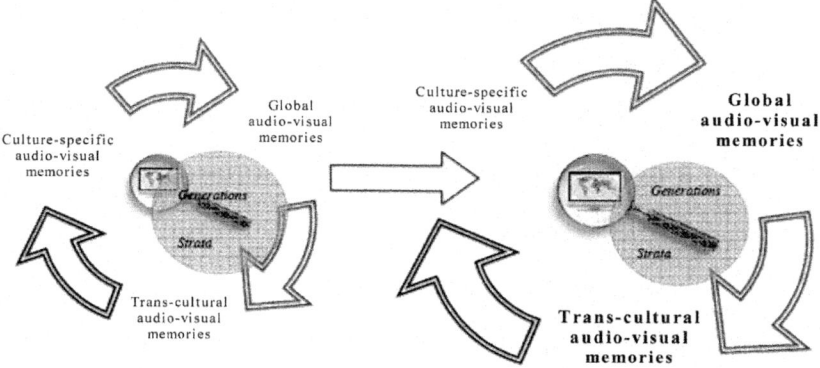

Figure 1: The interdependence of three major types of collective audio-visual memories and their transformation in time

Modern TV equipments such as digital TV, Home Theatre receivers and also the new audio-visual systems of conventional TV equipments permit to airing programs with high sound and visual quality that increasingly attract the auditive and optic senses of viewers/listeners. "More and more people apprehend more and more hours of TV programs and WWW streaming videos per day. The technical transmission quality of these pictures and videos constantly improves, while their origins and their presentation formats become more international and more transcultural. The production, distribution and use of these media visuals turn considerably more economical" (Ludes 2005: 22).

The concept of "Key Measures" can be applied to describe and qualify different procedures of audio manipulation (not only) on television. Key Measures elements encompass:

- Key elements of the most publicized visual narratives with music and sound-design and
- culture specific aspects and aesthetic similarities, which intend the elicitation of certain affective states.

They

- guide audio-visual memories and
- allow for co-orientation and coordination.

In general, the combination of entertainment and news becomes more spectacular. "It is certainly true to say that entertainment is one component of modern leisure culture, charged with the function of destroying superfluous time. However, within the context of a theory of the mass media, we shall stick to problems concerning the construction of reality and to the question of what kind of effects the coding information/non-information has in this case" (Luhmann 2000: 51).

Music on TV annual reviews works as a real compensation of deficits and neglects in TV production and reception. "It is evident that such quantitative extension of the musical background leads to qualitative changes of television" (Klüppelholz 2005: 172, our translation). In his contribution to: *Sound. Zur Technologie und Ästhetik des Akustischen in den Medien*, Werner Klüppelholz pointed out three main hypotheses concerning these changes:

- Music in the television programs serves the habitual compensation of deficits in production and reception;
- contemporary documentaries are transformed into some kind of fiction (or faction), also and exactly through music;
- the dominant principle of musical invention in television is imitation.

2   Audio-Visual TV Productions

"Music is certainly insidious and reaches the body even when distant from the source of its emission. For this reason, in some countries music is not welcome in public places, centres of purchases and supermarkets or even newscasts. It is, however, a fundamental means of accompanying moving images, and, in the majority of the cases, when it is absent; one perceives its merit and influence" (Boccia 2005: 74). However, audio-visual TV productions result in different kinds and modes of reception. The concurrent producers limit the time of the TV audio-visuals and the sound production on television usually must be achieved in a very short period of time. The audience share rates impose very fast time conditions. "The competition between journals, the competition between journals and television, the competition between television networks takes the form of a competition for the scoop, to be the first. [...] In short, there are objects which are imposed to the viewers because they are imposed to the producers and if they are imposed to the producers, it is because they are imposed through the producer's competition" (Bourdieu 1997: 38, our translation). Competition pressure is incisive for the production of music and sound design on television programs. Mostly, the post production and final editing process must be quickly concluded, sound editors give the final touch to the audio-visual products. But "sound design is a highly creative art. The careful recording of audio during production, as well as in post-production, can make a visceral impact on the project" (Kellison 2006: 132).

However, to edit music on visuals or strategically combine Key Measures and Key Visuals to a new multi-modal unit of Key Measure Visuals, it is important to be aware of the structure of the music. Not every audio-editor is a musician or composer and even has time enough to mix music and visual elements together. The results are frequently pastiches, strange collages or grotesque combinations, which disturb and change the visual messages, provoking a peculiar construction of reality. Many crisis and war news thereby become unreal or seem to be far away from the immediate present. This is often the case in the annual reviews of the Brazilian Globo Television Network, which use music and sound effects throughout the entire program, i.e. for more than one hour. Since its creation in 1973, Globo Reporter, the program in the context of which the annual reviews are shown, is one of the most important programs of Brazilian journalism. Originally, with the collaboration of film makers in 1967, the program had a more "documentary" character.

3 Brazilian and German TV Annual Reviews: Globo and ARD

In the annual review of Globo Television Network, the visuals of the night of March 20, 2003, when Baghdad was the target of violent attacks, become an aesthetic object of short duration to reach the best possible Brazilian audience share and to form the viewers' opinion. By means of melodic references and fade effects between noises and instrumental timbres, the program brightens up the raw ambience of the war. They are ethnic, classic and popular musical citations, which envelop the visual representation of the intense attacks, mitigating the perception of the explosions and its correlative information.

In its German counterpart, broadcast in the same month of the same year by ARD, no musical accompaniment is present during the reported events. Only diegetic sounds and journalist narrations accompany the visuals of the Iraq war and the news are transmitted without any "poetical" support. During the entire ARD annual review, music and sound effects are added on summaries ("Überblicke") only.

In fact, the structure of the German ARD annual review of 2003 seems to be edited with symmetrical rhythm and proportion between the parts. First, the short title theme on four main notes (D, C, F and G) introduces the program with timbres of synthesizer and drum. Then, the anchorwoman Susanne Holst presents the summary of events shown, at the same time, in pictures and titles on the background. In the entire ARD retrospective of 2003, the professional selection of "the most important images and stories of the year" is shown alternating the voices of the anchorwoman and that of the journalists in regular time proportions. Music and sound effects are added during the summaries, and diegetic sound ("Originalton") is frequently heard. Musical short pieces with percussion and synthesizer timbres are mostly originally composed for the review; nevertheless, diegetic' romantic songs, opera and world music are audible in the background of some reports. For the periodical summaries, a grave male voice narrates several events, accompanied by music and sounds.

The Globo report of Globo Television Network, however, is edited differently. The segment *Globo Reporter – Year of War* forms part of an end-of-the-year review of 2003, which has a total duration of 1:14:44 hrs. Of the entire program, the Globo Television Network dedicated 5:58 mins. to the subject of the beginning of the war in Iraq. The segment has the characteristics of an audio-visual spectacle which involves culture-specific, national and global musical themes. They are songs of diverse ethnic groups, selections of classical music and rock, in addition to sound effects that (re-)organize the moving images and add colour to the voice of the anchorman. The *Year of War* is preceded by a panoramic introduction accompanied by the title theme of the program. The anchorman Sergio Chapelin summarizes the issues to be broadcast that night, accompanied all the time by the title theme. A segment about national politics follows government programs, the president and his ministers, occupations and political demonstrations, a second block of sports topics, and a third one with brief topics of varying genre. In turn, after 17 minutes of the program and some additional minutes for commercial breaks, the segment about the beginning of the war in Iraq starts. Furthermore, during the analysis, after many hours of listening to the audio segments of this program, something incredible emerged between sounds, music and text; in response to the anchorman's question: "Does Saddam Hussein have the prohibited weapons?" another male voice affirms, whispering between chords, "He does!" (Listen for yourself at www.keyvisuals.org and see Boccia 2005.)

Is this a subliminal message to manipulate opinion? Or an editing mistake? Is this program a musical show which involves audio manipulations, a fruit of the lack of time to mix the program? Or is it an aesthetic object using spectacular means to raise the curiosity of the audience with considerable success, since audience shares are regularly far beyond fifty percent for the Globo network during primetime? In the block of *Globo Reporter – Year of War*, the images and sequence rhythms are mixed with several well-known musical songs and citations from classical to rock music. All musical citations are of famous songs and hits distributed all over the world. The musical citations are very short; parts of pieces of 'mass art' (Carroll) forming a nervous mosaic of sounds and melodies. In the second segment of *Year of War*, for example, W. A. Mozart's Symphony No. 25 in G minor (KV 183; the same piece that was used for the opening music of the film *Amadeus* [1984]), accompanies the visuals for 19 seconds and mitigates the images of President Bush reading the Iraq ultimatum. Here, the music hides the subliminal whispered message ("He does!"). A classical piece of musical art is turned into a mass art theme distributed all over the world, without any apparent relation, and recalled to form part of a new message, as a strategic element of an audio-visual composition in which music is selected in terms of how it can attract mass attention.

4 Mass Art as Citation

The success of musical themes turns melodies into national, trans-national and global mass art elements. Parts of them, as short citations, especially in the audio-visual construction of Globo Television Network annual reviews, work to get the attention of the audience, but also to corrupt the message of the visuals. What can Mozart's music recall when it is associated to the images of a contemporary war? It seems to be a strange (an-)aesthetical combination, but famous musical citations are very frequent elements of the sonorous strategy of Globo television audio producers to elicit emotional remembrances from the viewers/listeners in Brazil.

> In so far as mass artworks are formulaic, they are easy to follow, i.e., they accord with our expectation. And inasmuch as mass artwork are easy to follow, they are also apt to appeal to more and more people as suitable or appropriate objects with which to occupy one's leisure time. Of course, in order to command large audiences, mass artworks must be more than merely easy to consume. They must also invite or excite our interest. [...] However, the ease with which mass art is consumed is not a flaw, but rather a design element, which is predicated on the function of mass art as an instrument for addressing mass audiences. (Carroll 1998: 194/195)

To address mass audiences, well-known musical themes are great accomplices. In that sense, more and more music is added more frequently to different TV programs traditionally broadcast without any musical support. Lots and lots of people consume mass art, and mass delivery technologies have been fundamental to improve that. In modern "tele-audio-vision" post-production, the digital audio formats and their compression are elaborate with high quality and synchronic precision. Commonly, "audio that is recorded during production on sound stage or at a location is known as *production sound* and refers to all scripted dialogue, ambient sound, and background noise. If an unwanted sound creeps in, or the dialogue changes after the footage has been shot, most production sound can be recorded later in the post-production stage" (Kellison 2006: 135).

However, in the annual reviews of Globo, the musical citation and audio effects added in the final editing process encompass a major part of the entire program. In our analysis of Globo reviews from 2003 to 2006, this trend is confirmed. Examples from the Tsunami catastrophe, obituaries or the death of Pope John Paul II are shown on Globo and demonstrate that the audio-visual post-production construct is basically a preferred format. Furthermore, in comparison with its German counterpart of the ARD annual reviews, analogous music citations are based on different post-production conceptions. The death of Pope John Paul II is an example that may well expose such differences: The ARD example starts with a big bell and its symbolic chime. For the 38 seconds of the journalist's narration, only ecclesiastic chants sound in different audio levels from the back to the foreground. In the second part of this report, audio elements include journalist's commentaries on the enormous crowd of people coming to give a last tribute to the dead pope; in some part of the *production sound* one can hear Cardinal Ratzinger giving a sermon; no sound of the crowd can be heard.

In stark contrast, the example from the Globo review makes use of the last movement of Tchaikovsky's ballet *Swan Lake*, a very famous musical motive that accompanies the images of the crowd on the Vatican square and streets for 33 seconds. One male journalist narrates while walking trough the crowd. In the second part of this report, a female journalist continues narrating; the audio editing includes world music, jazz and parts of *production sound* where the crowd acclaims the result of the new pope election:

ARD (1:12 mins.)	*GLOBO (1:17 mins.)*
Big bell and ecclesiastic chants for 38 secs.	Last movement of *Swan Lake* for 33 secs.
Voice of a male journalist as narrator	A male journalist narrates, walking through the crowd
Internal images of St. Peter's Cathedral	A female journalist narrates from high above St. Peter's Cathedral; world music, jazz and parts of production sound
Production sound: Cardinal Ratzinger giving a sermon	The crowd acclaims the result of the election of the new pope

Table 1. The death of Pope John Paul II on TV: audio-visual components

Epilogue: Key Visual Measures in the Dialogues of Cultures

A new audio-visual combination reaches television audiences and viewers of the largest TV stations all over the world. Analyzing the annual reviews of the Globo and ARD television networks, it is possible to notice a global trend in the audio-visual construction of television programs. Music and sound design integrate the visuals of global news in a post production phase, however, not merely as an audio background accompaniment but as a part of the suggested meaning of the visuals shown. Annual reviews thereby become a spectacle for entertainment and recall very different memories and sensations. The short music citations selected from a huge pool of mass music pieces distributed from modern delivery technologies are very easy to follow and become an instrument for addressing mass audiences. In our analysis of the annual reviews of the ARD and Globo television networks, the comparison between the analogous programs and years of transmission show different final editing decisions, techniques and formats. But it is also evident that more and more music and sound bits or Key Measures were added to the programs during the last few years. The new post-production technology improves all the time and makes it easy to mix visuals and measures (parts of melodies) for a spectacular audio-visual construction of the new world languages of Key Visuals and Key Measures. They are partially integrated into Key Measure Visuals or Key Visual Measures, depending on whether the audio- or the visual components dominate.

Audio-visual conventions and strategies are implemented to achieve the attention of culture-specific, trans-cultural and global audiences. Trans-cultural visual, sound and musical patterns, rhythms and music of different eras usually back up to two centuries, but rarely including contemporary non-popular musical compositions, and 'realistic' contemporary visual narratives of a few seconds compose a reservoir of symbols to communicate national, international and global (media) events.

For the annual reviews of TV stations, parts of famous old musical themes as well as popular songs are selected to accompany "the most important images of the year", considered to be keys to more encompassing stories to be kept in collective audio-visual memories. Major companies and to a lesser degree parties and movements can make use of the sound-images they want to be associated with; they can even exploit the limited stock of highly positively evaluated Key Measures and Key Visuals for enhancing their own reputation.

At the speed in which global information, entertainment and attention are processed, there is no time for translations. The Key Visuals summarize various events, music and sounds as Key Measures to fill "the voids of the unspoken". Therefore, no time remains for reflecting the multimodal mediated experiences. The power of differences results first in hybridizations, but later in the agile fusion of visual and musical elements of a new technology. Audio-visual hegemonies therefore constitute major driving forces, frames, and goals of media specific publics and consumer markets. More and more, they are offered and accepted as symbols and have become parts of the (audio-visual) co-ordination of expectations, orientations, and actions. This hegemony of the audio-visual compared to the other components of multi-sensual experiences represents a global trend of the 20th century, which will most probably accelerate and increase its worldwide spreading in the first half of the 21st century. Fights for our eye-balls and ear drums, for our attention, amalgamation, and sometimes submission are increasingly carried out with mass-mediated audio-visual symbols.

In the contemporary multimedia and multi-modal age, a single medium can no longer be the message. This historic trend has already been interpreted in terms of intermediality. Key Measures and Key Visuals are – we propose – major nodes for connecting narratives, types of actors, situations, problems, and problem solutions or crises as well as multi-model imaginations of multi-sensual experiences across media types and formats, generations, and cultures. They require more attention than offered so far in mono-disciplinary research for they constitute, shape, and steer collective audio-visual memories and multi-sensual identity-formations. Thereby they form powerful networks of meaning or networks of powerful meanings, which are still vastly neglected in contemporary network analyses.

Bibliography

Boccia, Leonardo. *Choros da humanidade*. Salvador: Cian, 2006.

Boccia, Leonardo V. "Key Measures." *Over the Waves music in-and broadcasting*. International conference: Hamilton, Ontario, 2005: www.humanities.mcmaster.ca/~admv/overthewaves/

Bourdieu, Pierre. *Sobre a televisão*. Rio de Janeiro: Jorge Zahar Editor, 1997.

Carroll, Noel. *A Philosophy of Mass Art*. Oxford: Clarendon Press, 1998.

Huber, Hans Dieter. "Visuelle Musik in der Erlebnisgesellschaft." *Bilderfragen. Die Bildwissenschaften im Aufbruch*. Ed. Hans Belting. München: Fink, 2007: 119-131.

Kellison, Cathrine. *Producing for TV and video. A real-world approach*. New York: Elsevier; Focal Press, 2006.

Klüppelholz, Werner. "Musik im Fernsehen." *Sound. Zur Technologie und Ästhetik des Akustischen in den Medien.* Ed. Harro Segeberg, Frank Schätzlein. Marburg: Schüren, 2005.

Ludes, Peter. "Visual Hegemonies." *Visual Hegemonies: An Outline.* Ed. Peter Ludes. Münster: LIT, 2005: 9-69.

Ludes, Peter. *Medien und Symbole: Europäische MedienBILDung.* Siegen: UniVerSi, 2002.

Ludes, Peter. *Multimedia und Multi-Moderne: Schlüsselbilder. Fernsehnachrichten und World Wide Web - Medienzivilisierung in der Europäischen Währungsunion.* Wiesbaden: Westdeutscher Verlag, 2001. With CD-ROM: *Schlüsselbilder: Wissenschaft, Politiker und einfache Leute, Wirtschaft, Militär und Medien. Pressefotos, Spielfilme, Fernsehnachrichtensendungen und Informationsangebote im World Wide Web.*

Luhmann, Niklas. (2000) *The Reality of the Mass Media.* Stanford University Press.

Werner, Hans-Ulrich and Ralf Lankau. *Media Soundscapes II: Didaktik, Design, Dialog.* Siegen: MUK, 2007.

Wyatt, Hilary and Tim Amyes. *Audio Post-Production for Television and Film.* Third Edition, New York: Elsevier; Focal Press, 2005.

Zielinski, Siegfried. *Audiovisionen: Kino und Fernsehen als Zwischenspiele in der Geschichte.* Reinbek: Rowohlt, 1989.

Margret Schild

Text-Based Film Retrieval 2006

A New Concept to Index, Manage and Present Films, Their Content and Context

This paper will emphasize the perspective of a librarian and information specialist, being myself responsible for the museum libraries of the Film Museum and Theatre Museum at Düsseldorf. I deal with books, journals and other printed material within the library. Another department is responsible for other types of objects – photos, posters, handwritten material, films on reels, video tapes, etc. My task is to acquire printed material, to archive and preserve it, to record it and put it at the disposal of library users. Users are members of staff of the museum, free lancers and volunteers working on projects, and the interested public. The approach of Text-based Film Retrieval (TFR) 2006 was developed by the Institute of Terminology and Applied Knowledge Research (itaw),[1] located at Berlin and affiliated to the Humboldt University. The tool combines the experience of daily practical work with methods of knowledge structuring and presentation in order to organize information around film in an efficient way and to preserve it in the long term.

Information Flood / Chaos

Every time when a film is made, when visual media are produced, the development, the actual shooting and post-production are accompanied by rich textual material: scripts, results of information retrieval during the planning stages, collections of scientific, popular and technical information concerning the subject. When the film is distributed, more material is produced: advertising brochures, film stills, features for broadcasting on TV, trailers, websites on the Internet etc. Since film is not only seen as entertainment but as a cultural phenomenon and subject of special interest, the producers, the distributors, institutions dedicated to the cultural heritage and others try to make this textual material, acquired with great expenditure of human and financial resources, available for potential users (e.g. the audience of a film, film historians, teachers, students etc.). The materials enable users to get to know the process of

---

1 Further information concerning the institute and the project: www.itaw.hu-berlin.de/imb-prod.htm

film making, distribution and reception. Users and information specialists interested in the subject of film or media know that a lot of material of this kind exists, but is not easy to know how much there actually is and where it is available in the long term.

Currently, accompanying materials are normally issued by the industry, administrations, or public broadcasters. They address the general public as well as special target groups or mediators like teachers or instructors.

Problems

In the past, the material normally was split up into two parts: the film, archived on reels, video tapes, or as data files on the one hand; printed materials on the other. Fairly recently, a third group of materials emerged: digital information – e.g. information on CD or DVD, or websites on the Internet. In Germany, a lot of film-related collections exist: collections and archives for printed material, collections and archives for films, film libraries and information centres. The German National Library and its regional counterparts have the task to collect all printed and digital publications issued by publishers; however, neither brochures, leaflets and other film-related ephemera nor the films themselves fall under this rule. Actually, there is no institution in Germany that has the official task to collect and archive films and film-related materials.

Another problem lies in the difficulty to link between films and the textual or digital material about them, especially when the material refers to a particular image or scene. Especially when the film itself is stored by analogue means on celluloid or video tape, it is difficult to refer to particular places, or vice versa. With the development of DVDs and film presentations on multimedia-equipped computers, this has become much easier.

From the perspective of libraries and archives, the long-term preservation of information comes into focus. Because of technical changes and developments, some facilities have already disappeared (or will have in the near future), e.g. video recorders. Within the field of digital information, archives and libraries have to develop strategies in order to preserve the information in the long term, taking into consideration changing data formats, operating systems, and software, which are often not compatible to earlier versions. And we simply have no experience concerning the archival possibilities of CDs or DVDs. Within the archival community, we only have experience with microfilm and normal film.

The Concept of Text-Based Film Retrieval

TFR 2006 offers a way to present and edit moving images together with the textual material on the same level and on one shared platform – the computer screen. The accompanying material has not to be printed and dispatched. The complete material is available on the Internet without geographical or time limits. If the user wants to store the textual material, he is able to store it on his computer like any other information found on the Internet.

The greatest advantage of this concept is the possibility to link sequences of a film to relevant text parts or key words. It is also possible to add context information, for example by linking to the terms in a dictionary or other resources. The sequence of a film can be seen as a basic structure. By linking between film sequences and texts, the user can easily switch between the two, or navigate through the context of the film.

In TFR 2006, film images and textual materials are displayed simultaneously. Complex structures and highly organized information are presented through multimedia presentations. Different retrieval facilities with regard to the needs of the respective subject can be supplied. The accessibility and the view to the information can be defined free and open for everyone as well as restricted to special users or user groups through accounts and rights management.

The Technical Basis

Starting point was the development of multimedia implementations at the Humboldt University of Berlin. This means the integration of different types of information to achieve visualized content units. One media type is, of course, film.

The time code of a film is used to link film sequences with the relevant textual information. The time code allows the annotation and enrichment of film sequences by textual means. This additional information also enables the user to be directed quickly and precisely to a particular film sequence by free text search, field oriented search or index search. In order to realise this solution, the itaw MediaBase (iMB), an XML platform, was implemented and the Text-based Film Retrieval application was developed.

Within the application, the film files and the text files are stored strictly separate. They are only brought together for the presentation on the computer screen. The film format does not matter - every format can be integrated in the multimedia application: film on DVD (MPEG2), film via streaming (MPEG4 or ASF), or film as download.

The iMB offers tools to record, edit or import information as well as tools for the visualisation and for interactive facilities. The format of the textual files is XML. This format enables the user to copy and paste any part of the text in order to transfer it into his own database without any formatting problems, independent of the word processing software. The transfer of information can be reduced to the two commands "copy" and "paste" without the danger of loosing information.

Which Kinds of Film Can be Presented?

The concept is already used for different film genres. In the case of documentaries, additional information can comprise a lot of different aspects, for example the text of the commentary, original statements of the presented persons, additional information for a better understanding of the content and the presentation of associated subjects. The context is presented together with the content of the film. The necessary context information is normally acquired during the formation process of the film. This means: additional benefit can be achieved with little additional work (costs), using the existing knowledge (i.e. the context information). More images, short or long citations – from secondary literature –, historical or subject related additions can be integrated. The Internet and the internal linking options increase the multidimensional approach to the information.

In the case of movies, the text of the dialogue (or the complete script) and any other material, for example film-historical analyses, the literary model, or other film sequences for comparison can be brought together on one computer screen. The context information is the second level of information, displayed and presented parallel to the film itself (first level of information).

All parts of the presented film sequences can be linked to different levels of background information (context). The film presentation can be stopped at any point. All relevant text parts are presented now, even if there is more than one level of background or additional information available. It is also possible to use this the other way round: If a citation or the title of a chapter is marked, the linked film sequence will be found and displayed immediately. TFR 2006 can be used to provide access to scholarly and technical information about the medium film as well as to media-pedagogical solutions at schools, universities or museums.

Advantages

The information provider defines the structure and depth of indexing on the basis of his needs and the habits and needs of potential target groups. Because of the separate storage of the different kinds of data (text, image, film, sound), it is possible to follow the technical development for each type. Existing electronic information can be imported into the data base and controlled, using the rules defined within the document type definition (DTD) or the XML scheme for the data import. Forms can be used to record new data without knowledge about the hidden XML structure as well as guaranteeing consistency and quality for the data input. Different ways of information retrieval can be offered: free text search, field oriented search, the use of subject headings, the implementation of a thesaurus or a classification.

Some Examples

TFR 2006 was used in a project in cooperation with the public broadcaster Rundfunk Berlin-Brandenburg (RBB). A prototype was developed for the TV documentary *Deutsche und Polen* (Germans and Poles), a four-part history programme (see Figure 1 and dvd.deutsche-und-polen.de). The table of content on the left side allows direct access to a chapter or a special segment of a chapter by a mouse-click on the appropriate title. Playback of the film jumps to the new position as soon as another item is chosen. It is possible to search for terms in the field search. The result list of a search is presented on the left side; again, choosing one of the hits, the relevant film image is displayed on the right side screen. If the user prefers, he can read the text of the found segment (button "Text") rather than watch the part of the film. It is possible to switch between the search results, the relevant film segment and the text pertaining to that segment. The subject index on the left side enables the user to change directly to a special theme. These key words are linked to textual material, to images that are not part of the film, and to bibliographic references, as available on the Internet (context). After broadcasting, the film was commercially available as DVD-ROM. The user can insert the DVD-ROM into his computer drive and use it together with the information presented on the Internet.[2]

The Museum for Film and Television in Berlin has implemented TFR 2006 in its recently enlarged permanent exhibition – the history of broadcasting and television in Germany, especially in the program gallery. The visitor is invited to choose a film and get information about the film, the involved per-

---

2   In other cases, the film can be made available via streaming at different rates.

sons or institutions. The database with cinematographic information was a file maker data base that was exported within an XML structure. The information had to be combined with the process of choosing and the screening of the film on TV from the video tape.

Further examples:

- The movie *Bis zum Horizont und weiter* (1998, Peter Kahane) was published on CD-ROM together with different versions of the script (final printed version, realized version) as well as information about the making of and involved persons.

- A choice of documentary films was presented during the 50th International Festival of Documentary Film in Leipzig.

TFR 2006 can be implemented throughout the whole process of film making, film distribution and reception. It allows all information input to be documented and re-used for other purposes – resulting in an increasing information data basis, collecting all available and used material. It allows to combine different platforms and to combine finished parts of a project with not finished or additional material. The use of XML for data management and structuring enables the user to define the structures with regard to the content, the needed depth of indexing and to manage all types of information in an adequate way, following the development of the technological basis.

Figure 1. *Deutsche & Polen*

Rolf Kloepfer

How to Capture Offers of Filmic Effectiveness

AKIRA III as an Aid

1 Premises

My contribution[1] to the multi-faceted subject of this volume lies outside the usual purposes of digital tools, since I am not interested in recording singular aspects of films in an isolated way (e.g. the automatic detection of cuts, characters, faces, scenes, or developments of action). Quite the reverse, I am concentrating on film in its entirety as a work (of art) with a more or less complex composition.

The central question arises: what are the conditions under which digital tools can improve our cataloguing of the development of filmic effects of widely different sorts? I will be brief about the actual presentation of the software *AKIRA III*, which can be viewed on my website (www.phil.uni-mannheim.de/romanistik/romanistik3), in favour of an elaboration of the practical situations which the software has been developed to analyse:

An audio-visual text as a work of art is only effective or functions by means of its entirety ("Gesamtgestalt"). It is created in a more or less synergetic way according to the simultaneity of the perceptible and successiveness in time. According to "Gestalttheorie", the hypothesis, "the whole is more than the sum of its parts" is valid not only in detail for a melody, but generally for all phenomena of memory, imagination and will, for example. Fragments are also expanded to form a whole.

The degree of comprehensibility is correlated with a film's ability to motivate the spectator's realization, or even more his collaboration with the development of the "inner film." Central to this is the 'completion' which spectators make on their own, albeit guided by the film. Sign-directed participation beyond the automatic interpretation ("Umsetzung") of signs, which I called *sympraxis* (Kloepfer 1985), is above all based upon the motivating pleasure while watching a film.

Through this, unconscious forms of knowledge which the individual has more or less developed according to more or less common socio-cultural con-

---

[1] I would like to thank Rick Apgar and Birgit Olk for translating my text into English.

texts are activated. This gives rise to the problem of intersubjectively checkable determinations about the origins and consequences of filmic effects.

In this respect it is not a question of replacing the spectator's subjectivity by means of automatic digital tools, but rather to support it, to make it more profound, and – most importantly – to make it intersubjectively accessible and comprehensible for others. A tool serving this purpose is first of all a prosthesis for anyone who wants to record in a reflective way what is more or less unconsciously produced or may produce effects within us.[2]

These hypotheses imply a further dimension, which is known intuitively by anyone who has dealt extensively with effective forms of aesthetic communication or follows famous artists in the 20th century like Brecht, Eisenstein or Valéry, who correctly emphasize the fact: An approach, be it analytical, interpretive, or one that models the offer of effectiveness, does not destroy the effectiveness of a work of art, but possibly increases it according to a film's or text's complexity or the conditions of its reception. Therefore with regard to film or literary classics, pleasure gradually increases with time. The more the work of art succeeds, by means of its composition, in sympractically involving the spectator in the realization of the complex, semiotic text, the more economical its use of aesthetic means can be.[3]

A factor as basic as attentiveness makes clear that during reception conscious and unconscious, as well as voluntarily and involuntarily working faculties can be used and have to be considered if we want to model effects. Through attentiveness, processes of perception and cognition are selectively directed, activated and intensified, and by the transfer of units into different

---

2   Since G. Bateson (1973) we know that due to psycho-economical reasons our actions and their conditions can easily be transferred into a system of unconscious control ("habit" in Peirce's terms), the more important and therefore more frequently or significantly they are used. P. Wuss (1999) has discussed this phenomenon very thoroughly. Another example are stereotypes, which can be recognized automatically by a competent spectator, so that the film director can rely on the fact to create further effects.

3   This argument, which in theories of art can be traced back to antiquity, receives an extremely astute expression in the work of Jan Mukarovský, following the tradition of Russian formalism and Prague structuralism, with respect to the correlation between temporary aesthetic ends in themselves, the arrangement of all extra-aesthetic values employed by the work of art, and the offer made to the processing subject "to involve himself/herself" (1967: 103, 123). Periodically, the directed co-authorship of the addressee, already demonstrated by Plato in his *Symposion*, is rediscovered in the Age of Enlightenment (e.g. Diderot, Kant), Romanticism (Novalis, Baudelaire) or by authors influenced by phenomenology (Bakhtin, Merleau-Ponty, Sartre). See also Kloepfer/Landbeck (1991).

kinds of memory, they can be recalled in spite of a limited capacity for memory (e.g. by repeating a melody that evokes memories of a particular scene).

Finally, during the development of our tool a central problem arose: How can we model the simultaneity and successiveness of offers of effectiveness which appear in multiple visual and acoustic means in such a way that the potentially resulting complexity remains easily comprehensible?

2 Motivation: How to Make a Strong Intuition Provoked by a Film Comprehensible

It is often pointed out that even the best digital tools – including those discussed in this volume – can only serve as aids or supports which can help us to model filmic communication. Of course, eyeglasses, telescopes and cameras are – as far as they are compensating for weaknesses – nothing more than a "prosthesis", like script, gramophone or all kinds of pictography. At the same time functioning as media, they open up new dimensions of human productivity. This is also true with regard to the prosthesis introduced here, which may help us to heighten the potential of films. It is – or at least it is supposed to be – a means of enhancing the spectator's creative faculties.

The experience that initiated my interest, and from which the tool got its name, may illustrate my point. Disagreeing with usual interpretations of Akira Kurosawa's film *Rashomon* (1950), I repeatedly watched the film during the 1970s, searching for evidence against the predominant hypothesis, which considered it an early post-modern film that revealed four apparently incompatible views of the world (Kiefer 2002). At court, the three central characters – the robber, the knight, and his beautiful wife – each tell a different story of their common experience: the knight outwitted by the robber who more or less takes his wife through violence, and the knight's death. Which of the three killed him? Was it the robber at the end of a fair fight, his wife, no longer able to bear his contempt, or does he commit suicide in despair over the events? What they narrate is shown to the spectators in the images of their memories. There are actually four different stories, since a farmer, an accidental witness, also tells what he saw. Do these four people no longer live in a *common* world but in their exclusive constructs, in separate universes, as is maintained by the literature on the film? Suddenly I found a clue: in all key scenes the respective central figure and the leitmotif determining his or her life is characterized by different music. In the fight between the heroic knight and the witty robber for his noble wife, as observed by the farmer, there are only acoustic effects: the warriors lying in wait for each other, panting nearly like dogs, snapping at each other, biting and rolling in the leaves. At this point as well as at the end of the film, the different views collapse into the common, fundamental base of the inhumane or the primal.

This was my hypothesis: The music colours each view of the world with a corresponding belief or conviction. Each of the three stories has to prove itself true under the decaying gate of an ancient temple, if they are not – as a cynical tramp maintains – simple lies or subjective visions, shaped according to one's own interests (a very post-modern perspective). The robber, the knight, his wife, and the farmer tell their stories differently only with respect to the part that affects their pride. They seek respect and do not bear contempt. Their point of view is characterized by this premise. When it falls away, because they admit to their weaknesses – like the farmer who concealed his theft in court – the melody of destiny (Bolero motif), composed to characterize them and to create unbearable suspense ends. With this, Akira Kurosawa had directed my intuition. Unconsciously, I understood the borders of these increasingly compatible views. The melodic shading made the main characters' guiding motifs of life and the trajectory of their lives subliminally experienceable. This ultimately led to the new conviction: truth exists and there is goodness in people, who, unlike the three main characters, are not prisoners to a belief which leads to madness if they fail to admit the contradictions between it and real experience, and if they refuse to accept the possibility of change or reversal, rather seeing only murder or suicide as alternatives. But can I prove my view against the opposing interpretations?

Through acoustic characterization, Kurosawa directs, or even manipulates, both the characters and, according to their unconscious inclinations, the viewers. My entirely subjective "joining in the play" (Mitspielen) can easily be re-experienced intersubjectively, if one paradigmatically isolates each character's musical theme and listens to each successively. We are thus directed to experience the conditions which motivate the lives – more precisely the four trajectories – of these people and are called upon to accept these as possibilities and finally to overcome them. (Kloepfer 2007). T. S. Eliot maintains, "The end is where we start." And H. von Förster confirms: "The cause lies in the future."[4] A film's aim is the realization of our inner film, which – at least as far as successful traditional works are concerned – follows a hierarchy of goal determinations.

---

4   See Nadin (2002: 11 ff.) against all forms of "Cartesian determinism" and in favour of a theory following Peirce as far as the discovery of communicative "energies" is concerned.

3   From Aesthetic Theory to the "Prosthetic" Argument

How can we represent what we – guided by the filmic offer – perform simultaneously and successively in our consciousness? In the 1930s, Sergej Eisenstein answered this question by stating it should be written down in the same way as a musical performance is in a score. Should the film director proceed according to an aesthetics of production, like a composer who writes down the notes and their respective realization in terms of meter, melody, harmony and rhythm for the strings, drums, choir and soloists one beneath the other on a timeline? If this approach made sense, film directors of the last one-hundred years would have tried to do so. We can start, however, from an aesthetics of reception, i.e. from the perspective of the addressee. What are the "symphonically" experienceable "attractions" (Eisenstein in his early work) or effects and clusters of effectiveness? Eisenstein advises us to imagine this as a multi-dimensional spherically opening book, like a hypertext.[5] In contrast, we wanted to create a tool with which anyone – schoolchildren, university students, or film experts – is able to create one's own modelling of a film. At the same time, it was to allow the user to predefine score patterns for use or further development by others. Therefore we were not to presuppose any technical programming skills. The solution is demonstrated by Goethe on his journey to Italy: Whenever he reached the limits of his drawing abilities, he simply wrote on the spot in a tree something like "fantastic bird."

First of all it is important to add to the film a model of a possible score. Doing this, we start from the radical pragmatics of Peirce, who considers even the act of perceiving as a more or less complex, more or less unconscious drawing of conclusions according to anthropological universals and historical socio-cultural habits. We have learned them to be able to act in the world. They are equally necessary for our ability to understand a film, and for the aesthetic skills required for inter-medial energy exchange (e.g. knowledge of all kinds of literary, photographic, and musical traditions). This knowledge is used specific to genre and style and is gathered in key images or larger units building up to key scenes. To remember a film, we sometimes only need a few central images like those from *Rashomon* in Figure 1.

---

5   See Kloepfer (2003) on a semiotic approach of film theory, and Kloepfer (2002) on Eisenstein.

Figure 1. Central images from Akira Kurosawa's *Rashomon*

Like a soundtrack, all kinds of tracks can be arranged one below the other parallel to their succession in time. Units within the tracks – scenes, sequences and single takes – can be cut and marked by colours. So, after getting an insight into the fundamental structure of *Rashomon,* I thought: if an overview can be achieved in this way, then it immediately becomes evident what the four stories have in common, what is characterized by the "melody of life", what leads to self-deception, and under which conditions truth may be experienced. It is in the second part of the farmer's narration, in which the three "heroes" loose all their pride, in which they reveal their inner conflicts, are scared to death, no longer able to fight, and in a moment of insanity break down because of the burden. The fragments of narration and perception become transparent with regard to their correlation (their meaning) as well as with regard to their value (their sense), when we are able to communicate our unconscious intuitive co-acting. So, Akira Kurosawa guided me towards the concept of my annotation tool, which I started to develop decades ago with the help of skilled programmers and decided to call *AKIRA*.

In many respects, film studies have to deal with the same problems as literary studies or other areas of scholarship: how can the particular effect on the spectator, who perceives a work of art under more or less individual conditions, be "intersubjectively" communicated to others? All forms of art make particular use of human imagination, but while book readers can make notes of their observations directly in the book, there is no such way with film, even though its handling has recently become much easier. The ideal of every film scholar – the film editing tool – is now available to all. But does this provide us with appropriate means to raise the effects offered by films in order to make them communicable for analysis, interpretation or any form of teaching?

Therefore, *AKIRA III* has to make comprehensible the immense field between an "aesthetics of innovation" on the one side and an "aesthetics of repetition" (including stereotypes or even serial redundancy) on the other (see Lotman 1972, Wuss 1999).

Aesthetics of Innovation

Sometimes a film not only refuses any automatic kind of understanding of filmic, cultural or universal signs, but at the same time creates a kind of need or compulsion to fill the unknown or complete the gap (Kloepfer 1982). To illustrate this argument, let us consider the beginning of *The Sea Inside* (*Mar adentro*, 2004; dir. Alejandro Amenábar). It is a film about internal "filmic" narrations which form human memories and imaginations about the future, and which give meaning to our lives. The film opens with a black screen, slowly illuminated by an expanding rectangle. A voice invites us to imagine an ideal place.[6] The process of denying any deictic orientation regarding time and setting or causes, perpetrators and victims of the action, forces us to continue the process of reception, to suspend the attribution of meaning, and to stick with an unvarnished impression. Such a structure invites assumptions. It works like a question.

If we consider a film as an offer of effectiveness in the course of time, and therefore as a process, it is not appropriate to interpret such scenes with hindsight, from our knowledge of the end of the film. That would make us ignore the dynamics of effects, which may lead from frustration to curiosity, from uncertainty and dizziness to doubt and especially to the stimulation of our guessing instincts. The instinct called abduction was added by mediaeval philosophy as a fundamental complement to in- and deduction.

Apart from the usual navigational functions, we have to be able to mark certain scenes. While we are watching a film on our computer, *AKIRA III* allows us to set marks with the cursor or to save a corresponding image to the hard drive (see Figure 2). Moments experienced as particularly striking or strange for their departure from the norm can be summarized in a text window with brief or extended notes detailing assumptions or hypotheses. Simple marks or key images may later be corresponded to the complementary moment of uncertainty or recognition. They work like answers to our questions or fulfilment of our anticipation. This results in our first assumptions about the rhythm of a film. It is the area of guidable *intuition*, i.e. conclusions whose causes temporarily evade our reflexive interpretation, especially when our unconscious interpretation of affordances is in reality increased by aesthetic means. The habits of automatically drawing conclusions may use anthropo-

---

6 I discussed this film in more detail (Kloepfer 2007), partly because it plays with the possibilities of imaginations (remembering, interpreting, anticipating), which can make life to appear worthwhile or undignified, or even lead to the conviction that suicide can be considered the highest form of humanity.

logically universal or culture-specific codes as well as codes of arts and especially of film and its genres.

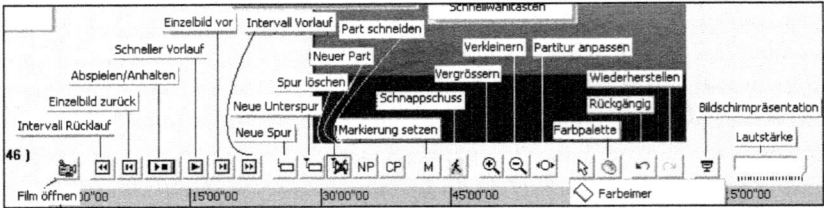

Figure 2. *AKIRA III* tool bar

Aesthetics of Repetition

On the other side of the spectrum, we can add scores of fulfilled norms. In many respects, the represented world, the intended forms of the addressee's participation with the extensive offers of effectiveness, and the central narrative procedures all correspond to the "Einfache Formen" (simple forms) of oral and literary narration (Jolles 1930/1972). Such norms concern above all the genre. When we hear or read, "Once upon a time . . ," we know that this is a fairy-tale. Art films are nearly without exception narrative. The terms for the different genres, however, were defined according to different premises, corresponding equally to the predominant dimensions of effects. They emphasize the represented world (e.g. *westerns*) or the dominant effect (e.g. *horror films*), or the means of creation (e.g. *animated films*). Analogous to the soundtrack mentioned above, we call the distribution in time of filmic offers like these *tracks*. Correspondingly, we developed a score-like structure which allows to differentiate between individual tracks (like in a musical score, where the string part may consist of violins, violas, cellos or double-basses). Illustrating this with the western genre, different sub-tracks can be registered:

- the meaningfully-constructed relationship between time and place (Bakhtin's "Chronotopos"), where forms of wilderness are confronted with those of security (town, saloon, etc.) and connected by paths (railways, wagon trails, etc.);
- the typical constellations in the course of time, the antagonists (the good and the evil) and their helpers in contrast with the undetermined people;
- the pattern of the action, with the five act structure known since Aristotle and taught in Hollywood (the apparently peaceful but nevertheless prob-

lematic starting point, the development of the conflict up to the crisis, the turning point and the solution as a result of the heroic deed).

Such patterns, which can be marked with different colours (which we cannot illustrate here), can be noted in a more or less detailed way in the form of parts from individual acts or chapters all the way down to scenes, sequences, takes or even single frames.[7]

For teaching purposes, especially with films that have unusual structures, *AKIRA III* allows to direct the learners' attention to genre and the styles of particular epochs or directors: everything that can be arranged in front of the camera, microphone and at the editing table, starting with casting, make-up, even down to the scenery.

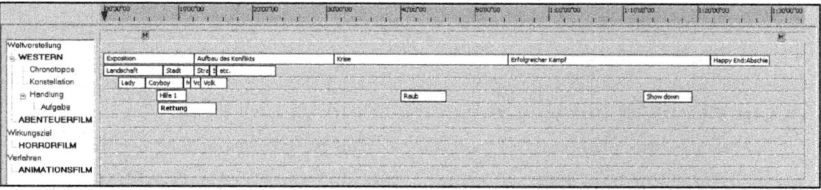

Figure 3. *AKIRA III* score pattern: genres

4 Dynamics of Film Semiosis: The Economics of Co-Production of the Inner Film

It may have become apparent that *AKIRA III* can be helpful for teaching film. With the help of tracks and parts it is easy to mark sequences and visualize and communicate their filmic, dramatic or diegetic aspects of composition, as well as their offer of effectiveness. Depending on the goal, the division (creating of parts) of the different tracks may range from a rough survey to a detailed analysis (e.g. individual sequences). In this connection the structure and hierarchy of the tracks (for example by creating sub-tracks) can correspond to the concentration of aesthetic means or offers of effectiveness in the form of clusters. Teachers have the opportunity to formulate assignments for their students in individual tracks. The answers to these tasks can be given in additional tracks which can be accessed via a password. The penultimate, in my opinion decisive, advantage for teaching film is the possibility of transferring tracks (including their parts and texts) from one analytical file into another. This not only facilitates working in groups, but over the course of time the analysis of a

---

7   We chose the MPEG-1 video format, which allows work with individual frames.

film can proceed up to more elaborate subdivisions. In this way, collective knowledge can be integrated into tracks and parts (for example research in intermediality or cut frequency, see Yuri Tsivian's paper in the present volume). As already mentioned above, every user can adapt the analysis pattern to his or her individual needs, to expand or change tracks, parts or texts, to use different colours to highlight something striking like rhythms, etc. Perhaps the most interesting feature of *AKIRA III* is the screen presentation, which allows the user to create play lists of selected parts, playing them in any desired order, which means to reorganize them to a certain extent. This simplified "editing tool" helps the user to test how and in which order aesthetic means have effects, e.g. on montage sequences, turning points, etc.[8] That way, as far as the film's central theme is concerned, the effect of the montage within the complete work is revealed. The presentation function also facilitates lectures, permitting the speaker to present scenes illustrating or emphasizing the argument in the order of ones own choice. The screen presentation can be interrupted, for example for comments, and later continued.

Guiding the consciousness of individuals which according to their sociocultural background constitute a film's audience is effected on the micro level by clusters that impress the spectators' short-term memory. The simultaneity of filmic means appealing to sensory perception, which can be stored in working memory for only a matter of "seconds up to minutes," can deeply intensify their effectiveness through concentration ("chunks", see Birbaumer/Schmidt 1996: 527 f., 571 ff). The transfer into long-term memory can again be increased through repetition, consolidation and controlled handling. This explains for all art forms, especially those operating in multiple dimensions of space and time, why the appropriate methods have to be created, tested, researched and why ultimately new models have to be established. This leads us to the opposite extreme, the area deliberately excluded from film analysis as "intuitive" and "subjective."

More important than the assistance of *AKIRA III* in the detection and teaching of automated and codified filmic processes is the revelation of successful, unconscious processing. Naturally, the size of this area depends on the level of developed competence. Processing can happen implicitly (procedural) or explicitly (declarative); the borders between the two vary according to the chosen theory of memory or processing system. Put more simply, we notice perhaps that something occurs within us, but in most cases we are not able to put into words what was or still is going on within us. We *are* involved in the

---

8   See Kuchenbuch (2005: 178 ff.) for an analysis of *High Noon*.

process of semiosis, but cannot *have* it – especially not in a reflected way. This leads us back to the beginning.

Our inner film depends on our systematically motivated will to supplement the film's perception and processing by our personal (individual) contribution. The "moving picture" only makes the pictures "move" because the number of frames per second exceeds our ability to separate them. Our imagination surrenders to the "attractions" of works of art, but only if we do not refuse and look away. Vice versa, the desire to be attracted, to draw conclusions, or to get involved, to immerse oneself in a stimulation that stirs up the deepest layers of our memory, can itself be stimulated, directed or even manipulated. As Bateson (1973) noted nearly a century ago: it is only by deep crises or great works of art that the deepest habits can be changed. This is the reason why we have chosen the challenging film *The Sea Inside*. Very few people have reflected on the growing problem of suicide with the necessary depth. Especially out of the experience of euthanasia and suicide in the face of brutal, dictatorial violence in Nazi Germany or the Soviet Union, and nowadays at Guantanamo Bay and elsewhere, there is great reluctance to break through the orthodoxy, for instance of Christian associations, in dealing with this subject.

All the film's characters are against the wish of the central character Ramón Sampedro to bring his life to an end after 28 years of total immobilization from the neck down. With each character, the film in an unbroken rhythm makes an offer to stop short for some seconds. What is his or her relationship to Ramón? Why is his behaviour time and again surprising to them? Why does their affection for him become more intense in new ways all the time? When we highlight these scenes only, it becomes evident why especially the four women that love him are for such a long time unable to respect his decision, let alone help him end his life. The director puts us into the role of "creative co-producer" to get an idea of their motivating visions, which we may experience by our inner performance. This permits us to view things from their perspective and to behave according to their values. This is only valid according to the aesthetic premises of freedom and competence.

The simple marking or labelling of images that correspond to moving, astonishing, puzzling, baffling, and unsettling scenes reveals in a completely evident way the distinctive features and a framework:

- The musical characterization of the life story of each figure (track 1) builds up, together with particular camera effects (track 2 with sub-tracks), colour effects and montage, an intensive priming. The creation of our expectations is closely linked to an intensive detection of structures; the priming, however, always begins with music.

- Since the disabled main character can only use his mouth and his eyes as direct means of communication, his mediated "prostheses" play a central role: an apparatus that enables him to write with his mouth, a telephone he is able to dial and answer via a rope that he can grasp in his mouth, communication in the house by whistling, and finally a radio and television which are used interactively in the film and up to the climax of his filmed death when he addresses the legal authorities and us directly (track 3).

Figure 4. *AKIRA III* score of *The Sea Inside*.

- The film is determined by mediated performances in the multiple sense of the word: What caused (visualized in memory) his accident? What could love be like between him and Júlia, who is equally affected by an incurable degenerative illness, if only ...? Consequently, on the screen there are three kinds of envisioned images (track 4): in an unmarked way we participate in the daily scenes of a village in Galicia, in Barcelona and in the little seaport of Beuro as well as on the paths between them. His memories are multiple, always linked to the sea and particularly the accident up to the fulfilment of his death and his translocation to the ideal: a gorgeous beach on the Seychelles and the desired encounter with Júlia.

According to the rich tradition of rhetoric and especially the work of Bakhtin (1930: 70 f., 163 f.), the subject matter of an artwork is the dynamic task to which we are enabled by the semiotic process. Therefore, the "technical apparatus" of its realization is more than the sum of its informative (referential) meanings in the strict sense of the term, but at the same time encompasses our individual, sign-directed actions (sympraxis), which include the dimensions of evaluation and sense. Only by this are we able to explain why especially in successful aesthetic communication all dimensions of the mind (emotion, will, reason) are used in a synergetic way. In Amenábar's extraordinary film, the images direct us towards the performance of our inner film, during which we may change our convictions. It is not a matter of suspending the taboo of death and dying, but to accept active support of a death with dignity as an important act of humanity. We are thereby directed to tolerate the extreme contrast in the hero's life, the disparity between his mental vitality, attraction, dignity, and affection for the widest variety of people and his physical immobility. Precisely because of Ramón's love for the life he imagines for himself, and for people – infinitely deep, vast and multiple like the sea, the origin of all life – and because of the strength of his imagination, his family and friends have difficulty accepting his personal sense of a lack of dignity.

The composition corresponds to a complex association with our imaginative capabilities in such a way that we are directed through the figures and the aesthetics down into the microstructure to a "learning by imitation or modelling" (Städtler 2003). The larger the gap between us and the psyche of the protagonist in his existential decision, the greater, more intense, more effective the following must be:

a) the concentration of means to provoke the spectator's transference into someone else's situation in the form of imaginative sympathy (lovers, friends) or antipathy (legal authority, church, "big brother" with his orthodox moral) and

b) the filmic offer of elicitors and with these cues that provide the spectator the possibility of freeing himself from "persuasive stereotypes," of tolerating uncertainty, and finally of confirming acceptance of the voluntary termination of life. In the score these scenes show a highly functional load.

From the scenes in which the spectator's conditioning is assumed and he or she is led into a first moment of insecurity or even doubt, up to the sequences of explicit confirmation, there is an ever-increasing intensity of the filmic offer, to immerse oneself into someone else's situation, to develop tolerance and adopt external conditions and finally to expect a positive ending.

5 Conclusion

In conclusion, I would like to briefly sketch the composition tracks that comprise the now relatively easily groupable filmic offers:

- The immersion by means of primary emotional qualities into different dimensions of evaluation plays with different forms of sympathy and antipathy, for our attitudes change – in so far as we can, want, or permit ourselves to get involved – dynamically and adaptively.

- Offers of effectiveness involving the will with possible effects ranging from curiosity to the unconscious development of hypotheses (abduction) are in most cases paired with an initial moment of astonishment, like in the scene when Ramón suddenly seems to move his hand, gets up, moves to the corridor, takes a run-up ... and – like he always does – flies out of the window above the hills to the sea.

- The cognitive conclusion is carried out equally through distinctly exacting offers from simple riddling situations up to refined consequences, which presuppose a certain degree of learned competences. Ramón's father, for example, appears only a few times and very briefly, but judging from the few seconds of farewell, when his hand touches the imprint of his son in the deserted bed, we can understand that he accepted the final turn of destiny.

I call this film polyvalent, because it offers, depending on the different conditions of the addressee, a similar, yet also variably rich or deep gesture to be carried out. This also implies that it fulfils the "autodidactic" principle providing the spectator with the clues for its comprehension during the course of the film. Therefore it can be assumed that in all probability *The Sea Inside* will become a film classic that will still be effective when our societies have perhaps decided to create the conditions for death with dignity.

Bibliography

Bakhtin, Michail (publ. as Vološinov, Valentin). *Marxismus und Sprachphilosophie*. Berlin: Ullstein, 1975 (1930).

Bateson, Gregory. „Style, Grace and Information in Primitive Art." *Steps to an Ecology of Mind*. Gregory Bateson. London: Paladin Books, 1973: 126-132.

Birbaumer, Niels und Robert F. Schmidt, Biologische Psychologie, Berlin: Springer, [3]1996.

Jolles, André. *Einfache Formen. Legende, Sage, Mythe, Rätsel, Spruch, Kasus, Memorabile, Märchen, Witz*. Halle (Saale), 1930 (Tübingen: Niemeyer, [4]1972) .

Kiefer, Bernd. "Rashomon – Das Lustwäldchen." *Filmklassiker*. Ed. Thomas Koebner. Stuttgart: Reclam, [4]2002: Bd. II 95–101.

Kloepfer, Rolf. "Escape into Reception. The Scientific and Hermeneutic Schools of German Literary Theory." *Poetics Today* 3.2 (1982): 47–75.

———. "Mimesis und Sympraxis: Zeichengelenktes Mitmachen im erzählenden Werbespot." *Narrativität in den Medien.* Ed. Rolf Kloepfer and Karl-Dietmar Möller. Mannheim /Münster: MANA/MAKS, 1985: 141–181.

———. "Cultures de langues philosophiques. Les traditions françaises de la Troisième critique de Kant." *Kants Ästhetik / Kant's Aesthetics / L'esthétique de Kant (Colloque de Cerisy 1993).* Ed. Herman Parret. Berlin / New York : de Gruyter, 1998 : 748–764.

———. "La puissance des prémisses anthropologiques dans la théorie du film de Sergej M. Eisenstein." *Eisenstein – L'ancien et le Nouveau.* Ed. Dominique Château, François Jost and Martin Lefebvre. Paris: Publications de la Sorbonne, 2002.

———. "Semiotische Aspekte der Filmwissenschaft: Filmsemiotik." *Semiotik=Semiotics. Ein Handbuch zu den zeichentheoretischen Grundlagen von Natur und Kultur,* Band III. Ed. Roland Posner. Berlin / New York: de Gruyter, 2003: 3188–3211.

———. "Film als Dialog – Östliche Semiotik (Bachtin, Jakobson u. a.) und fernöstliche Praxis (Kurosawas *Rashomon*)." *Strukturalismus. Osteuropa und die Entstehung einer universalen Wissenschaftskultur der Moderne.* Ed. Johann S. Koch et al. Heidelberg: Synchron, 2008.

———."*The sea inside*: On the Principles of one's own performance of the other." *Narration and Spectatorship in Moving Images (collection of essays selected from the proceedings of the conference).* Ed. Joseph Anderson and Barbara Fisher-Anderson. Cambridge: Cambridge Scholars Press, 2008.

Kloepfer, Rolf and Hanne Landbeck. Ästhetik der Werbung. Der Fernsehspot in Europa als Symptom neuer Macht. Frankfurt a. M.: Fischer, 1991.

Kuchenbuch, Thomas. Filmanalyse. Theorien – Methoden – Kritik. Wien/Köln/Weimar: Böhlaus (UTB), ²2005.

Lotman, Juri. Die Struktur literarischer Texte. München: Fink, 1972.

Mukařovský, Jan. Kapitel aus der Poetik. Frankfurt a. M.: Suhrkamp, 1967 (1948).

Nadin, Mihai S. *Anticipation: Die Ursache liegt in der Zukunft.* Wuppertal: Lars Müller, 2002.

Städtler, Thomas, *Lexikon der Psychologie. Wörterbuch – Handbuch – Studienbuch.* Stuttgart: Kröner, 2003.

Wuss, Peter. Filmanalyse und Psychologie. Struktur des Films im Wahrnehmungsprozess. Berlin: Sigma, ²1999.

ZfK – Zeitschrift für Kulturwissenschaften

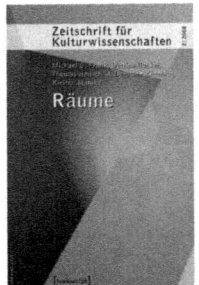

Michael C. Frank, Bettina Gockel,
Thomas Hauschild, Dorothee Kimmich,
Kirsten Mahlke (Hg.)

Räume

Zeitschrift für Kulturwissenschaften,
Heft 2/2008

Dezember 2008, 160 Seiten, kart., 8,50 €,
ISBN 978-3-89942-960-2
ISSN 9783-9331

ZFK – Zeitschrift für Kulturwissenschaften

Der Befund zu aktuellen Konzepten kulturwissenschaftlicher Analyse und Synthese ist ambivalent: Neben innovativen und qualitativ hochwertigen Ansätzen besonders jüngerer Forscher und Forscherinnen steht eine Masse oberflächlicher Antragsprosa und zeitgeistiger Wissensproduktion – zugleich ist das Werk einer ganzen Generation interdisziplinärer Pioniere noch wenig erschlossen.

In dieser Situation soll die **Zeitschrift für Kulturwissenschaften** eine Plattform für Diskussion und Kontroverse über Kultur und die Kulturwissenschaften bieten. Die Gegenwart braucht mehr denn je reflektierte Kultur, historisch situiertes und sozial verantwortetes Wissen.

Aus den Einzelwissenschaften heraus kann so mit klugen interdisziplinären Forschungsansätzen fruchtbar über die Rolle von Geschichte und Gedächtnis, von Erneuerung und Verstetigung, von Selbststeuerung und ökonomischer Umwälzung im Bereich der Kulturproduktion und der naturwissenschaftlichen Produktion von Wissen diskutiert werden.

Die **Zeitschrift für Kulturwissenschaften** lässt gerade auch jüngere Wissenschaftler und Wissenschaftlerinnen zu Wort kommen, die aktuelle fächerübergreifende Ansätze entwickeln.

Lust auf mehr?

Die **Zeitschrift für Kulturwissenschaften** erscheint zweimal jährlich in Themenheften. Bisher liegen die Ausgaben Fremde Dinge (1/2007), Filmwissenschaft als Kulturwissenschaft (2/2007) und Kreativität. Eine Rückrufaktion (1/2008) und Räume (2/2008) vor.

Die **Zeitschrift für Kulturwissenschaften** kann auch im Abonnement für den Preis von 8,50 € je Ausgabe bezogen werden.
Bestellung per E-Mail unter: bestellung.zfk@transcript-verlag.de

www.transcript-verlag.de

Medienumbrüche

SIGRID BARINGHORST, VERONIKA KNEIP,
ANNEGRET MÄRZ, JOHANNA NIESYTO (HG.)
Politik mit dem Einkaufswagen
Unternehmen und Konsumenten als Bürger
in der globalen Mediengesellschaft

2007, 394 Seiten, kart., 28,80 €,
ISBN 978-3-89942-648-9

ALBERT KÜMMEL-SCHNUR, JENS SCHRÖTER (HG.)
Äther
Ein Medium der Moderne

April 2008, 404 Seiten, kart., zahlr. Abb., 33,80 €,
ISBN 978-3-89942-610-6

RAINER LESCHKE, JOCHEN VENUS (HG.)
Spielformen im Spielfilm
Zur Medienmorphologie des Kinos
nach der Postmoderne

2007, 422 Seiten, kart., 33,80 €,
ISBN 978-3-89942-667-0

Leseproben, weitere Informationen und Bestellmöglichkeiten
finden Sie unter www.transcript-verlag.de

Medienumbrüche

DANIEL MÜLLER, ANNEMONE LIGENSA, PETER GENDOLLA (HG.)
Leitmedien
Konzepte – Relevanz – Geschichte

Band 1
Februar 2009, ca. 250 Seiten, kart., ca. 25,80 €,
ISBN 978-3-8376-1028-1

Band 2
Februar 2009, ca. 250 Seiten, kart., ca. 25,80 €,
ISBN 978-3-8376-1029-1

RALF SCHNELL (HG.)
MedienRevolutionen
Beiträge zur Mediengeschichte
der Wahrnehmung

2006, 208 Seiten, kart., 23,80 €,
ISBN 978-3-89942-533-8

JÜRGEN SORG, JOCHEN VENUS (HG.)
Erzählformen im Computerspiel
Zur Medienmorphologie digitaler Spiele

April 2009, ca. 500 Seiten, kart., ca. 39,90 €,
ISBN 978-3-8376-1035-2

**Leseproben, weitere Informationen und Bestellmöglichkeiten
finden Sie unter www.transcript-verlag.de**

Medienumbrüche

MANFRED BOGEN, ROLAND KUCK,
JENS SCHRÖTER (HG.)
Virtuelle Welten als Basistechnologie für Kunst und Kultur?
Eine Bestandsaufnahme
Februar 2009, ca. 130 Seiten, kart.,
zahlr. Abb., ca. 16,80 €,
ISBN 978-3-8376-1061-1

JÖRG DÖRING,
TRISTAN THIELMANN (HG.)
Mediengeographie
Theorie – Analyse – Diskussion
Februar 2009, ca. 500 Seiten,
kart., zahlr. Abb., ca. 35,80 €,
ISBN 978-3-8376-1022-2

RAINER GEISSLER,
HORST PÖTTKER (HG.)
Integration durch Massenmedien/ Mass Media-Integration
Medien und Migration im internationalen Vergleich
Media and Migration: A Comparative Perspective
2006, 328 Seiten, kart., 27,80 €,
ISBN 978-3-89942-503-1

MARCUS HAHN,
ERHARD SCHÜTTPELZ (HG.)
Trancemedien und Neue Medien um 1900
Ein anderer Blick auf die Moderne
Februar 2009, ca. 300 Seiten, kart.,
ca. 29,80 €, ISBN 978-3-8376-1098-7

WALBURGA HÜLK, GREGOR SCHUHEN,
TANJA SCHWAN (HG.)
(Post-)Gender
Choreographien/Schnitte
2006, 236 Seiten, kart., 24,80 €,
ISBN 978-3-89942-277-1

INGO KÖSTER, KAI SCHUBERT (HG.)
Medien in Raum und Zeit
Maßverhältnisse des Medialen
Februar 2009, ca. 300 Seiten, kart.,
zahlr. Abb., ca. 29,80 €,
ISBN 978-3-8376-1033-8

ANNEMONE LIGENSA,
DANIEL MÜLLER (HG.)
Rezeption
Die andere Seite der Medienumbrüche
Februar 2009, ca. 200 Seiten, kart.,
ca. 25,80 €,
ISBN 978-3-8376-1026-0

MICHAEL LOMMEL,
ISABEL MAURER QUEIPO,
VOLKER ROLOFF (HG.)
Surrealismus und Film
Von Fellini bis Lynch
Juni 2008, 326 Seiten, kart., 29,80 €,
ISBN 978-3-89942-863-6

MICHAEL LOMMEL,
VOLKER ROLOFF (HG.)
Sartre und die Medien
März 2008, 228 Seiten, kart., 23,80 €,
ISBN 978-3-89942-816-2

ISABEL MAURER QUEIPO,
NANETTE RISSLER-PIPKA (HG.)
Dalís Medienspiele
Falsche Fährten und paranoische Selbstinszenierungen in den Künsten
2007, 416 Seiten, kart., 36,80 €,
ISBN 978-3-89942-629-8

DANIEL MÜLLER, ANNEMONE LIGENSA,
PETER GENDOLLA (HG.)
Leitmedien
Konzepte – Relevanz – Geschichte,
Band 1
Februar 2009, ca. 250 Seiten,
kart., ca. 25,80 €,
ISBN 978-3-8376-1028-4

Leseproben, weitere Informationen und Bestellmöglichkeiten finden Sie unter www.transcript-verlag.de

Printed by Printforce, United Kingdom